Lecture Notes in Computer Scie

Edited by G. Goos, J. Hartmanis and J. van L

Springer

Berlin
Heidelberg
New York
Barcelona
Budapest
Hong Kong
London
Milan
Paris
Singapore
Tokyo

Boris Magnusson (Ed.)

System Configuration Management

ECOOP'98 SCM-8 Symposium
Brussels, Belgium, July 20-21, 1998
Proceedings

Springer

Series Editors

Gerhard Goos, Karlsruhe University, Germany
Juris Hartmanis, Cornell University, NY, USA
Jan van Leeuwen, Utrecht University, The Netherlands

Volume Editor

Boris Magnusson
Lund Institute of Technology, Department of Computer Science
P.O. Box 118, SE-221 00 Lund, Sweden
E-mail: boris.magnusson@dna.lth.se

Cataloging-in-Publication data applied for

Die Deutsche Bibliothek - CIP-Einheitsaufnahme

System configuration management : proceedings / ECOOP'98 SCM-8 Symposium,
Brussels, Belgium, July 20 - 21, 1998. Boris Magnusson (ed.). - Berlin ;
Heidelberg ; New York ; Barcelona ; Budapest ; Hong Kong ; London ; Milan ;
Paris ; Santa Clara ; Singapore ; Tokyo : Springer, 1998
 (Lecture notes in computer science ; Vol. 1439)
 ISBN 3-540-64733-3

CR Subject Classification (1991): D.2, K.6, K.4.3

ISSN 0302-9743
ISBN 3-540-64733-3 Springer-Verlag Berlin Heidelberg New York

© Springer-Verlag Berlin Heidelberg 1998
Printed in Germany

Typesetting: Camera-ready by author
SPIN 10637998   06/3142 – 5 4 3 2 1 0   Printed on acid-free paper

Preface

Configuration Management is the discipline of managing the evolution of families of systems. It involves supporting versioning, composition, and generation of all relevant configuration items, as well as controlling and supporting related team activities. It is central to any large engineering project and requires a significant amount of system support. These problems have been studied in parallel, in the *Software* domain and in the general product domain (*PDM*). With this year's conference we have attempted to create a forum for interaction between these two communities. As a consequence the abbreviation *SCM* now means *System Configuration Management*.

Earlier, seven SCMs were organized as workshops, but with a growing community of researchers and practitioners in the field the format has this year been changed to a regular conference. Despite this change, and a growing number of attendees we hope the meeting can maintain some of its character with lively discussions and its special flavor with participants from industry, academia, and tool vendors. Earlier SCMs were organized in conjunction with Software Engineering conferences. This year's shift to join a conference dedicated to object orientation hopefully creates a new blend of people with backgrounds in Software CM, PDM, and OO – areas which have interesting common problems.

Much of the currently growing interest in SCM can be traced to the CMU/SEI CMM model with its focus on 'repeatability' and SCM as a key process, as well as the availability of networks and the need for new distributed solutions their use demands. Papers in the parts on *Cooperative Systems and Web Based Applications* in particular illustrate this research trend. Several papers in the parts on *Experimental Systems and Formal Approaches* can also be read in this light. We are happy to see that almost half of the papers come from industry, including all the papers in the *Industrial Experience* part. And finally, the papers in the *PDM and SCM* part contains comparisons that will hopefully help people from both domains to understand the relation between the fields, as well as a paper that illustrates the relation between SCM, PDM and OO.

Having SCM-8 organized as an open conference (rather than a workshop with limited attendance as before), and in conjunction with ECOOP, where CM has not been a central issue, we expect an unusually high number of new participants. The conference therefore started with an invited *tutorial*, by Susan Dart, which was also open for ECOOP participants. You will find an extended abstract of this presentation at the end of the proceedings.

As the program chair, I would like to express my gratitude to all the authors who submitted papers, the program committee doing a wonderful job in reviewing and selecting the program. Also, I thank all the authors who bore with me in getting the papers in a suitable electronic format (with page numbers and running heads) which still is surprisingly tedious when different document processing systems are involved.

Lund, May 1998   Boris Magnusson, SCM-8 Program chair

Organization

SCM-8 was organized in connection with the European Conference on Object Oriented Programming, ECOOP'98, this year taking place in Brussels, Belgium. Relying on the local organization for ECOOP has saved us from having to deal with the local organization for which we are most grateful.

Conference chair: Annita Persson, Ericsson Microwave AB, Sweden
Program chair: Boris Magnusson, Lund Institute of Technology, Sweden

Program Committee

Geoffrey Clemm, Rational Software, USA
Reidar Conradi, NTNU, Trondheim, Norway
Susan A. Dart, Dart Technology Strategies, USA
Prasun Dewan, University of North Carolina, USA
Jacky Estublier, University of Grenoble, France
Andre van der Hoek, University of Colorado at Boulder, USA
Boris Magnusson, Lund Institute of Technology, Sweden
Chris Marlin, Flinders University, Australia
Annita Persson, Ericsson Microwave AB, Sweden
Ian Sommerville, University of Lancaster, United Kingdom
Walter F. Tichy, University of Karlsruhe, Germany

Previus SCM Events

SCM-1 1988, Grassau, Germany
SCM-2 1990, Princeton, USA
SCM-3 1991, Trondheim, Norway
SCM-4 1993, Baltimore, USA
SCM-5 1995, Seattle. USA
SCM-6 1996, Berlin, Germany
SCM-7 1997, Boston, USA

Contents

Formal Approaches

Cooperative Systems

Web Based Applications

Tutorial

Introducing ClearCase as a Process Improvement Experiment

Jens-Otto Larsen[1] and Helge M. Roald[2]

[1] Norwegian University of Science and Technology,
Department of Computer and Information Science,
N-7034 Trondheim, Norway
jensotto@idi.ntnu.no

[2] Sysdeco GIS AS, Postboks 433, N-3601 Kongsberg, Norway
Helge.Roald@sysdeco.no

Abstract. This paper describes the experiences gained in the CMEX project, an ESSI Process Improvement Experiment on revising the change control system in one department of Sysdeco GIS AS, a Norwegian software house. The aim of the project was to install ClearCase, a configuration management system, and to measure and evaluate the impact of the new system on processes and products. This paper describes the company background, CMEX, and some quantitative and qualitative results of the project.

1   Introduction

This document describes the experiences gained and results achieved during the CMEX project. CMEX was a *process improvement experiment* (PIE) within the ESPRIT ESSI, *Software Best Practice*, initiative. A PIE should measure and report on the effect of one specific process improvement step in one company. Process improvement experiments could be to introduce new methods, techniques, tools, or process and organizational changes. The measured results are reported to ESSI and should also be disseminated to a wider community.

CMEX has been concerned with revising the change control system of the graphic tools department of Sysdeco GIS AS (SGIS), a Norwegian software house in the GIS sector (Geographic Information Systems). The earlier configuration management (CM) system, which was based on SCCS and Make, was replaced with ClearCase [3,2], and the change processes, especially those concerned with management of change requests and defect reports were slightly revised. The new CM system was expected to improve the quality and efficiency of the change processes, and to reduce the number of CM-related problem reports and defects. The initial process improvement goals of CMEX were to reduce the number of CM-related defects by 10% and increase the relative development effort by 5%.

The CMEX project was carried out by SGIS in cooperation with the Norwegian University of Science and Technology, assisting in process modeling, measurements, CM system evaluation, and dissemination. The project started early 1996 and went on for 22 months and was recently concluded. ClearCase has been

B. Magnusson (Ed.): ECOOP 98, SCM-8, LNCS 1439, pp. 1–12, 1998.

successfully installed and is being used in development as well as in maintenance of a released product version. The measurement activities have focused on product quality and the maintenance and delivery processes. The project has been successful in meeting the initial goals by a good margin.

In the following sections we will present the company, their products and the current CM practice. We will then describe the motivations for introducing a new change control system and the process of introducing ClearCase. We will then shortly describe the measurement activities within the project, and show some preliminary results, followed by a conclusion.

2   Background

2.1   Company and Products

Sysdeco GIS makes end-user systems for different mapping areas such as topographic mapping, utility mapping, systems for power plants, fleet management (GPS) etc. The customer data base consists of national mapping organizations, power plants, local authorities, utility companies, insurance companies, software houses, etc. Consultants from Sysdeco GIS build end-user applications using a tool-kit made by the graphic tools department at SGIS. However, Sysdeco also sells the tool-kit to other companies. This puts strong requirements to the tool-kit regarding robustness and documentation.

SGIS has around 150 employees in Europe and Asia and 40-50 at the main office in Norway. The graphic tools department is a small product group, consisting of 1 director, 8-10 developers, and 3 persons working on technical support, software building and system administration. Sales and first line support is handled by SGIS.

The graphic tools department delivers two main products: Tellus and Tellus Vision. Tellus, which was originally developed for various UNIX environments in the late 1980's, provides developers with a hybrid raster and vector tool-set for layered color maps and includes a proprietary programming language (TCL) for application dependent code. Tellus is supported on seven different UNIX platforms (HP/UX 9.05, HP/UX 10.01, DEC Ultrix, DEC OSF/1, SUN Solaris, SunOS and IBM AIX) with four database connections (Oracle, Sybase, Mimer and Ingres).

The newest product is Tellus Vision, which in addition to offering Tellus on a PC platform, couples Tellus with QBE Vision, a Microsoft Windows-based 4GL tool-kit. This is also a Sysdeco product. This combination not only makes Tellus available to PC users, but also integrates QBE Vision's 4GL and DBMS functionality as well as the QBE Basic programming language. Tellus Vision is targeted as the main development effort in the future. It is available for Microsoft Windows NT and Windows 95 and supports Oracle, Sybase, Informix, SQL*Server and ODBC databases.

2.2 Configuration Management Practice

The Tellus family of products has been delivered in more than 25 different configurations depending on platform (UNIX, Windows) and database system. This variability has been managed with conditional compilation.

The amount of source code was around 650,000 lines (C, SQL, etc.) in more than 5000 files. In addition, the build system consists of ca. 500 Makefiles, averaging 200 lines. At the start of the project, 3 main versions were supported and new ones were under development. The older versions had undergone more than 30 revisions the two years before the start of CMEX. Except from maintaining an older product version for a single customer, no variants of the source code were developed or maintained.

The source code is organized in modules and each developer is responsible for a number of modules (development, maintenance, unit testing). Product builds, system tests, and deliveries are the responsibilities of the production group. Each developer manages the development source code in the respective modules. When a new version is released, the source code is frozen and entered into source code control. SCCS and strict change control procedures were used for management and version control of source code in released versions.

The maintenance process has been developed along with the product and is functioning well. Change requests and error reports are collected by the development coordinator and recorded in a database, circulated for identification and work-estimation, and then queued. The development coordinator regularly initiates change-jobs in the development group; each job resolving a number of reported errors and implementing other changes. Most likely the change job will also include building and delivering the new product revision on a number of platforms.

When the change-job is finished in the development group, the system administrator takes over, includes the corrected code in the official version and generates the new official release (and a new product revision). This is sent to the QA responsible for testing. When the new revision is accepted, an official version is produced on the appropriate media and shipped to customers requesting the changes.

2.3 Background Summary

The existing change control system worked satisfactorily for the UNIX products, but when the Windows products were introduced, there was no formal configuration system used for the Windows products. The lack of a supporting CM system resulted in a situation where development was depending on manual procedures that easily led to errors and inconsistencies. This was a major technical weakness of the development process.

Another issue has been observed during the project. For the latest version, the products have been rewritten in the C++ programming language. This has resulted in a completely new program structure with some central source files, new dependencies between subsystems, and new patterns of change propagation in the source code. The new structure would have been very difficult to manage with the existing system or with manual routines.

3   The CMEX Project

The overall objective of the project was to measure the effect of introducing a revised formal configuration management and version control system in the software development process. The project was conducted in the graphic tools department at the SGIS main office. The existing tools for configuration management and accompanying routines had been in place for some years.

The project had three phases, *preparation, experiment,* and *evaluation.* The preparation phase carried out at the start of the projects had three main activities: process modeling, measurement of the initial process and product, and CM-system installation. The experiment phase consisted of system introduction and training, system usage and mid-term process adjustments. The evaluation phase measured the improvement results and reported these.

In the following we will briefly discuss some aspects of the project.

3.1   Process Modeling

This activity in the first project phase was concerned with modeling and understanding the work process, suggesting process changes, finding process parameters to be used to evaluate the effects of the new system, and with finding out which measurements were needed and how to perform them.

The maintenance process in SGIS was well defined and mature at the start of the project. The process was documented, and this part of the experiment consisted of collecting process documentation and editing a process model. The model is mostly textual with a number of figures for overviews and clarity of the presentation.

We did not change the work process itself, but changed some of the forms used in the process to be able to measure some aspects that were not recorded in the current process support databases.

3.2   Measurements

To be able to quantify improvement results in CMEX we needed a set of metrics and measurements at the start and the end of the project. We used a GQM-like process [1] to establish candidate metrics, resulting in 16 possible metrics for the products and processes. These were concerned with defect report characteristics, process performance, effort, customers, and change size.

We then reviewed possible data sources to find which measurements could be based on these. The customer database, the defect report database, project databases, and the source code under SCCS all provided good background data for the two previous years, and could be used directly for 7 metrics. Data for 6 process performance metrics were gathered from the system used for following up deliveries, following small adjustments to this. After a dialogue with the development coordinator, it was decided not to use the remaining 3 metrics, all detailing defect characteristics. This was due to the need for a data set covering a longer period than what could be measured during the early phases of the project.

In the initial assessment of the situation, 6 months after the start of the project, we had established data sets for 13 metrics, resulting in a good picture of the product quality and process performance at the start of the project. The results are presented in the next section of the paper. The number of metrics used in the final assessment was further reduced to 5, due to either insignificant data sets or changes that made data incomparable, e.g. a full rewrite of the software and new policies on process follow-up.

3.3   Configuration Management System

The state of the SGIS organization at the start of CMEX could be summarized as follows:

- Long experience with SCCS and a strict change control process.
- Lack of source code control under Windows NT, and an acknowledgment of the fact that a new system was needed.
- Acknowledgment of the needs for more advanced CM functionality, especially for rebuilding former product revisions and handling product variants.
- Acknowledgment of problems with the build and delivery systems.
- Some skepticism towards the performance and cost/benefit of ClearCase, mostly based on reviews and rumors from other companies.

ClearCase had already been chosen as the CM system when the project application was submitted. However, as a part of the process of motivating the personnel for a new CM system, we stated the requirements to a new system, and ran a brief evaluation of a simpler system, Microsoft Visual SourceSafe, and ClearCase.

The evaluation considered functionality, performance, scalability, cost and user confidence. The conclusion was in favor of ClearCase and the evaluation helped remove the initial skepticism.

System Introduction The steps followed in introducing ClearCase were the following: Training of the system administrator, who would act as the ClearCase administrator. Using ClearCase on a pilot-project, a smaller product add-on to Tellus. Then the source code was gradually transferred to ClearCase while working contexts for developers were established. Training of developers was done internally in a very short time, mostly due to the fact that the system was easy to use through a good integration with the development environment, Microsoft Visual C++.

The first part of this phase took considerably more time and resources than expected, mostly due to problems with timing and arranging training of the system administrator. A fortunate side-effect of the delay was that we could start using a new and more user-friendly version of ClearCase. We believe that the new version of ClearCase made the transition simpler. Once the system was put into use, developers embraced the new system. This is partly due to the user-friendliness and a better than expected performance, but also the acute need of a CM system in the development of the new C++ version of the tool-kit.

The installation of ClearCase also required extensive upgrades of the technical environment, both workstations and servers. It also soon became apparent that more licenses were needed than the 5 that were originally purchased. The final configuration has one license for each of the 8 developers using ClearCase.

4 Results and Analysis

An important part of ESSI projects is to gather and analyze results from the project and report these. In our case we used the following metrics to measure the process improvement:

- *Defect report arrival rate:* number of defect reports received per month. The metric was used for externally reported defects as well as internal ones, i.e. defects reported by the development group or the testing teams.
- *Defect report priority:* distribution of reports between the 5 priority levels used in SGIS.
- *Defect fix time:* Average number of days used to fix high-priority defects.
- *Resource usage:* resource usage for main activities.
- *Maintenance effort:* detailed resource usage for maintenance-related tasks.

In addition to the quantitative results measured by the metrics above, a questionnaire to the users was used to get an impression of the human factors of introducing a new system in a well-established development department.

The overall aims for the CMEX project was stated in the application to "Introducing a formal change control system is believed to improve the process, resulting in 5% shorter time-to-market and a 10% reduction in error reports for the software products". The measurement results show a significant improvement, higher than what was planned. In the following these results of the data analysis will be elaborated and discussed.

4.1 Technical

The main quantitative results from the projects are:

- *Defect report arrival rate:* The arrival rate of external defect reports went from 12.1 reports/month during 1995/96 to 7.8 in 1997, a reduction of 36% (high-priority reports went down 31% while the rate of lower-priority/change requests went down 45

  The arrival rate of internally reported defects increased by 132%, mostly due to the testing of a new product version. But an increase in urgent reports by 40% also indicates that more defects were found internally.

An interesting observation was that 11% of the external reports were in fact not defects, but user misunderstandings etc. 3.5% of the reports were duplicates, reporting the same defect.

- *Defect report priority:* The share of high-priority reports (the two highest priority levels) was nearly constant, rising from 61% to 64% of the reports received.
- *Defect fix time:* The average time taken to process and fix urgent defects went down 6%
  For internally found defects the reduction was 54%, most probably as a result of a reduction of the workload.
- *Resource usage:* The total resource usage for the graphic tools department was nearly constant during 1996 and 1997, with only a few personnel changes. Comparing figures for 1996 and 1997, we find that the share of resources spent on development has increased by 22%, while maintenance work went down by 33%. More resources were also made available for external projects. This change is mainly due to the lower arrival rate of defect reports, and the consequence has been that more functionality than planned was included in a new tool version.
- *Maintenance effort:* A more detailed study of the 33% decrease in maintenance effort, shows the expected decrease in effort spent on correcting defects, and that more effort has been spent on support and testing. However, significantly less effort has been spent on system building, deliveries and system maintenance, the exact areas where ClearCase was expected to contribute to the improvement.

In summary, fewer external defect reports are received and the effort spent on maintenance is correspondingly reduced. More effort is spent on testing, resulting in a higher number of defects being found internally. This indicates that the desired shift in the process has been achieved. The original goals have been met with a very good margin. In addition, ClearCase has helped in automating source code and system management as well as making the building step more efficient.

In terms of qualitative improvements we will mention:

- The process modeling activities at the start of the project resulted in a better understanding of the maintenance process, and, following a discussion, a number of process changes, mostly concerning responsibilities and use of report forms. SGIS has been following a quite formal maintenance process for some time, and this experiment activity played an important role in clarifying some of the loosely defined parts of the process.
- When installing ClearCase, SGIS also revised its Make-based production and delivery systems and this activity resulted in improved quality of the production and delivery services of Sysdeco GIS.
- The introduction of ClearCase has resulted in an increased ability of reconstructing previous product revisions.
- The measurement activities have resulted in a better understanding about the performance of the maintenance processes and the costs involved. SGIS

continues to assemble process data and uses the metrics as a basis for further process improvements, leading to a higher process maturity of the company.

The reported improvements can not be attributed to the introduction of ClearCase alone. We should state that 1996 was an exceptional year in terms of changes: in addition to work on introducing ClearCase, the company was restructured, and a number of product versions were released on new platforms. We do believe that the experiment has triggered an increased awareness of the importance of the maintenance process, and that improvements to some degree can be attributed to the whole project.

4.2 Business

The major business outcomes of the experiment has been a significant improvement of the quality and efficiency (cost and time) of the maintenance services and process. There has been a 33% decrease of maintenance effort, mostly corresponding to the fewer defect reports. As a result, significant resources have been made available for development activities, an increase of 22% from 48% of the total human resource usage in 1996 to 58% in 1997. Defining "time-to-market" in terms of available development effort, we have achieved an improvement much higher than what was expected.

We have also saved significant maintenance costs. ClearCase is expensive compared to a simple version control system. The costs of purchase, training, installation and administration are high. A mature development group with a size similar to our, with a well-founded change process will need to allocate 100-200 kECU (European Currency Unit) to acquire ClearCase and get the system up and running. ClearCase by itself can not be expected to improve the product quality, but accompanied by a formal change management process improvements might be expected.

One way to calculate the return of investment is to compare the costs mentioned over with the reduced costs for correcting errors. This can be done by using the formula $R = I/(P*N)$, where R = number of months to regain the investment I, I = invested capital, P = price to correct an error, N = reduction in number of errors/month. In our case we have reduced the number of errors by 4.3/month (=N), from 12.1/month to 7.8/month. The cost for correcting an error (P) has been estimated in average to be 5000 ECU (40 man-hours at 125 ECU/hour). Seemingly high, the figure however includes first line support of the customer (usually abroad), as well as second line support, correction, testing and shipment. By applying the formula above, we regain an investment of 150 kECU in 7 months.

4.3 Organization

The experiment has so far only had a very small impact on the organizational environment. The maintenance process has undergone some changes in terms of more clearly defined responsibilities and tasks, and introduction of some additional forms to support the change process. The reason for this might be that SGIS is a mature organization with a long experience in product change management and in using simpler version control and production systems. The process changes connected to the experiment have been perceived as a natural part of the continuously ongoing discussion of the company's processes.

There was some initial skepticism towards introducing a large and complex system as ClearCase, but when exposed to the functionality of ClearCase the system was acknowledged as superior to the alternative of keeping the existing system. This is mainly due to the following factors:

1. The existing software was ported from UNIX to NT, where the old configuration management system was not available.
2. Given the number of platforms and database systems, the product matrix has become complex to manage.
3. The transition to an object-oriented design has dramatically changed the propagation of source code changes and requires a new way of managing source code; something that has been helped by using a sophisticated system.

At the end of the project all personnel involved in the project answered a questionnaire about various aspects of the process of introducing ClearCase. The general opinion was acknowledged need for a new CM-system, some dissatisfaction with the process of selecting ClearCase and with training, and a very positive reception of ClearCase once in use. The users clearly stated that they have better CM system and that it has improved the working environment and cooperation within the group.

5   Key Lessons

5.1   Technological Point of View

ClearCase Introduction ClearCase is a large system and requires in-depth training of system administrators and source code managers before it is installed. It is of crucial importance to plan for a long introduction period and use the time to prepare the organization. One possible introduction process is to make the involved personnel define the problems and requirements to the new process and support tools, and then evaluate candidate tools.

Training of the users is also required and more time should have been spent on this. Also the number of software licenses must be relevant from the start of the introduction. Our experience is one license for every user. Although the system allows sharing of licenses, it makes the system unusable.

It has also become evident that the management of product changes is far more dependent on a rigorous and accepted work process than on the tools used to support the process. The success of the experiment so far is largely dependent on the fact a work process was already in place. In another setting, the experiment might have failed or taken considerably more effort.

We believe that it is important that the ClearCase system administrator is given enough time to get acquainted with the system so that the installation is stable when other personnel start using the system. Otherwise, the attitude towards the new system could quickly have become negative. In terms of technology, ClearCase has many advanced features, and these should be taken into use gradually.

A related issue is that the management of defect reports and other change-related items is equally as time-consuming and error-prone as the management of file versions. The lesson regarding this issue is that support tools for managing defect reports, orders, and product revision availability lists might also be a cost-effective investment.

Process Modeling Defining the work process is a time-consuming task, which should be paid much attention to. It is important to assure that one ends up with an agreement on how the work is going to be carried out. The different groups involved in the work process might have quite different views on what is done at each process step and whose responsibility it is. The process modeling activity is an excellent opportunity to discuss these views and arrive at an agreement or even revised process definitions.

Measurements The measurement activities have required far more effort than originally planned. This is due to the facts that existing data do not lend themselves to direct use in measurement, and that parts of the data required to measure success are not present. To get a relevant data basis one has to measure the process over a period of time.

We have also learned that new measurement efforts are useless unless the data collection is an integral part of the ordinary work process. In our case we have solved this by extracting data from new and existing lists and databases used for managing defect reports and orders.

Another issue is that metrics based on error reports will have an inherent delay in showing the effects of a process or technology change. The time from an improvement step is implemented to the product is in use at customer sites yielding defect reports may take as long as 3-5 months

5.2   Business Point of View

The major business outcomes of the experiment has been a significant improvement of the quality and efficiency (cost and time) of the maintenance services and process. As a result, significant resources have been made available for development activities and we have been able to bring new functionality to the market earlier than expected. The configuration management system is not expected to improve product quality by itself, but the increased focus on maintenance (costs and resource usage) has lead to fewer product defects.

From a business point of view, ClearCase, would not have been the obvious choice since this system is more expensive than other systems. Our most obvious alternative would have been Visual SourceSafe from Microsoft that cost about 1/7 of ClearCase's. ClearCase is a complex system to understand and it takes time to understand the advantages over simpler systems in our setting. This was not obvious at the beginning of the project, but is clear now. The cost of the system has proven to be insignificant in comparison to the potential for improvements.

Due to the cost, ClearCase may initially seem more suited in larger companies supporting several products on a variety of platforms. However, we do believe that ClearCase is a good investment for a group of 8-12 people developing and maintaining medium-sized products, both in business terms and in improving the process and working environment. We also believe that CMEX will have internal effects in Sysdeco GIS by setting an example that may encourage other leaders to focus on the complexity of the development issues and economics of tool investments.

5.3   Strengths and Weaknesses of the Experiment

The most obvious strength of the experiment has been the maturity of the organization and the fact that the involved personnel had acknowledged the need for a new change control system. The process of motivation the personnel for using ClearCase was a distinct phase, but it was simplified by these facts.

The most obvious weakness has been the lack of background statistics over the last few years. This has lead to much effort being spent on data collection and analysis. Another issue has been the extraordinary events during the experiment: a company restructuring, change of primary development and supply platform, along with unusually frequent product releases has left small and fragmented time-frames for training, installation and deployment of ClearCase.

CMEX has also been an example of cooperation between a university and industry. NTNU has contributed with knowledge on configuration management, process modeling and measurements, and gained valuable experience in using techniques and tools in practice.

6   Conclusions

This paper has described the background of CMEX, and experiences gained so far in a two-year project evaluating the benefits of revising the change control system in a small, but mature software enterprise. The experiment introduced ClearCase to the graphic tools department of Sysdeco GIS AS, Norway, developing software for the mapping industry or GIS sector.

The company has a strictly defined change process that has been based on the use of SCCS and a few process support/follow-up systems. Over the last year, the development platform has changed and the lack of CM support on the new platform has had consequences for the quality of the change process.

The goal of the experiment was to reduce the number of error reports by 10% and the "time-to-market" by 5%. The experiment shows significant better results than these goals: The number of defect reports received per month has been reduced by 36%, urgent defects are fixed in 6% less time, and the development effort has increased by 22%. The latter two improvements contributing to bring new products quicker to the market.

In addition, the effort spent on maintenance has been reduced by 33%, although more effort is spent on testing and more defects are found internally. System building and management functions have been automated and made more efficient. The user confidence in the system is high, and the new CM system has also helped improve cooperation in the group.

Apart from the result above, the key lessons from the experiment have been:

- The costs of introducing ClearCase were recovered in a short time, less than a year, much less than expected.
- To introduce the new configuration tool, ClearCase, was more difficult than anticipated. Careful planning and experimenting took more time than planned and caused more problems for the developers than expected.
- Well-established routines for handling errors and an experienced development group both significantly contributed to the success of the experiment.
- Relevant background data to measure the improvement was harder to collect than anticipated. It took more time and required also more effort to analyze than expected.

The success of the experiment makes it evident to continue to use the new system in our development and maintenance of our products. It has become evident that tools to support the change request management parts of the process are important in terms of quality and efficiency. The acquisition and deployment of such tools will be considered as a next improvement step. We have also identified new areas for improvements and we will in the near future start a similar experiment introducing automatic testing tools.

This experiment is relevant for SMBs planning to introduce new tools in their development department, especially configuration management tools.

References

1. Basili, V., Caldiera, G., Rombach, H.D. Goal Question Metric Paradigm. In Encyclopedia of Software Engineering. John Wiley & Sons, (1994).
2. http://www.rational.com/products/clearcase
3. Leblang, D.B. The CM Challenge: Configuration Management that Works. In [4], chapter 1, pages 1–37. John Wiley & Sons (1994).
4. Tichy, W.F., editor: Configuration Management (Trends in software). John Wiley & Sons (1994).

Industrial Experiences from SCM Current State Analysis

Tua Rahikkala[1], Jorma Taramaa[1], and Antti Välimäki[2]

[1] VTT Electronics and
INFOTECH OULU, Software Process Improvement Research Action Laboratory
(SPIRAL)
Kaitoväylä 1, P.O.Box 1100
FIN-90571 Oulu, FINLAND
E-mail: {Tua.Rahikkala, Jorma.Taramaa}@vtt.fi
www: http://www.ele.vtt.fi

[2] Valmet Automation Inc., Lentokentänkatu 11, P.O. Box 237
FIN-33101 Tampere, FINLAND
E-mail: Antti.Valimaki@valmet.com
www: http://www.valmet.com/automation

Abstract. This paper describes a systematic approach for collecting and analysing software configuration management (SCM) requirements. The analysis is based on Pr2imer, *Pr*actical *Pr*ocess *Im*provement for *E*mbedded *R*eal-Time Software, which is a framework for process improvement. Pr2imer applies interviews for qualitative analysis and assessment, such as BOOTSTRAP, for quantitative analysis. It also includes a Goal/Question/Metrics (GQM)-based approach for identifying goals for new practices. An industrial experiment employing SCM requirements analysis has been carried out in the VISCOUNT[1] project. The results of requirements analysis, and the advantages of the approach are presented, including a plan for future, work where virtual software corporations will be supported by advanced SCM systems.

1 Introduction

Large, multi-site, multi-organisation, software development projects in virtual software corporations (VSC) [3, 6], and their special needs with respect to managing the SCM process and supporting project team activities, are challenging tasks. In many cases, organisations try to solve their SCM problems by acquiring SCM tools,

---

[1] VISCOUNT (*Vi*rtual *S*oftware *Co*rporation *Un*iversal *T*estbed) is an EU/Esprit project 25754. The core technical objective of the VISCOUNT project is to develop a configuration management tool for use in a geographically distributed environment. The tool development is based on software configuration management (SCM) process analysis, modelling, improvement and measurement in industrial organisations [12].

B. Magnusson (Ed.): ECOOP 98, SCM-8, LNCS 1439, pp. 13-25, 1998

and often they have a large list of requirements for such tools [5]. One of the reasons that problems do not disappear by tool acquisition can be traced back to not understanding the SCM process and its links to other processes, and thus, the real requirements of the organisation [1, 5, 15]. Therefore, a systematic approach for SCM requirements analysis is needed.

The framework used in our industrial case is Pr2imer, *Practical Process Improvement for Embedded Real*-Time Software [10], which is an approach to process improvement developed at VTT Electronics. Pr2imer uses the goal-oriented measurement paradigm GQM (Goal/Question/Metric) [2] to analyse and define the current state and problems, improvement goals, and metrics of software processes. In this work, the focus of the Pr2imer approach is on SCM. Therefore, we call our approach **SCM-Pr2imer**.

Chapter 2 of this paper describes the industrial context of the work and explains the background and goals for SCM requirements analysis. Chapter 3 briefly analyses the SCM-Pr2imer framework, SCM concepts, and SCM-Pr2imer's view to requirement analysis. Chapter 4 presents the current state analysis in the industrial case, and chapter 5 includes the conclusions and lessons learned.

2   The Approach

In the figure below, the SCM-Pr2imer framework and the main SCM concepts are briefly described.

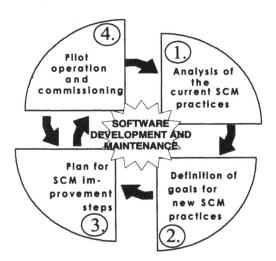

Fig. 1. SCM-Pr2imer.

2.1   The SCM-Pr2imer Framework

Practical Process Improvement for Embedded Real-Time Software [10] is a systematic approach to improving the quality of the software process. It fully integrates software process analysis, modelling, improvement, and measurement techniques. SCM-Pr2imer addresses the SCM-related activities of the software process by supporting the four steps described in Figure 1.

An important step towards successfully adopting SCM tools is to understand the processes that the tools and methods should support. In this paper, the first step of SCM-Pr2imer is proposed as a method for analysing and collecting industrial requirements for SCM.

The analysis of the current SCM practices consists of both quantitative and qualitative analysis (Fig. 2). Quantitative analysis is carried out by the use of, for example, SCM-focused parts of the BOOTSTRAP [11], SPICE [9] or CMM [7] assessment methods.

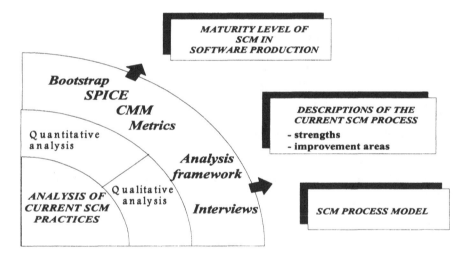

Fig. 2. The first phase of SCM-Pr2imer.

Qualitative analysis is done by follow-up of the actual work and by using the analysis framework, which can be applied by an assessment consultant or by the company itself. Qualitative analysis results in the description of the current SCM process.

2.2   SCM-Pr2imer Concepts

SCM processes are classified in various standards, e.g., ISO/IEC 12207 [8] and ISO/IEC 15504 (SPICE-project) [9]. Both standards have the so-called support process category, which includes the configuration management process. SCM processes are typically categorised and described as follows [1, 4, 12]:

Table 1. SCM processes.

SCM processes	Description
Version control	〈 Identifying and defining the configuration items for the product (configuration identification). 〈 Recording and reporting the status of configuration items and change requests (configuration status accounting).
Configuration audit	〈 Verifying and validating completion and correctness of these items.
Change control	〈 Controlling all changes to these items throughout the product's life cycle.
Manufacturing	〈 Software manufacturing based on conventional builders (traditional compiling and linking technique)
SCM-planning	〈 SCM described as a defined process.

The SCM processes have, however, links to other processes, and it is vital to understand the entire SCM-related process area for developing, improving, measuring, and automating SCM. In this work, we used the SPICE process categories as a basis for SCM classification:
〈 Customer Supplier category   (CUS)
〈 Engineering process category   (ENG)
〈 Support process category (SUP)
〈 Management process category   (MAN)
〈 Organisation process category   (ORG).

The purpose of the analysis of the current state of SCM is to consider all processes in the context of the SCM-Pr2imer framework (Fig. 3). The functions of different processes are evaluated and described, if they are essential for understanding the SCM view. This aspect is one of the main features of the SCM-Pr2imer analysis framework.

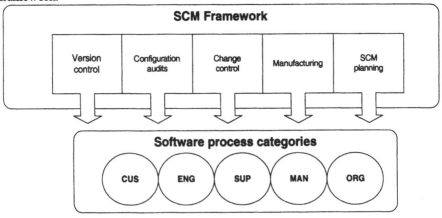

Fig. 3. SCM framework and software process categories.

3   Industrial Context

The software engineering environment of Valmet Automation, Inc.[2] (later referred to as VAT) has been changing over the past few years. There are many parallel development and maintenance projects, which operate in a distributed environment, and product supply has also been disseminated [14]. Examples of product specific features are that the systems must work in a multi-platform environment and that customer-specific variations are required.

The software processes and environment of VAT were evaluated against the SPICE standard a while ago. According to this assessment and other analyses, the improvement of the SCM process and SCM-related processes were seen as important at VAT. An SCM-Pr2imer based improvement program was started in the VISCOUNT project [13].

4   Experiences

In the following, the progress and results of analysis of the current state of SCM at VAT are described. The analysis was undertaken in the following phases:

1. Analysis planning
2. Interviews
3. Feedback session I
4. Quantitative assessment
5. Feedback session II and planning of work continuation

4.1   Analysis Planning

At the beginning, a planning meeting was held for the purpose of defining the goals and developing a work plan for the analysis. The participants of the planning meeting were representatives of VAT and the SCM-Pr2imer team.

The analysis was limited to maintenance projects, development projects, the logistics department and the management of these activities. In the planning meeting, the projects and the individuals to be interviewed were selected. It was important to select the different views of projects, such as those of project leaders, designers, programmers, quality assurance people, and test managers.

---

[2] Valmet Automation, Inc. is a part of Valmet Corporation. It develops and supplies control and management systems for, pulp and paper industry, chemical and petrochemical industries, and power and desulphurisation plants. These control and management systems are complex and software-intensive products in a very demanding market, where high reliability and quality are key competitive factors. VAT has manufacturing, engineering, sales, and customer support units in 27 countries in Europe, North and South America, Africa, Asia, and Australia.

4.2   Interviews

The qualitative analysis of SCM-Pr2imer was made by using a structured interviewing technique. The earlier SPICE assessment results were available. The SPICE SUP2 (Perform configuration management) process was assessed on the project level and, based on the assessment, some improvement actions were presented. The interviews were held in four sessions. Before each session, the purpose and goals of the analysis were reviewed with the interviewees. During the interviews, the workflows (e.g. the personal processes of the engineering category of the SPICE standard) of all interviewees were examined, but the focus was on SCM (Fig. 3) and VSC. Examples of the SCM focused questions used at the project engineering (SPICE engineering category) level are presented in Table 2. The questions are based on the definition of SCM processes and SCM Pr2imer framework, as well as our experiences in the application area and BOOTSTRAP assessments.

Table 2. Examples of SCM focused questions.

SCM element	Questions
Configuration identification	〈 How is the source code managed and identified? Is there any support tool? 〈 Are all the required documents described (e.g., templates)? 〈 Do identification standards exist? 〈 Are there any roles for product labelling? 〈 How are version numbers formed? 〈 Test material identification (especially in critical cases). 〈 How are the requirements for the configuration items (CI) stated and how is the design is documented? 〈 Are process baselines clearly defined? 〈 Are practices for information changes described? 〈 Do documents meet the needs?
Configuration status accounting	〈 Is there any method for recording and reporting the status of configuration items (source code, documents, etc.)? Is there any tool support? 〈 Error follow-up. 〈 Is there any method to follow the status of errors and proposed changes? 〈 The implementation status of approved changes.
Configuration audits	〈 Are functional configuration audits defined? 〈 Is there any method to verify that the CI conforms to the technical documentation that defines it? (physical audits) 〈 Is the SCM process established in an organisation being followed? Are improvements needed?

Change control	⟨ Are persons responsible for changes identified (approval/disapproval of changes)?
	⟨ Are methods/practices used to trace changes defined?
	⟨ Are there any links between various information and the configuration items?
	⟨ Is there any formal method or explicit practices for the registration of information changes (e.g., error messages from different places)?
	⟨ Is there any tool support to manage changes?
	⟨ Is the change process formally described?
	⟨ Is the error registration process formally described?
	⟨ Is there any method to manage change proposals?
	⟨ Is there any method to manage interface changes?
	⟨ How is parallel development managed?
	⟨ Are there formal methods or rules for managing test information (test plans, test cases, test results, etc.)?
	⟨ Is the supply process of documents described? Are responsible persons defined?
Software manufacturing	⟨ Are there mechanisms or methods for software manufacturing? Tool support?
	⟨ How are releases managed?
SCM plan	⟨ Are the base instructions and practices described?
	⟨ Are there other common standards or practices?
	⟨ Are the responsibilities clear?
	⟨ Do the practices vary depending on a person or a situation?
	⟨ Are the standards fully in use?
	⟨ Is there a project level SCM plan?

The corresponding classification of questions was used, when the representatives of the logistics department were interviewed, but the SPICE process view used was the Customer-Supply category. The management process of the SPICE standard includes the following processes: manage project, manage quality, manage risks, and manage subcontractors. In the SPICE standard, each of these processes is estimated in the context of configuration management. The basic question for each process is (SPICE: Level 2): 'Are the configuration of process work products managed?'. The objective is to ensure the integrity of all work products.

The processes of the management process category (MAN) were evaluated in the context of the above question, and be employing the SCM-Pr2imer framework during the interviews. In Table 3, some questions for each process are described.

Table 3. Examples of the SCM questions in the context of the MAN process category.

Management process category	Questions
Manage the Project	⟨ Are base practices and work products for projects defined? ⟨ Are there any common rules for the documents of the project management process? ⟨ Can the documents be identified? ⟨ Is the status information of the documents defined? ⟨ In-process audits? ⟨ Is information of the version history defined? ⟨ Where are the documents stored? ⟨ Are the responsible persons of the documents defined?
Manage quality	⟨ Are the quality goals defined and identified? ⟨ Are the metrics of the quality goals defined? Is there any method for measurement? ⟨ Are the responsible persons defined?
Manage risks	⟨ Are the practices and methods of risk management described? ⟨ Is the risk information updated (the identification of the risk information and the risk actions)? ⟨ Are the risks followed? ⟨ Are the persons responsible for specific risks named?
Manage subcontractors	⟨ Are the managing practices for subcontractors described? ⟨ Management of contracts? ⟨ The identification and status of contracts? ⟨ Are there other documents for managing subcontractors? ⟨ The management, identification, and status of other work products? ⟨ Are the responsible persons of subcontractor management named? ⟨ Are reviews of the subcontractors conducted?

After the interviews, an analysis report was written and sent to the interviewees for their comments.

4.3   Feedback Session I

Requirement analysis included two feedback sessions. Both sessions employed the following steps:

1. Data aggregation and preparation of slides (SCM-Pr2imer team)
2. Slide evaluation and selection for presentation (SCM-Pr2imer team)
3. Slides distribution to interviewees
4. Feedback session
5. Evaluation of the feedback session together with interviewees
6. Evaluation of the feedback session (SCM-Pr2imer team).

The first feedback session was held after the comment round and document correction. The purpose of this session was to make sure that the SCM-Pr2imer team had understood all answers and comments and that all relevant information was presented. Another aspect of the first feedback session was to classify preliminarily the main problems and improvement areas for further work.

4.4   Quantitative Assessment

The quantitative assessment was made in three phases:
1. Analysing the results of the earlier SPICE assessment
2. Current state assessment by use of the SCM-Pr2imer questions
3. SCM-focused BOOTSTRAP assessment.

Analysing the Previous Assessments
At the beginning, the SCM-Pr2imer team obtained the results of the earlier quantitative assessments that had been carried out at VAT. The SCM problems and potential improvement areas were collected and their current state was evaluated.

Current State Assessment by Use of the SCM-Pr2imer Framework
The first quantitative assessment was made by evaluating the current SCM practices through the use of the SCM-Pr2imer questions lists and the previous qualitative analysis. An example of the evaluation, based on one interview at VAT, is shown in Table 4. The strengths and weaknesses of each of the analysed practices were evaluated by using the following estimation levels: N = Not achieved, P = Partially achieved, L = Largely achieved, F = Fully achieved, NA = Not applicable.

Table 4. Example of the evaluation process.

+ Practices are OK.
− Situation is seen as a problem by project participants.
? Practices should be identified and/or defined more accurately. The influence of the current situation on the SCM process is unclear, and it can cause problems later.

SCM element	Strengths/Weaknesses and remarks	Level
Configuration identification	+ Source codes are managed and identified by a CM tool (Clear Case).	F
	+ The types of configuration documentation required for each CI are determined (Quality Manual).	
	+ Version numbering standard is described.	
	+ Documents are updated and identified.	
	− At the development phase, no formal project level instructions or rules for labeling exist.	
	− Test material identification (in critical cases)?	
	− Change history information in the development phase?	
	? The right level for the change history information (code and documents)?	

Configuration status accounting	+ CM tool support (recording and reporting the status of the versioned elements) + The Quality Manual includes a list of the required documents. + Documents are updated and reviewed after each development phase. ? Recording and reporting the status of the documents during the development phase? ? Status of proposed changes? ? The implementation status of approved changes?	L
Configuration audits	+ Functional configuration audits are defined. ? Verification to that the CI conforms the technical documentation that defines it (physical audits)? ? In-process audits (is the SCM process established in the organisation being followed? Improvements needed?).	L
Change control	+ The responsible persons have been determined (product manager, project manager, etc.). + Parallel development is managed by the CM tool. + The responsible persons for each element are defined (not formally). + Tool support for fault management. + The responsible persons for fault management are defined. − The information process for changes is not formally described. − Formal descriptions of practices are missing in many cases. ? The traceability of the changes (automation?).	L
Software manufacturing	+ ClearCase tool support. − The version manufacturing process is not effective. Lacks are found in almost every product version after its building, and the time spent on the building process is too long.	L
SCM plan	+ The Quality Manual includes the basic instructions + There are also some other instructions, such as naming standards, programming recipes, etc. + The standard development process is described. − The practices vary depending on the person or situation (there are need for more formal instructions and rules in many cases). ? Are the standards fully in use? ? The project level SCM plan?	F

The kind of quantitative evaluation results shown in Table 4 were put together at VAT, and the final results and remarks were reported and documented. The main improvement areas of VAT were identified:

1. The version manufacturing process is not effective. Lacks are found in almost every product version after they are built, and the time spent on a building process is too long. This is an even bigger problem when sub-product versions are built at different sites.
2. When working in the VSC, VAT's information sharing between project participants is not effective in all cases, and the practices vary depending on projects and individuals. This causes rework and misunderstandings.
3. Changes are not always documented, and the documentation practices are not clear. The traceability of changes is not complete. Formal instructions and methods are needed. Practices for remote sites should be planned and defined more accurately.
4. The special requirements and properties of SCM within VAT's VSC are not really known or identified. This causes uncertainty and raises questions about whether VAT's SCM tools and the ways of using them are effective and adequately useful.

Focused BOOTSTRAP Assessment
The SCM-focused BOOTSTRAP assessment was madefor both the project and the logistics department. The BOOTSTRAP results and the earlier evaluations were along the same lines as the SCM-Pr2imer results.

4.5   Feedback Session II and the Planning of the Continuation Work

The second feedback and planning session was held after the quantitative results were completed and documented. The purpose of this session was to present the assessment results to the interviewed persons team and to propose the preliminary plan for continuation work.

5   Conclusions and Lessons Learned

SCM-Pr2imer is a GQM-based approach to the analysis and improvement of the SCM processes and SCM related processes. The first step towards implementing successful software development tools and using them in an organisation *is to understand the software development process that the tools should support*. In this paper, we have presented the first step of SCM-Pr2imer, which aims at analysing and describing the SCM practices, problems, and objectives for improvement. The benefits of the systematic approach are visible when analysing and collecting requirements to improve SCM. We have assembled the benefits and remarks in the following list:

1. The analysis is based on the needs and problems of the *real projects and organisation units*. Therefore, the planned improvement actions affect the real processes.
2. The representative persons of the organisation are being involved from the beginning in the improvement cycle. Therefore, *commitment* to the actions is strengthened.
3. The *awareness* of SCM and its influence on process and product quality increases inside the organisation.
4. All software processes cannot be improved at the same time. The SCM-focused improvement program *restricts the improvement area,* so that the actions easier to focus on, measure, and follow.
5. The SCM-Pr2imer framework uses *well known process classifications and standards*. Therefore, the framework is familiar to the representative people of the organisations, and the evaluation and assessment results can be fully exploited, e.g., SPICE assessments and ISO certification.
6. SCM-Pr2imer offers *an approach for further work, result analysis and measurement*.
7. The *formal instructions and methods* play an essential role in SCM.
8. The *information process* is critical within VSC, and therefore, e.g., SCM process descriptions, well defined practices, and SCM tool support are needed.

The SCM process improvement of VAT is continuing. The next actions will be:
⟨ The SCM process and the SCM related processes are modelled by using the use case technique. The purpose of the use case models is to document the processes and the roles the users play in the organisation. The ultimate goal is to support understanding and communication in organisations within the VSC.
⟨ The improvement goals, actions, metrics, and measurement methods are planned by using the GQM method. The plans are based on the results of the current state analysis.
⟨ The revised SCM practices, methods, and tools are adopted in pilot projects, and the improvements are measured according to the GQM-based measurement plan.
⟨ The pilot projects exploit the described use cases. At the same time, the SCM tools, especially Lifespan[3], are being tested and analysed.
⟨ The results of the piloting phase and measurements are analysed carefully and the SCM-Pr2imer cycle may start again.

Acknowledgments

We are grateful to Mrs. Anne Lilja, Mr. Tapio Hautala, Mr. Hannu Koistinen, Mr. Markku Tyynelä, Mr. Jouko Vuorenpää, Mr. Janne Miettinen, Mr. Kari Heino, Mr. Juha Viljamaa, Mr. Kari Kieloaho, Mr. Kari Lehtiranta, and Mr. Tapani Syrjänen of

---

[3] LifespanTM is a trademark of BAeSEMA Ltd. Lifespan is an SCM tool which will be developed further in the VISCOUNT project.

Valmet Automation Oy for their contribution to the current state analysis and to Mr. Lawrence M. Brown for language checking. Special thanks to Prof. Veikko Seppänen of VTT Electronics for his comments.

References

1. Auer, A., Taramaa, J. Experience Report on the Maturity of Configuration Management for Embedded Software, In: I. Sommerville (ed.), The 6th International Workshop on Software Configuration Management (SCM6), Berlin, Germany, March 1996, Published by Lecture Notes in Computer Science 1167, Springer Verlag, Heidelberg, Germany, pp. 187-197.
2. Basili, V.R., Caldiera, G. and Rombach, H. D. The goal question metric approach, in Encyclopedia of Software Engineering, John Wiley & Sons, 1994.
3. Boldyreff, C., Newman, J., Taramaa, J. Managing Process Improvement in Virtual Software Corporations, In: Proceedings of the 5th Workshops on Enabling Technologies: Infrastructure for Collaborative Applications (WET ICE '96), Stanford, California, June 1996, IEEE Computer Society Press, pp. 142-147.
4. Dart, S.A. Concepts in Configuration Management Systems, In: Feiler, P.H. (ed.), Proceedings of the 3rd International Workshop on Software Configuration Management (SCM3), Trondheim, Norway, June 1991, ACM Press, Baltimore, Maryland, pp. 1-18
5. Dart, S.A., Adopting an Automated Configuration Management Solution, the Eight International Workshop on Computer-Aided Software Engineering (CASE'95), Toronto, Ontario, July 1995, an invited speech, 15 p
6. Davidow, W.H. and Malone, M.S. The Virtual Corporation: Structuring and Revitalizing the Corporation for the 21st Century. Harper Business, New York, 1992, 294 p
7. Humphrey, W.S. Characterizing the Software Process: A Maturity Framework, IEEE Software, Vol. 5, No. 3, 1988, pp. 73-79
8. ISO/IEC 12207. Informational Technology - Software Life Cycle Processes, International Standard, ISO/IEC Copyright Office, Geneva, Switzerland, 1995, 57 p.
9. ISO/IEC 15504. SPICE - Software Process Assessment - Part 5: Construction, Selection and Use of Assessment Instruments and Tools, Version 1.00, ISO/IEC Copyright Office, Geneva, Switzerland, 1995, 130 p.
10.Karjalainen, J., Mäkäräinen, M., Komi-Sirviö, S. and Seppänen, V., Practical process improvement for embedded real-time software. Quality Engineering, Vol. 8, No. 4, 1996, pp. 565-573.
11.Kuvaja, P., Similä, J., Kraznik, L., Bicego A., Saukkonen S. and Koch, G. BOOTSTRAP: Europe's Assessment Method, Blackwell, Oxford, UK, 1994, 149 p
12.Tichy, W. Tools for Software Configuration Management, International Workshop on Software Version and Configuration Control, Grassau, Germany, January 1988, In: Winkler J.F.H. (ed.), the German Chapter of the ACM, Vol. 30, Teubner Verlag, pp. 1-31.
13.VISCOUNT, EU/Esprit project 25754 Project Plan Version 4.1 - 21 July, 1997.
14.Välimäki, A., Confmanag - Enhancing software configuration management for the process control system, MID-TERM report, EU/ESSI project 23891 - 28.11.1997.
15.Wein M., MacKay S.A., Stewart D.A., Gauthier C.-A., Gentleman W.M. Evolution is essential for software tool development, Proceedings of the Seventh International Workshop on Computer-Aided Software Engineering, Toronto, Ontario, Canada, July 10-14, 1995, pp. 196-205.

Change Measurements in an SCM Process

Ivica Crnkovic, ivica@sw.seisy.abb.se, ABB Industrial Systems, Västerås, Sweden

Per Willför, dat95pwr@idt.mdh.se, Mälardalens Högskola, Västerås, Sweden

Abstract. An SCM database contains data which can be used as input for Software Metrics. Both data for Size-Oriented Metrics, and information for Process-Oriented Metrics are available from SCM systems. This paper describes measurements taken from an SCM database used at ABB Industrial Systems. The SCM tool is change-oriented and collects information about changes in Change Request (CR) documents. As CRs are under version control, the measurements taken on them give information not only about the amount and type of changes but also about the change process behavior. The measurements, generated from CRs by a tool, are used during the development process and in the final analysis of the project. The paper presents some of the measurements showing typical cases of lifecycle models.

1 Introduction

There are a number of different Software Metrics and they can be classified in relation to the relevant development process, products or resources [1]. Typical product metrics are size metrics (number of lines of code, number of documents, etc.), quality metrics, etc. Process metrics are a result of measurements related to the different phases of the development process. Process measurements help us to understand the processes concerned, to control them, improve and predict them [2].

Can SCM tools provide information for process metrics? The answer is yes for tools which integrate a Process Management with SCM, for example ClearGuide [3]. Change-oriented tools provade information about changes which can also be used as input to process measurements.

This paper describes a metrics tool and measurements performed on a change-oriented SCM tool, designated Software Development Environment (SDE), developed and used at ABB Industrial Systems [4]. Different metrics showing the behavior of development projects are presented.

B. Magnusson (Ed.): ECOOP 98, SCM-8, LNCS 1439, pp. 26-32, 1998

2 Change Management in SDE

2.1 SDE Basic Characteristics

SDE is a software package intended for use in the development of large systems. SDE is based partly on RCS[5]. Using slightly modified RCS commands and certain new commands related to RCS files, SDE enables easy and fast browsing through the hierarchical system structures and versioned files. The SDE and RCS commands are encapsulated in GUI-applications.

2.2 Change Management

SDE provides support in the management of Software Development Processes. Change Management is a part of the support. Any change in SDE is under change-set control. A basic item of SDE Change Management is a Change Request (CR), an entity which describes a logical change to be made in a software system. Change Requests are created from Requirement Specifications or from defect reports. During the development process CRs collect information about physical changes made in the system: When a developer checks in a file, he/she refers to a related CR. The file name, file version and log message are registered in the CR. The final version of a CR includes both a description of a logical change and information about all modified file versions. The references between CRs and changed files are controlled by the SDE tools. No change can be introduced in the software without referring to a CR.

A Change Request passes through different states during the development process. When a CR is created it is in the state *Init*. During the work sessions it passes through other states, such as *Exp, Implemented, Tested* and reaches the *Terminated* state. The CRs integrated in a product release are in the state *Released*. Figure 1 shows different states of a CR in a development process.

Change Requests are under version control. Each time a CR is changed it is automatically checked out and after the modification, checked in. CRs are saved in an RCS directory located in a CR library which contains all logical changes of a software version. As a versioned file under RCS control, a CR includes not only the change description and list of changed file versions, but also attributes from RCS: a state, a responsible user (author) date of change and other RCS attributes.

Change Requests are implemented as text files which follow a specific syntax. The header part of a CR includes keywords such as Priority and CR Type, creation date and termination date. A list of files being checked in follows. The body part includes a description of the change and log messages of the files checked in.

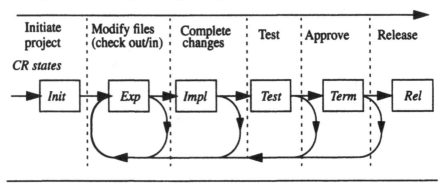

Fig. 1. Change Requests in a development process

3 CR Metrics

The main purpose in using CR metrics is to increase the predictability of the behavior of software development projects. The second purpose is to obtain an overview of the current project status. To achieve these objectives we need answers to the following questions:

- How many changes and types of changes have been made, how many changes should be made?

- What is the dynamic of the changes? How often are further changes required and how does the project respond to them?

- How are changes distributed among developers? What is the current state of change per developer? How many changes has a developer to implement?

- How did the change process look in the projects completed previously?

CRs contain data which can be used for providing the answers. The number of changes, their states, classification according to priority, type or function, number of changed files, etc. is one type of possible metrics. Since CRs are under version control, the history of every change is also available. The states of all changes are available for the whole period of the development process. The state changes data in a time period is input to another type of metrics - process metrics. There is also information about the authors of changes introduced in CRs. It is therefore possible to obtain metrics for the entire development project and also for every member.

A CR-Metrics application collects data from CR libraries, by parsing CRs. Information about every CR version is taken and saved in a spreadsheet. The measurements are displayed as embedded Excel objects [6] in the form of different graphs. All measurements are performed in a similar way. All versions of all CRs are parsed and different criteria are used for extracting data. The CR-Metrics application presents the following measurements:

Current status	The states of the latest CR versions for each period are shown.
Accumulated CRs	Completed and incomplete CR are sorted according to date.
New CRs	The graph shows the number of new CRs in a time interval.
Latest Changes	The CRs being changed during a given period are presented.
New and completed	The number of new and the number of completed ("input" and "output") CRs per time interval are shown.
CR life length	A distribution of CR life lengths is shown.
CR Type	CRs are classified according to CR types (Error, Improvement, etc.).
Priority and State	A classification according to the change priority for completed and incomplete CRs is shown.

4 Measurements

Some of the metrics for a development project designated WinSDE 1.1-0 are presented here. The graphs show characteristics of the development process, i.e. the dynamics of change introduction and their completion.

The WinSDE 1.1-0 project uses a development model which is a combination of the spiral model and the evolutionary prototyping model [7]: The development is performed as a number of iterations, each consisting of several phases: prototyping, evaluation of different alternatives, refining the prototype, developing and building the deliverables and a plan for the next iteration. An implication of this model is a constant growth of the number of CRs - new requirements are defined during each iteration (refinements) and at the beginning of the new iteration (new functions). In the last iteration the number of new CRs describing new functions declines, but new CRs related to the release activities are still being created. The test activities with CR termination become more intensive at the end of each iteration, but especially at the end of the project. The unsolved CRs are postponed to a succeeding release.

The current status graph (Figure 2) shows the number of CRs created during the project. CRs are classified according to their states. The graph shows how many changes have been completed and how many remain open.

The example in the graph shows that the number of new CRs grows constantly. The number of completed CRs also increases. The number of open CRs is approximately the same during the entire project except during the last phase. Some steps in completing CRs can be seen - when the time for a new deliverable approaches, many CRs are terminated.

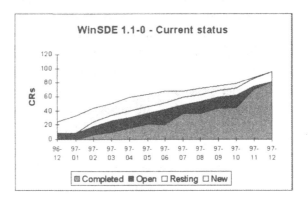

Fig. 2. Current states of CRs for a project using the Spiral model

Figure 3 shows the same type of graph for another project which followed the Water-fall model. In the project initiation phase, all the requirements have been defined and CRs have been created. The graph shows how the work has improved. The number of open CRs increases, and in the final, test phase, the CRs are being completed.

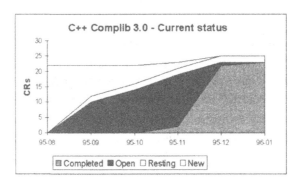

Fig. 3. Current states of CRs for a project using the Waterfall model

Figure 4 shows the distribution of the times taken in making changes. The time on the X-axis is the time interval between the reception of the CR and the completion of the change. The Y-axis shows the number of changes which are completed in the specified period. The graph indicates that most of the CRs are completed within six months, and it suggests that it is acceptable to deliver the product modified in that period without waiting further six months for making the remaining changes planned in the project..

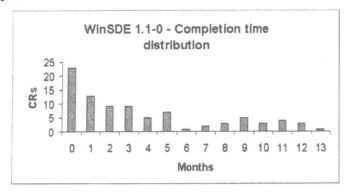

Fig. 4. Distribution of times for making changes

5 Conclusion

The measurements shown in this paper illustrate the possibility of using an SCM database not only for size metrics but also for process metrics. The process metrics should lead to a better understanding of development processes and help in making appropriate decisions in process management. Experience in the use of the CR-Metrics tool at ABB Industrial Systems remains limited because of its recent development. However, a case study has shown very similar patterns of metrics: Three projects for the development of similar products using the Spiral model have been measured, and the results from CR-metrics have shown surprisingly many similarities. The total number of CRs was three times greater than the number of CRs at the outset. The number of postponed CRs was approximately 20% of the total number of CRs (which suggests a weakness in the project planning). The number of open, i.e CRs being processed was constantly about 6 per developer during the development process in all projects. The most interesting fact is that the shapes of the curves in all projects were similar.

The idea is to use CR-metrics during execution of the project when both the project manager and project members can follow up the project status. The final measurements can be taken at the completion of the project. The metrics can be compared with those from other projects and related to other facts. One advantage of the tool is the possibility of collecting data from earlier projects, as all data concerned is under SCM control.

References

1. The Software Measurement Laboratory, University of Magdeburg,
   http://irb.cs.uni-magdeburg.de/sw-eng/us/metclas/index.shtml

2. William A Florac, Robert E. Part, Anita D. Carleton - Practical Software Measurement: Measuring for process management and Improvement, *Software Engineering Institute, Carnegie Mellon University, CMU/SEI-976-HB-003, April 1997*

3. David B. Leblang, Managing the Software Development Process with ClearGuide, *Software Configuration Management ICSE'97 Workshop, Boston, May 1997, proceedings, Springer Verlag, ISBN 3-540-63014-7*, pages 66-80

4. Ivica Crnkovic, Experience with Change-Oriented SCM Tools, *Software Configuration Management ICSE'97 Workshop, Boston, May 1997, proceedings, Springer Verlag, ISBN 3-540-63014-7*, pages 222-234

5. Walter F. Tichy, RCS -A System for Version Control, S*oftware and Practice Experience*, 15(7):635-654, 1985

6. Microsoft Visual Basic 5.0 ActiveX Controls Reference, 1997, ISBN 1-57231-508-3

7. Steve McConnell, *Rapid Development: timing wild software schedules*, Microsoft Press, 1996, ISBN 1-55615-900-5

PRCS: The Project Revision Control System

Josh MacDonald[1], Paul N. Hilfinger[1], and Luigi Semenzato[2]

[1] University of California at Berkeley, Department of Electrical Engineering and
Computer Sciences, Berkeley CA 94720, USA,
[2] National Energy Research Scientific Computing Center, Lawrence Berkeley
National Laboratory, Berkeley CA 94720, USA

Abstract. PRCS is an attempt to provide a version-control system for
collections of files with a simple operational model, a clean user interface, and high performance. PRCS is characterized by the use of project
description files to input most commands, instead of a point-and-click
or a line-oriented interface. It employs optimistic concurrency control
and encourages operations on the entire project rather than individual
files. Although its current implementation uses RCS in the back-end,
the interface completely hides its presence. PRCS is free. This paper describes the advantages and disadvantages of our approach, and discusses
implementation issues.

1 Overview

PRCS is an attempt at producing a version control system for collection of files
that is competitive with existing commercial and free systems with regard to
ease of use, implementation, and maintenance. PRCS borrows freely from well-
established concepts and ideas in this area, but re-engineers them into a small
set of orthogonal features, a clean version model, and a simple yet powerful user
interface based on text editing.

The design and development of PRCS was partly motivated by the authors'
dissatisfaction with existing systems. Commercial systems tend to be large,
feature-laden, and expensive. They often have fancy graphical user interfaces,
which can make many operations intuitive, but typically present a sharp thresh-
old beyond which even conceptually simple operations become exceedingly cumbersome. CVS (Concurrent Version System)[1], the standard non-commercial
solution, is widely used but we find that many aspects of its operation, administration, and user interface are unnecessarily complex, mostly because of its
choice of version model and its explicit dependency on RCS.

CVS and several other systems are designed around the idea that version
control for a group of files can be achieved by grouping together many single-file
version-control operations. PRCS defines a project version as a labeled snapshot
of a group of files, and provides operations on project versions as a whole. Our
experience shows that focusing on this model results in a cleaner system than a
model cast explicitly as groups of single-file operations.

One notable difference between PRCS and other systems is its user interface.
In the PRCS model, each version of a group of files contains one distinguished file,

B. Magnusson (Ed.): ECOOP 98, SCM-8, LNCS 1439, pp. 33–45, 1998.

called the version descriptor. This file contains a description of the files included in that particular version. All user-controlled project settings are entered and manipulated through this file. Indeed, many user-interface issues become text-editing problems from the start, rather than requiring a graphical user interface or numerous command-line utilities for maintaining project state.

Additionally, PRCS includes several novel features, including an improved keyword replacement mechanism and a flexible way of incorporating PRCS into external programs.

In the remainder of this paper, we provide a small example (§3), and discuss the system design and operational model (§2), related work (§4), branch control (§5), distinguishing features (§6), implementation considerations and implications for back-end storage management (§7), and future work (§8).

2   Operational Model

PRCS presents the user with the abstraction of named *projects*, which are collections of *project versions* (or simply *versions*), each of which is a snapshot of a set of files arranged into a directory tree. Every project version is labeled with a *version name*, which is unique within that version's project. Finally, a PRCS *repository* contains a group of projects.

Each version contains one distinguished file in its top-level directory, known as its *project-version descriptor*, or simply *version descriptor*. This is an ordinary text file that identifies the version and contains a list of the version's constituent files. When a file is added to a project version for the first time, it is assigned a unique, internal identifier, which follows the file through its history, even as it is renamed. This identifier is known as the *internal file family*. The version descriptor contains a mapping between internal file families and file names. We give more detail in §6.1.

Users modify directory structures of files independently of the repository. We use the adjective *working* to distinguish these files and directories from those that are stored in the repository: thus *working version, working file,* and *working version descriptor*. When we say that a project version is a snapshot of a directory structure, we typically mean a snapshot of such a working project version.

Before any working version is *checked in* (the usual term for "taking a snapshot") PRCS modifies its descriptor to reflect the new (repository) version. In particular, the resulting version descriptors contain a record of the identity of the versions from which they were derived, thus inducing a partial order on versions that serves to define ancestry.

Within this framework, PRCS provides the following major operations:

Checkin deposits a labeled snapshot of a working version in the repository.
Checkout reconstructs any project version, identified by project and version label.
Diff compares project versions.
Merge reconciles two project versions interactively by modifying the working project version. PRCS uses the notion of ancestry described above to

determine a common ancestor version that allows it to determine the proper handling of many inconsistencies between the versions being merged.

As you can see from this list, there is no operation for locking a project, version, or file. Instead, PRCS employs optimistic concurrency control. Users are expected to merge changes prior to check-in when conflicts occur, and are informed when this is necessary.

3   An Example

This section presents an example of basic use of PRCS to give some flavor of the interactions involved. Consider two programmers, Jack and Jill, performing maintenance on a system we'll call WaterWorks. For illustrative purposes, we'll assume that WaterWorks is not initially under source-code control. Jack therefore acquires some directory structure of files. He places it under PRCS's control with the following commands (lines beginning with a jack% or jill% prompt are user input).

```
jack% prcs checkout WaterWorks
prcs:  Project not found in repository, initial checkout.
prcs:  You may now edit the file 'WaterWorks.prj'
jack% prcs populate
prcs:  245 files were added.
```

Jack now has a version descriptor file for the new project, WaterWorks.prj, containing the names of all files in and below his current directory. Nothing has been added to the repository yet. Jack edits the version descriptor to add descriptive text about the project, if desired, and to remove any uninteresting files from the list. He then performs the command

```
jack% prcs checkin
```

which takes a snapshot of the collection of listed files, and labels it '0.1' in the repository. He performs a set of edits, adding new files to the version descriptor, if needed, and then

```
jack% prcs checkin -rJack
```

which takes a snapshot of the current state of his working version of the project, and names this version 'Jack.1'. Jack can how continue editing, performing periodic checkpoints with

```
jack% prcs checkin
```

Meanwhile, Jill gets her own copy of the WaterWorks project with

```
jill% prcs checkout -r0 WaterWorks
```

which retrieves the version Jack started with, 0.1. Jill makes modifications, creates her own branch with

```
jill% prcs checkin -rJill
```

and performs a cycle of edits and checkins, just as Jack did.

Eventually, Jack has completed a coherent set of modifications, and checks it into the main branch (labeled '0' here), with

```
jack% prcs checkin -r0
```

creating a snapshot of the project named '0.2'. When Jill attempts to do the same with, say, her version Jill.5, PRCS tells her that the latest version in the main branch is not an ancestor of the one she is checking in. She is thus alerted to look at the changes made since she branched off:

```
jill% prcs diff -r0.1 -r0.2
```

and eventually to *merge* her changes with those in 0.2, using

```
jill% prcs merge -r0
```

This commences a dialog in which PRCS asks how to deal with each conflict between changes from version 0.1 (the common ancestor of 0.2 and Jill.5) and 0.2 versus changes between 0.1 and Jill.5. When this is complete, and Jill has made whatever edits are needed to reconcile her changes with Jack's, she can perform the checkin

```
jill% prcs checkin -r0
```

Jack and Jill can continue indefinitely with this cycle of edits, checkins, and merges. Most interactions with PRCS on the command line are as simple as these.

4   Related Work

The list of available version control and configuration management systems is quite long. Two systems deserve special attention: the Concurrent Version System (CVS) because it is a *de-facto* standard among free systems; and the commercial system Perforce[tm] [4], because it shares with PRCS similar approaches to several problems. In §5, we compare these three systems with respect to two features: labeling of sets of file versions, and branch control.

Research in software evolution and CASE tools has focused on augmenting traditional entity-relation design and analysis techniques with version histories and dependencies. One such attempt is the PROTEUS Configuration Language (PCL) [5]. PCL allows for the description and control of software variability by tracking changes in the requirements and tools required to build the each variation, where variations may include different hardware platforms, releases, or customer configurations.

5   Branch Control

Much of the variation between SCM systems found today can be reduced to their differing notions and definitions of branches, labels, and change numbers. A branch is a division in project development, a logical split occurring when a particular ancestor has more than one descendent. Branches are typically used to manage and help reintegration of variants in a project's development. Easy and fast operations on branches are essential for exploiting a version control system to its full potential. This section defines the common approaches to branch management and discusses their limitations and implications for ease of use.

5.1   Labels vs. Change Numbers

To use Perforce's terminology, both labels and change numbers are mechanisms for naming sets of revisions of files contained in a project.[1] A *label*—also known as a *tag* in RCS or CVS—names an arbitrary set of file revisions chosen by the user. The file revisions named by a label may change at any time, and may consist of revisions that were created at different times and by different developers. A *change number* or *labeled change* refers to a set of revisions that were committed during a single transaction. Although CVS provides allows one to group operations atomically, it not have a mechanism for naming each transaction and later retrieving the contents of the project at the moment changes were committed. One can simulate change numbers with CVS tags, but this is not directly supported. Perforce supports both mechanisms and allows the user to construct views of the project named by either label or change number.

CVS cannot reconstruct change numbers from its repository. Since CVS treats each operation as a group of operations on individual RCS files in the repository, information such as this can only be obtained by check-in-time clustering or by carefully applying an immutable label at each commit.

The issue of labeling each change to the project is of great importance. Without these labels, later reconstruction of the project's history is not as straightforward as one might think. For example, with CVS it is difficult to request an operation such as: "display all changes made by user A during his last commit." One must examine the logs of all affected files, search for changes by user A, and then request a list of all differences in the project between some time before and some time after the commit occurred. By contrast, this operation is simple in Perforce and in PRCS: look for the last change by user A, request to view the changes at that change number.

PRCS only supports change numbers, which we call *version names*. All version names have the form $M.N$. Here, M is the *major version name*, a string chosen by the user (0, **Vendor-2.2**, and **broken-branch** are typical examples),

---

[1] We use the term *project* to refer to the Perforce depot, the CVS module, and the PRCS project.

and N is the *minor version name*, a positive integer numeral assigned consecutively by the system. The user is free to ascribe any desired semantics to major version names. This labeling scheme has proved satisfactory; so far, we have no evidence that a system without labels is any worse for not having this feature.

5.2   Branching with Labels and Change Numbers

In CVS, branching is accomplished by first creating a label for the branch point, which is then used to name the new branch. Each file in the repository must be tagged with the new label—expensive for a large repository.

In a system supporting change numbers, branching is much simpler. A branch may be created during a transaction, when the change number is assigned. The notion of the parent or predecessor of a version is straightforward to define and therefore, in contrast to CVS, a version history—a tree of project versions—is easy to construct.

In PRCS, major version names can serve to identify branches. There is no explicit notion of a hierarchy of branches; the user is free to adopt any desired scheme for reflecting relationships between branches in their names. In fact, minor versions within a branch are just as independent of each other as any arbitrary pair of versions.

6   Features

This section describes in more detail some distinguishing features of PRCS.

6.1   Version Descriptors

The syntax of the version descriptor file is a slight variant on Lisp syntax. Figure 1 displays a sample project descriptor. Most project settings are entered by editing this file before a check-in. Some fields are provided by PRCS at check-in time. For example the Project-Version, Parent-Version, Version-Log, Checkin-Time, and Checkin-Login identify the project version. Others allow users to supply arbitrary information about a version. For example, anything may be placed in the New-Version-Log field before a check-in, and it becomes the Version-Log of the next version.

The Project-Keywords field contains a list of keyword-value pairs to be added to the standard set of keywords during keyword replacement. Keyword replacement is described in §6.3.

The Files entries contain lists of files, symbolic links, and empty directories contained in the version. Their main function is to associate the name of each file (as seen by the user) with its internal identification in the repository. For example, the line

```
(src/parser.c (1_parser.c 1.3 644))
```

in Figure 1 indicates that the file named src/parser.c is associated in this version with data in the repository whose internal label is (1_parser.c 1.3 644). The next line,

```
(src/lexer.c ())
```

indicates that the working file src/lexer.c is not yet in the repository, but is to be added when the current working version is checked in.

```
(Project-Version P Vendor 5)
(Parent-Version P Vendor 4)
(Project-Description "Sample Project")
(Version-Log "Version log for Vendor.5")
(New-Version-Log "Version log for working changes (eventually
Vendor.6).")
(Checkin-Time "Wed, 14 Jan 1998 23:24:44 -0800")
(Checkin-Login jmacd)
(Populate-Ignore ("~$" "\\.o$"))
(Project-Keywords (Release "2.2") (PatchLevel "6"))
(Files :tag=sourcefile :difftool=prcs-ediff :mergetool=prcs-emerge
  (src/main.c (0_main.c 1.5 644))
  (src/parser.c (1_parser.c 1.3 644))
  (src/lexer.c ())
)

(Files :no-keywords :tag=image
  (img/logo.jpg (2_logo.jpg 1.2 444) :difftool=jpg-diff)
  (img/icon.gif (3_icon.gif 1.1 444) :difftool=gif-diff)
)

(Files
  (lib () :directory)    ; Include a lib directory, even if empty
  (core (/dev/null) :symlink)
)
```

Fig. 1. A Sample Working Version Descriptor

From the user's point of view, the internal file labels are simply arbitrary label strings having a somewhat unusual form and a simple semantics: each uniquely identifies a particular file snapshot. The same internal label in two different version descriptors of the same project denotes the same file contents (modulo keywords; see §6.3). Check-in automatically updates the internal labels of all modified files in the version descriptor when a check-in occurs. Files in a working directory that are not mentioned in the Files entries are not included in snapshots of the directory.

The Files entries may also attach a set of attributes to any file. The ':tag' attribute allows arbitrary labels to be attached to files. The ':no-keywords' attribute turns off keyword replacement for the file in question. The ':difftool' and ':mergetool' attributes set the programs which are used to display files differences and perform three-way file merging, respectively. As illustrated, Files lists allow files to be grouped by common attributes for brevity.

A particularly elegant result of this design is that because version descriptors are simply text files in a format that is intended to be readable, numerous operations needed for version control reduce to text editing. Adding, subtracting, and renaming files (including moving them across directories) is accomplished by editing the working copy of the version descriptor file before checking in the new version. For example, the file list in the version descriptor of a project consisting of the files hello.c and hello.h might look like the following.

```
(Files
  (hello.c (0_hello.c 1.1 644))
  (hello.h (1_hello.h 1.1 644))
)
```

Suppose that in our working version, we (1) rename hello.h to greetings.h, moving it to a new include subdirectory, (2) add a new file, include/cards.h and a new empty directory, doc, and (3) delete hello.c. We would modify the working version descriptor as follows.

```
(Files
  (include/greetings.h (1_hello.h 1.1 644))
  (include/cards.h ())
  (doc () :directory)
)
```

Assuming that we do not change the contents of the former hello.h, PRCS will, on check-in, modify this list into something like this for the new version it creates:

```
(Files
  (include/greetings.h (1_hello.h 1.1 644))
  (include/cards.h (0_cards.h 1.1 644))
  (doc () :directory)
)
```

The internal label associated with include/greetings.h does not change, since it reflects a particular file contents, independent of the name.

Suppose that we later decide to re-introduce the file hello.c into a still-later version, renaming it to greetings.c. It is possible to do this by adding the line

```
(greetings.c ())
```

to the working descriptor's Files list, but PRCS also allows us to establish the association of this file with the previous hello.c by copying one of the latter's internal labels, as in:

```
(greetings.c (0_hello.c 1.1 644))
```

The effect of doing so is to put **greetings.c** into the same file family as **hello.c**, which means that when versions containing these files are compared or merged, PRCS can recognize the relationship between them. Old internal labels can be recovered by checking out earlier versions of the version descriptor.

Creating the first version of a project is a special case. One creates a working descriptor file by checking out a project not yet in the repository. This file has an empty Files list. One can fill this as we've done so far, with entries having '( )' for their internal label. To avoid tedium and error, PRCS provides a convenience command, **populate**, that finds files under the current directory and generates new Files entries for each of them. Editing the resulting working descriptor will remove any that are not wanted.

PRCS does not, of course, implicitly trust the contents of working version descriptor, and subjects them to verification before check-ins. Indeed, it may seem dangerous to allow the user to directly modify administrative information that, in other systems, is kept hidden behind an appropriate GUI. However, our experience shows otherwise; users do not show any tendency to hang themselves, and the consistency checks suffice to prevent accidents.

The use of a text editor for project administration is admittedly controversial. However, we have found it surprisingly effective. The most common use, after all, consists of adding a log entry—a simple exercise in text insertion, as is the addition of files. Deleting files from a project or changing their names likewise correspond to standard editing operations.

6.2   The execute Command

The PRCS **execute** command facilitates efficient, open-ended extension to the functions provided by PRCS. Its command syntax allows another command or script to be executed with the name of each file and directory in the project. Regular expressions may be used to filter the list of files, allowing selection or exclusion by file name, extension, or attribute. The special ':tag' file attribute has no special meaning to PRCS, and is simply included to allow grouping of files according to relevant characteristics.

Various options allow many elaborate commands to be constructed. When run against a project version in the repository, PRCS can also supply a checked-out copy of each file. Instead of executing the command once per file or directory, PRCS can execute the command just once for all affected files. Finally, PRCS can supply the contents of the file to the command on the standard input. For example, the command:

```
prcs execute --pipe --match \\.cc$ P -- wc
```

pipes each file in the working version of project P with the .cc extension to the wc command.

6.3   Keyword Replacement

PRCS, like many other version control systems, allows keyword replacement in selected files. Abstractly, we may think of this replacement as being performed upon check-in of a file. Internally, PRCS actually does not do so, in order to avoid having to store changes of keywords as part of the change information for a file.

Within files in a version, PRCS recognizes two forms of keyword instance: simple and formatted. Simple keyword instances (as in RCS) have one of these forms:

> $*keyword*$
> $*keyword*:   *value*$

and on check-in, such instances are replaced by an instance of the second form, with the appropriate value.

Sometimes, one needs keyword replacement data without the leading "$*keyword*:" and trailing '$'. A novel feature of PRCS, the *formatted keyword instance,* allows this. When PRCS encounters the text

> *arbitrary text* $Format: "*format-string*"$ *arbitrary text*
> *current-string*

at check-in time, it replaces the line reading *current-string* with *format-string,* after first substituting simple keywords in the latter. The line containing the "Format" instance itself is not altered. For example, Figure 2 illustrates the contents of a file before and after formatted keyword replacement for project version 0.4.

Before replacement:

```
    /* $Format: "char* version = \"$ProjectVersion$\";"$ */
char* version = "x.x";
```

After replacement:

```
    /* $Format: "char* version = \"$ProjectVersion$\";"$ */
char* version = "0.4";
```

Fig. 2. Formatted Keyword Replacement

There are 13 predefined keywords that have values dependent on the project version and individual file version. Many, such as Date and Author (the date at which a modified version of a file was checked in and the identity of the user checking it in), will be familiar to users of RCS. Others are project-related, such as ProjectDate and ProjectAuthor (the date of a check-in and the identity of the user doing it). In addition, users may introduce their own keywords in the project descriptor, as was illustrated in Figure 1.

6.4 Subprojects

PRCS has no explicit facilities for managing *subprojects*—one or more PRCS-controlled projects within another *super-project*. Nevertheless, it is possible to get much of the effect, in a typically minimalist fashion, simply by including version descriptor files for the subprojects among the files included in the super-project. Checking in the super-project consists of first checking in the subprojects (if needed), and then checking in the superproject. On checking out this version, one gets the subproject descriptor files. These uniquely identify the constituent subproject versions, so checking out any of the subprojects based on its descriptor (a simple operation in PRCS) recovers the subproject. It is not clear to us that this simple recursive process represents something sufficiently common and error-prone to really need explicit support. While automated support process is conceivable, furthermore, it is not clear what the best policy is for mapping operations on the super-project onto the sub-project. For example, when branching the super-project it may or may not be desirable to create a new branch in the sub-project. Questions like this and our lack of experience with sub-project management has kept automated support for sub-projects out of our current design.

7 Implementation

PRCS is implemented using RCS as a back-end storage mechanism. While this helped in the quick implementation of a robust prototype, it has several limitations as a long-term strategy.

- Starting a new process for a revision control operation on each file is expensive.
- RCS calling and locking conventions make interfacing a higher-level version control systems to RCS unnecessarily complicated.
- Binary files are not well supported.
- The branching mechanism of RCS has unexpected performance implications, and it is difficult to optimize its use, either automatically or with user intervention.

These and other problems make RCS a less-than-ideal back-end tool. The process startup costs would be avoided by an implementation of RCS as a set of thread-safe library routines, but this would not fix its interface problems. The current implementation of PRCS, for example, is complicated by code to manage locking and unlocking of RCS files and placing or linking files into the correct path before performing batch check-ins. Additionally, the delta mechanism of RCS is out-of-date. New delta algorithms have been developed that outperform LCS-based delta algorithms, and handle binary files as well as text files, as demonstrated by Hunt *et al* [2].

Finally, the RCS branching model is inappropriate for higher level tools. RCS forces each version to be placed in a tree. Its location on the tree greatly effects the performance of operations on it. Experience with PRCS has shown that it is difficult for a high-level version control tool to place these versions well.

PRCS makes extensive use of timestamps and MD5 checksums to minimize file I/O and RCS invocations. The MD5 optimizations, though complicated by keyword replacement, reduce I/O greatly in situations where timestamps alone do not prevent a comparison.

8   Future Work

Upon completing the system, we immediately identified the need for distributed, multi-user version control, involving some sort of client/server structure. A design for distributed version control architecture can make many reductions in data transfer by carefully caching data and transmitting only changes. The problem of efficiently distributing version-control repositories has been nicely addressed by Polstra's CVSup (CVS Update Protocol) [3]. Work on a client/server implementation is currently underway.

As we introduce distributed PRCS repositories, we are planning to allow users to distinguish between *local* and *network* check-ins. Often, users of a global, shared repository feel uncomfortable checkpointing their progress with extra, possibly off-branch versions because of the shared nature of the repository. Personal, possibly local modifications do not belong in the global repository. Users are forced to use multiple repositories, one for their local work and one for shared, group work.

We plan to address this problem by allowing certain branches to be marked local. Local branches are not shared with the global repository and are invisible to other user of the repository. Operations on local versions in the network context treat other local versions as transparent, following their ancestry until a network version is found. This allows, for example, a user to check out the latest version on the network branch, check in several versions on a local branch for intermediate checkpoints, then return his work to the network repository by checking in the next version, possibly after a merge against the head of the network branch. A merge between the head of the network branch and the local working version would treat original network version as its immediate parent.

We have also investigated replacement delta algorithms similar to the Vdelta algorithm and improvements on RCS that avoid the branching problems mentioned above. Conceptually, to get rid of RCS-like branching and retain the "deltas are computed between a file version and its parent" aspect of RCS, we have devised a version-control library that computes a reverse delta between the new file and the entire version file. The most recently checked in version is always the "head", in RCS terms. It is always the quickest and easiest to extract. For a repository with N versions, version I requires the application of $(N - I)$ deltas, regardless of how the set of versions are related. This type of construction leads to a versioned storage format without the performance problems associated with branches, yet with similar storage efficiency. Branches are avoided by using the content of previous deltas in addition to the most recently checked-in file.

9 Conclusion

PRCS began as a study in engineering a conceptually simple solution to the version control problem, making good reuse of an existing tool—the text editor—to simplify operations from the user's point of view. It has evolved into a system that, we believe, is easy to use, presents a simple, abstract model to the user, and whose design is uncompromised by the ease or difficulty of a particular implementation.

We have observed that the snapshot, labeled-version model of project versions works well and is simpler than mechanisms that treat version control on groups of files as grouped operations on individual files. We conclude that a system with only one version labeling paradigm—change numbering—is adequate and sufficiently powerful to meet the needs of a sophisticated version control tool, yet is simpler than many competing approaches.

Availability. Information about PRCS and its source and binary distributions are available at `http://www.xcf.berkeley.edu/~jmacd/prcs.html`. The experimental RCS replacement and delta algorithm implementation described in (§8) is available at `http://www.xcf.berkeley.edu/~jmacd/xdelta.html`.

Acknowledgement. We wish to thank the National Automated Highway System Consortium, which helped to fund initial development of PRCS under Cooperative Agreement DTFH61-94-X-00001 with the Federal Highway Administration.

References

[1] BERLINER, B. CVS II: Parallelizing software development. In *Proceedings of the Winter 1990 USENIX Conference, January 22–26, 1990, Washington, DC, USA* (Berkeley, CA, USA, Jan. 1990), USENIX Association, Ed., USENIX, pp. 341–352.

[2] HUNT, J. J., VO, K.-P., AND TICHY, W. F. An empirical study of delta algorithms. *Lecture Notes in Computer Science 1167* (July 1996), 49–66.

[3] POLSTRA, J. Program source for CVSup. ftp://ftp.cvsup.freebsd.org/pub/CVSup, 1996.

[4] SEIWALD, C. Inter-file branching — A practical method for representing variants. *Lecture Notes in Computer Science 1167* (July 1996), 67–76.

[5] TRYGGESETH, E., GULLA, B., AND CONRADI, R. Modelling systems with variability using the PROTEUS configuration language. *Lecture Notes in Computer Science 1005* (1995), 216–240.

Multi-Grain Version Control
in the Historian System

Makram Abu-Shakra and Gene L. Fisher

Department of Computer Science
California Polytechnic State University
San Luis Obispo, CA 93407
{mabushak, gfisher}@csc.calpoly.edu
http://www.csc.calpoly.edu

Abstract. This paper describes Historian, a version control system that
supports comprehensive versioning and features to aid history navigation. Comprehensive versioning is supported through frequent and automated creation of versions which typically results in a large number of
versions. To reduce user overhead in history navigation, the hierarchical
structure present in most documents is utilized to support fine-grained
version control. The series of document editing operations is also organized hierarchically and can be used for navigation as well.

1   Introduction

This paper describes the Historian editor-based version control system. Historian
supports fine-grain version control of documents, with an end-user interface that
provides efficient and convenient version retrieval. A document is a collection of
structured text, where the structuring is defined on a document-specific basis.
For example, a prose document is structured as paragraphs within sections within
chapters; a program is structured as declarations within functions within files.

A number of existing systems provide features similar to those available in
Historian, notably COOP/Orm [10] and Orwell [19] The contributions of Historian compared to these systems are:

a. support for comprehensive version control at multiple levels of granularity
   along both structural and temporal lines
b. a graphical user interface for convenient historical navigation and low-overhead version retrieval

Structural granularity is based on the natural hierarchical organization of a
document. For example, versioned items in an object-oriented program range
from functions, to classes, to modules, as described well in [7] Temporal granularity is based on the frequency of version creation during document editing.
For example, the frequency of version creation can range from saving at each
individual edit operation, at the document save operation, or at each document
check-in operation.

B. Magnusson (Ed.): ECOOP 98, SCM-8, LNCS 1439, pp. 46–56, 1998.
© Springer-Verlag Berlin Heidelberg 1998

The support of different levels of granularity for both types provide unique advantages to the software configuration process. While our approach focuses on the effects of granularity on viewing the evolution of documents, existing systems have explored its effects on other areas such as merging alternatives and group awareness.

The focus of Historian is notably more narrow than many full-feature configuration management systems. From the end user's perspective, Historian appears as a largely standard text editor, with specialized features for version navigation and retrieval. In this sense, the end-user look and feel of Historian are much like groupware editors such as PREP [13,14] and SEPIA [5] Historian can be aptly viewed as a specialized component that can be integrated into a larger CM environment.

The term fine-grain version control appears first to have been used by the authors of Orwell [19] to refer to the version control of individual program methods (i.e., functions) as opposed to files or modules in an object-oriented program. This is fine-grain on the *structural* level. In COOP/Orm [11] the term is extended to mean frequent creation of versions as well. This is fine-grain on the *temporal* level. While a number of other good systems have addressed fine-grain version control on one or both of these levels, none has focused on convenient and low-overhead retrieval, which we view as an important issue. Historian provides version control that is comprehensive, fully automatic, efficient, and supports focused retrieval.

The motivation for Historian has come from our own frustration as authors when changes to a document eliminate versions that we might later wish to retrieve. Such frustration arises when working alone, and is amplified when working collaboratively with other authors, as reported in [3] for example. While version control systems have always addressed this problem to some extent, systems typically keep track of changes only when files are checked in, or at other explicitly invoked user operations. Comprehensive and fully automatic version control introduces the security that any version of a document is retrievable, without the user having to request version saving explicitly.

There are two major problems with comprehensive version control: excessive use of storage space and the high overhead of navigating through a large number of versions. Solutions to storage problems such as file compression and differencing algorithms are well known and are utilized in Historian to keep memory usage at a minimum. User interface solutions to the latter problem are largely unaddressed in CM systems, and the primary focus of Historian. In order to keep comprehensive version navigation practical, features are introduced to aid the user in searching for desired versions. In our experience, version navigation in most CM systems is already awkward and time-consuming; saving a comprehensive set of versions makes matters even worse.

We began our research with the assumption that reducing user overhead in navigation will make version retrieval a more common practice in software development and will thus increase productivity. In our experience using RCS [20] or RCS-based systems, we have found that saved versions were very rarely retrieved, even when they might be quite useful in undoing a design or implementation change that did not succeed as expected. That version retrieval becomes more common is fundamental to realizing the importance of reducing version retrieval overhead. In our experience using the current Historian prototype, we have observed that different versions have been retrieved as often several times per hour. This high frequency of retrieval typically occurs during the later development stages of programs. It is at these stages when history is most valuable because changes are often made to "code that already works" and is therefore more likely to be retrieved.

In addition to the quantitative increase in version retrieval, we have observed a number of qualitative improvements in program development with the use of Historian. The user gains a sense of security because no data are ever lost and a certain sense of bravery when modifying code. In addition, the multiple undo feature found in text editors is effectively replaced by Historian's features for very fine-grain version control. We will further elaborate on these effects later in the paper.

In the discussion of Historian, we will distinguish between two types of overhead: system-time and user-time. User overhead is what we consider being the amount of time spent in trying to find a specific version in mind. Version retrieval can be categorized into two fundamental types. The first type is the retrieval of a version whose id is already known, i.e., the version of a system release. This type typically involves little user overhead. The second type involves retrieving a version whose id is not known, when the user must search through history to find the version in mind. Historian aims to reduce the overhead of the latter type. Henceforth in this paper, we assume that the identifier is not known.

2   Related Work

Of relevance to Historian, there are four broad categories of tools that have been used to support document version control:

1. First generation tools developed primarily for software engineering, such as SCCS [16] and RCS [20]
2. Second generation configuration management tools that focus on fine-grain version control, such as COOP/Orm [10,11] Orwell [19] POEM [7] and CAMERA [8]
3. Conventional text editors with certain features that support version control, notably Emacs [18] and Microsoft Word [12]
4. Tools designed specifically for collaborative editing not necessarily in a software environment, such as Quilt [4] PREP [15,13,14] MILO [6] SEPIA [5] and DIVA [17]

Discussion of the relationship between Historian and these tools follows.

2.1   First and Second Generation CM Tools

RCS and SCCS are very well known in the CM community, having been the basis of use and/or comparison for very many later CM systems. The pros and cons of first-generation systems have been discussed extensively elsewhere, notably by Conradi and Westfechtel in [1] and [2] RCS is of direct relevance to Historian since we use the RCS engine in the Historian implementation, although the end user is completely unaware of this.

The second generation CM system with features most comparable to Historian is COOP/Orm. Multiple granularity is supported for both structural and temporal levels. While their approach does not focus on version navigation, granularity levels are utilized for the purposes of group awareness and unifying the approaches to version control of documents and configurations. Group awareness is supported at a temporally fine level by making visible incremental document changes to all users concurrently editing the document. Awareness is also supported at a coarse level.

Multiple structural granularity is supported in both COOP/Orm and Historian because both fine and coarse granularity have disadvantages when supported without the other. For example, if only fine granularity were supported, configurations would result in a large number of version combinations, though finer grained versioned items make more sense from the version control point of view because they limit the effects of changes.

The representations of fine-grain versioning used in the CAMERA and POEM systems are comparable to Historian, however the focus of both systems is different. In the case of CAMERA, the system is designed to support powerful techniques for merging different document alternatives. The major focus of POEM is the unification of the logical representations used in normal program development with the representations used for configuration management. Neither focuses on version navigation as in Historian.

2.2   Standard and Collaborative Text Editing Systems

Features to support version control are found in some conventional text editors. These features can be grouped into the following general categories:

1. automatic version saving
2. version comparison
3. undo/redo commands

As representatives of "conventional" editors, consider Emacs and Microsoft Word. Emacs provides all three of these features. Word supports the second and third, with partial support for the first..

What is common to Historian and conventional editors is the concept of a *basic action*. While the precise definitions of basic action differ between the editors, the concept is fundamental. The editor defines what constitutes a primitive editing action, representing the smallest level of granularity at which changes are recorded. Historian automatically archives changes at this level, whereas conventional editors only support non-archived undo/redo at this level.

Among systems designed specifically for collaborative work, MILO and DIVA provide limited forms of version control. MILO provides time-ordered views of a document, based on time-stamped notes attached to document elements. The

MILO user can traverse the note history, and filter the history based on the contents of notes. The DIVA system provides a catch-up facility that allows users to view document changes from an historical record. The user interface includes animated replay of document changes.

Historian provides a considerably larger degree of support for version control than in MILO or DIVA. In particular, Historian versions are not limited to time-stamped notes or other document attachments.

The Quilt and SEPIA systems focus on version control specifically. Version control in Quilt is less comprehensive, and requires users to define cooperative roles to enable versioning. The most recent SEPIA system [5] does provide comprehensive version control. In comparison to SEPIA, Historian is significantly more focused on the domain of textual documents. SEPIA is a full-scale hypertext system, in which version control is supported at the level of hypertext objects and tasks. While focused retrieval is supported at this level, it is less specifically focused than in Historian, where users concentrate on the textual content of a document, not on more general hypertext objects.

The existing system most closely related to Historian is the PREP editor [15,13,14] PREP allows users to focus on version changes at conventional levels of document organization, such as sentence and paragraph. It also supports flexible comparison between arbitrary version pairs. The contributions of Historian vis a vis PREP are fully automatic version archiving, combined with flexible version search and retrieval. PREP's side-by-side comparison interface is more elaborate than in Historian, but both PREP and Historian convey fundamentally the same comparative information. The advantage in Historian is that versions can be compared incrementally by traversing the archived history. In the broader area of cooperative work, the overall scope of the Historian system is considerably smaller than that of PREP. In particular, support for inter-author communication based on tunable parameters is beyond the current focus of the Historian system.

3   Overview of Historian

This section of the paper presents an overview of the Historian model. The interface and functionality described are somewhat beyond the capabilities of the current working prototype. Precise details of prototype limitations are presented in Section 5.

Historian supports multiple structural granularity by recognizing and utilizing the hierarchical structure of documents. In terminology presented in [10] the smallest versioned item of a document is called an *information unit*. For example, in a C file information units are functions and in a prose document information units are paragraphs. Larger versioned items, called *composite units*, are composed of zero or more information units. In a prose document chapters and sections are typical composite units; chapters consist of sections and sections consist of paragraphs. The largest composite unit versioned by Historian is the entire file.

From a version navigation standpoint, structural fine-grain support enables focusing a search on a particular section of a document. If the user is only interested in the evolution of a function, retrieving versions at the file level will typically involve retrieving versions that do not show changes in the function of interest. The user must also search for the section of interest in every version retrieved. Consider the following scenario: Functions f1, f2 and f3 exist in a file and the user modifies f1 and checks in the file, modifies f1 again and checks in, then modifies f2 only and checks in, and finally modifies f3 only and checks in. If the user wants to retrieve f1's earlier version, then traversing back in time at the file level retrieves three versions that do not show a change in f1. By focusing a search on f1 via fine-grain support, these three uninteresting versions are not retrieved.

Historian implements change propagation as defined in COOP/Orm [11] A change to an information unit also constitutes a change to the composite unit(s) of which it is a part. Thus, all changes are reflected in all the different levels of structural granularity and the user can switch granularity views at any point including in the middle of a search through history. An early version of a function, for example, can be used to bring up the corresponding version of the entire file.

In order to keep track of the hierarchical structure of a document and its modifications, Historian has been implemented as an extension of the XEmacs text editor. Figure 1 shows an example of the Historian user interface.

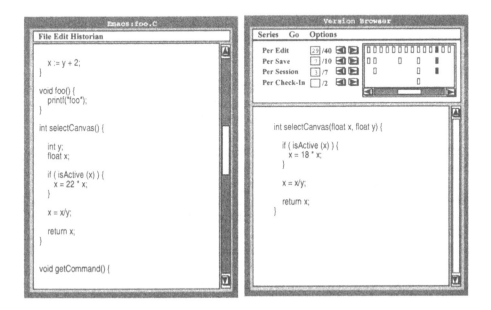

Fig. 1. Historian User Interface

The window on the left is the regular text editing window used to modify files. The window on the right is the version browser. The text editing window is used to specify the unit whose versions will be retrieved in the version browser. In this example, a C file is being edited and the versions of one of its functions (an information unit) are being browsed.

Versions are generated automatically by Historian as the user modifies the file. In order to support temporally fine-grained version control and to keep a comprehensive set of versions, Historian generates a version at every edit operation. This granularity can be compared to the change granularity typically supported by the multiple undo features in text editors.

Instead of generating only one series of versions for each unit, several series of versions are generated, each series differing significantly in size. Only one series contains a comprehensive set of versions and versions for the other series are generated less frequently. In this manner, Historian supports multiple temporal granularity. By choosing the series through which to traverse, the user can choose between executing a thorough inspection of a unit's history versus executing a quick and skimming search.

The size of a series is controlled by the type of user action that triggers a version save for that series. In our example, four series are generated where each of the following user actions triggers a version save for its corresponding series:

· The Per Edit series: An edit operation.
· The Per Save series: The file is saved.
· The Per Session series: The file is closed.
· The Per Check-In series: The file is checked in.

Note that a version is only saved if the unit has been modified..

The Per Edit series typically contains the largest number of versions since edit operations occur more frequently than file saves, file closes, and file check-ins. Conversely, the Per Check-In series typically contains the least number of versions.

Our example shows the four series in the version browser. For each series the number of the currently displayed version and the total number of versions in the series are shown. Forward and backward arrow buttons are used to sequentially step through the series. One can also retrieve versions by clicking on the version boxes inside the version graph. Versions that are vertically aligned in the version graph represent a single version shared between more than one series.

In our example, the versions of a single function (an information unit) are being browsed. If the versions of the entire file were being browsed instead, the four types of series will still be shown but they will typically be much larger in size since they will contain all of the changes made to the file. This represents a combination of the histories of all the information units of which it is composed.

The number and types of series used for a particular file are configurable by the user. For example, if a temporally fine-grained version control is not desired, only the Per Check-In series need be used.

In addition to the series in our example, other options are available such as the Per Compile (for compilable documents such as C files) and a Marker series.

Versions are generated for the Per Compile series whenever the file is successfully compiled. Traversing this series ensures that every version retrieved is correct to the degree that the compiler ensures correctness.

Versions are generated for the Marker series explicitly by the user to mark specific versions that are deemed important. Adding a version to the Marker series grants quicker access to that version in the future, a form of user-explicit sifting of uninteresting versions. For example, if a programmer is about to make major changes throughout a file, changes which may need to be undone in the future, marking the current file version allows the programmer to make these changes without worry since they can all be undone easily. The Marker series is especially useful for rapid development and exploratory programming.

As with structural granularity, the user can switch temporal granularity at any point during a search. A typical case is one in which the desired version of a unit exists somewhere early in its history and the user wishes to traverse back in time incrementally. This is done using the arrow buttons, starting from the most current version instead of starting at a random point in history. Instead of traversing a series with a comprehensive set of versions, the user would begin with a coarse-grained series such as the Per Check-In series for a skimming traversal. Once the general proximity of the desired version is found, the user would switch to a fine-grained series for a more thorough evolutionary inspection.

4   Technical Details

Historian's implementation is tightly integrated with the XEmacs text editor [9] in order to support fine-grained version control of both types. The use of XEmacs as the base editor has facilitated the continuous monitoring of changes made to a document. Structurally fine-grain version control requires maintaining the boundary locations of each information unit within a file and the awareness of which units the user modifies. Temporally fine-grain version control requires monitoring the user's actions and triggering version saves of modified units when appropriate.

Only the versions of information units are physically saved; composite unit versions are created from those of their information units. Due to change propagation, each change in an information unit reflects a change in the composite unit of which it is a part. In order to minimize overhead and memory, new versions are generated for changed information units only, and the current versions of unchanged information units are shared. Specifically, composite units are represented as collections of pointers to information units. Our approach is similar to the revision tree model defined in [11]

Versions are also shared along the different levels of temporal granularity since the same version can exist on more than one series. A version in one series is equal to a version in another series when a version is saved for the second series before any further modification is made to the unit since the version was saved for the first series. In our C example, the three coarser grained series always share all their versions with the finest grained series, the Per Edit series, since modifications always trigger a new version for that series. However, not all versions of a coarse-grained series share their versions with the finer grained series. In that sense, multiple temporal granularity differs from multiple structural granularity in that the structural type has the property of inclusion between the different levels whereas the temporal type does not.

5   Current Status and Future Work

A working prototype of Historian has recently been developed and only a small number of users have worked extensively with the system. Through this limited experience we have made observations on the effects of using Historian. We have observed a significant increase in the frequency of version retrieval with the use of Historian when compared to other version control systems. Also, the user gains a sense of security from the fact that no data are ever lost and that whatever changes are made, they can be undone quickly. This, in turn, enables the user to modify code that already works yet needs to be changed with less hesitation or worry, supporting rapid development and exploratory programming. Code is seldom commented out for later reference, but rather deleted instead to increase code readability. Finally, the multiple undo feature of XEmacs is effectively replaced by Historian, as discussed earlier.

The current implementation supports a limited number of features of the model discussed in this paper and we plan to continue development. Most importantly, structural coarse-grain support has been designed but not yet fully implemented. Structural fine-grain support and the different levels of temporal granularity are provided. Also, the user interface shown in the example is slightly more sophisticated than the one implemented. Specifically, the version graph is not present in the prototype and the series information is presented in a textual form. Otherwise, the interface of the prototype is as presented in Figure 1. In terms of supported document types, the prototype has been used on C, Lisp, HTML, and UNIX Troff.

A problem with structurally fine-grain version control which needs to be addressed deals with the relationships between units that arise when two units are merged together, one unit is split apart, or a significant portion of one unit is pasted into another. During traversal, the user might want to follow the history unit section that becomes part of the history of another unit as a result one of these operations. For example, if a large block of code were cut from one function and pasted into another, traversing forward in time through the history of the original function would suddenly indicate the disappearance of that block of code, even though its evolution continues elsewhere. Without special support from the version browser, the user would have to bring up the file version which corresponds to the function version displayed, and search for the new function that contains the desired block of code. Only then could the user resume inspecting the evolution of the block of code. There is still no guarantee the section can be found in the file version because the cut and paste operation could have been executed over a sequence of actions spanning version saves.

While splitting and merging units are relatively rare operations in programming compared to cutting and pasting, splitting and merging paragraphs in prose documents is common. Following the evolution of a paragraph can become quite confusing if proper navigation support is not provided. To the best of our knowledge, this issue has not been addressed by existing systems that implement structurally fine-grain version control, which is understandable because the overhead of version navigation has never been of primary focus. We have a number of user interface ideas each of which solves this problem but we have yet to decide upon which one to implement.

6 Conclusion

This paper has presented the Historian system for multi-grain version control and navigation. Our experiences to date with Historian have been quite positive. We have observed the hoped-for benefits of Historian – that overhead in version retrieval is reduced given multi-grain access to document histories at both structural and temporal levels.

It should be noted that the benefits for experimental programming provided by Historian, in particular the security to make rapid changes to an evolving program, are done in a context that also supports sound software engineering. That is, rapid development is done by an individual during the course of program evolution. When versions are to be shared by colleagues, they are checked in, and become stabilized by the normal mechanisms that lock-out changes to version that have been declared stable.

Our experience with the current Historian prototype is limited to use by its development team and a small number of other software engineers. We plan to conduct a controlled usage study that will provide additional data to help quantify the benefits we have observed in our use of the research prototype.

References

1. CONRADI, R., AND WESTFECHTEL, B. Configuring versioned software products. *Software Configuration Management, ICSE '96 SCM-6 Workshop* (March 1996), 87–109.
2. CONRADI, R., AND WESTFECHTEL, B. Towards a uniform version model for software configuration management. *Software Configuration Management, ICSE '97 SCM-7 Workshop* (May 1997), 1–17.
3. CROSS, G. A. A bakhtinian exploration of factors affecting the collaborative writing of an executive letter of an annual report. *Research in the Teaching of English 24, 2* (May 1990), 173–203.
4. FISH, R. S., KRAUT, R. E., AND LELAND, M. D. P. Quilt: a collaborative tool for cooperative writing. *Proceedings of the ACM SIGOIS Conference on Office Automation Systems* (1988), 30–37.
5. HAAKE, A., AND HAAKE, J. M. Take cover: Exploiting version support in cooperative systems. *Proceedings of the ACM SIGCHI Conference on Human Factors in Computing Systems* (April 1993), 406–413.

6. JONES, S. Milo: A computer-based tool for (co-)authoring structured documents. In *Computer-Supported Collaborative Writing*, M. Sharples, Ed. Springer-Verlag, 1993, pp. 185–202.

7. LIN, Y.-J., AND REISS, S. P. Configuration management in terms of modules. *Software Configuration Management, ICSE SCM-4 and SCM-5 Workshops* (1995), 101–117.

8. LIPPE, E., AND VAN N. OOSTEROM. Operation-based merging. *Proceedings of ACM SIGSOFT '92* (December 1992), 78–87.

9. LUCID. *Xemacs 19.14*, June 1996.

10. MAGNUSSON, B., AND ASKLUND, U. Fine grained version control of configurations in coop/orm. *Software Configuration Management, ICSE '96 SCM-6 Workshop* (March 1996), 31–48.

11. MAGNUSSON, B., ASKLUND, U., AND MINOR, S. Fine grained version control for collaborative software development. *Proceedings of the First ACM SIGSOFT Symposium on the Foundations of Computer Science* (December 1993), 33–41.

12. MICROSOFT. *Microsoft Word, The World's Most Popular Word Processor, Version 6.0*, 1994.

13. NEUWIRTH, C. M., CHANDHOK, R., KAUFER, D. S., ERION, P., MORRIS, J. H., AND MILLER, D. Flexible diff-ing in a collaborative writing system. *Proceedings of the ACM SIGCHI and SIGOIS Conference on Computer-Supported Cooperative Work* (November 1992), 147–154.

14. NEUWIRTH, C. M., KAUFER, D. S., CHANDHOK, R., AND MORRIS, J. H. Computer-support for distributed collaborative writing: Defining parameters of interaction. *Proceedings of the ACM SIGCHI and SIGOIS Conference on Computer-Supported Cooperative Work* (October 1994), 145–152.

15. NEUWIRTH, C. M., KAUFER, D. S., AND MORRIS, R. C. J. H. Issues in the design of computer-support for co-authoring and commenting. *Proceedings of the ACM SIGCHI and SIGOIS Conference on Computer-Supported Cooperative Work* (October 1990), 183–195.

16. ROCHKIND, M. J. The source code control system. *IEEE Transaction on Software Engineering, 1 (4)* (April 1975), 255–265.

17. SOHLENKAMP, M., AND CHWELOS, G. Integrating communication, cooperation, and awareness: The diva virtual office environment. *Proceedings of the ACM SIGCHI and SIGOIS Conference on Computer-Supported Cooperative Work* (October 1994), 331–343.

18. STALLMAN, R. M. *The GNU Emacs Reference Manual*, 1995.

19. THOMAS, D., AND JOHNSON, K. Orwell a configuration management system for team programming. *Proceedings of OOPSLA '88* (September 1988), 135–141.

20. TICHY, W. F. Rcs – a system for version control. *Software – Practice and Experience 15, 7* (July 1985), 637–654.

High-Level Best Practices
in Software Configuration Management

Laura Wingerd
Perforce Software, Inc.
wingerd@perforce.com

Christopher Seiwald
Perforce Software, Inc.
seiwald@perforce.com

Abstract: When deploying new SCM (software configuration management) tools, implementers sometimes focus on perfecting fine-grained activities, while unwittingly carrying forward poor, large-scale practices from their previous jobs or previous tools. The result is a well-executed blunder. This paper promotes some high-level best practices that reflect the authors' experiences in deploying SCM.

1   Introduction

„A tool is only as good as you use it,‚‚ the saying goes. As providers of software configuration management (SCM) tools and consultants to software companies, we are often asked for sound advice on SCM best practices – that is, how to deploy SCM software to the maximum advantage. In answering these requests we have a bounty of direct and indirect SCM experience from which to draw. The direct experience comes from having been developers and codeline managers ourselves; the indirect experience comes from customer reports of successes and failures with our product (Perforce) and other SCM tools.

The table below lists six general areas of SCM deployment, and some coarse-grained best practices within each of those areas. The following chapters explain each item.

Workspaces, where developers build, test, and debug.	〈 Don't share workspaces. 〈 Don't work outside of managed workspaces. 〈 Don't use jello views. 〈 Stay in sync with the codeline. 〈 Check in often.
Codelines, the canonical sets of source files.	〈 Give each codeline a policy. 〈 Give each codeline an owner. 〈 Have a mainline.
Branches, variants of the codeline.	〈 Branch only when necessary. 〈 Don't copy when you mean to branch. 〈 Branch on incompatible policy. 〈 Branch late. 〈 Branch, instead of freeze.

B. Magnusson (Ed.): ECOOP 98, SCM-8, LNCS 1439, pp. 57-66, 1998
© Springer-Verlag Berlin Heidelberg 1998

Change propagation, getting changes from one codeline to another.	⟨ Make original changes in the branch that has evolved the least since branching. ⟨ Propagate early and often. ⟨ Get the right person to do the merge.
Builds, turning source files into products.	⟨ Source + tools = product. ⟨ Check in all original source. ⟨ Segregate built objects from original source. ⟨ Use common build tools. ⟨ Build often. ⟨ Keep build logs and build output.
Process, the rules for all of the above.	⟨ Track change packages. ⟨ Track change package propagations. ⟨ Distinguish change requests from change packages. ⟨ Give everything and owner. ⟨ Use living documents.

2 The Workspace

The workspace is where engineers edit source files, build the software components they're working on, and test and debug what they've built. Most SCM systems have some notion of a workspace; sometimes they are called „sandboxes,‚‚ as in Source Integrity, or „views,‚‚ as in ClearCase and Perforce. Changes to managed SCM repository files begin as changes to files in a workspace.

The best practices for workspaces include:

⟨ *Don't share workspaces.* A workspace should have a single purpose, such as an edit/build/test area for a single developer, or a build/test/release area for a product release. Sharing workspaces confuses people, just as sharing a desk does. Furthermore, sharing workspaces compromises the SCM system's ability to track activity by user or task. Workspaces and the disk space they occupy are cheap; don't waste time trying to conserve them.

⟨ *Don't work outside of managed workspaces.* Your SCM system can only track work in progress when it takes place within managed workspaces. Users working outside of workspaces are beached; there's a river of information flowing past and they're not part of it. For instance, SCM systems generally use workspaces to facilitate some of the communication among developers working on related tasks. You can see what is happening in others' workspaces, and they can see what's going on in yours. If you need to take an emergency vacation, your properly managed workspace may be all you can leave behind. Use proper workspaces.

⟨ *Don't use jello views.* A file in your workspace should not change unless *you explicitly* cause the change. A „jello view‚‚ is a workspace where file changes are caused by external events beyond your control. A typical example of a jello view is a workspace built upon a tree of symbolic links to files in another workspace –

when the underlying files are updated, your workspace files change. Jello views are a source of chaos in software development. Debug symbols in executables don't match the source files, mysterious recompilations occur in supposedly trivial rebuilds, and debugging cycles never converge – these are just some of the problems. Keep your workspaces firm and stable by setting them up so that users have control over when their files change.

⟨ *Stay in sync with the codeline.* As a developer, the quality of your work depends on how well it meshes with other peoples' work. In other words, as changes are checked into the codeline, you should update your workspace and integrate those changes with yours.

As an SCM engineer, it behooves you to make sure this workspace update operation is straightforward and unencumbered with tricky or time-consuming procedures. If developers find it fairly painless to update their workspaces, they'll do it more frequently and integration problems won't pile up at project deadlines.

⟨ *Check in often.* Integrating your development work with other peoples' work also requires you to check in your changes as soon as they are ready. Once you've finished a development task, check in your changed files so that your work is available to others.

Again, as the SCM engineer, you should set up procedures that encourage frequent check-ins. Don't implement unduly arduous validation procedures, and don't freeze codelines (see Branching, below). Short freezes are bearable, but long freezes compromise productivity. Much productivity can be wasted waiting for the right day (or week, or month) to submit changes.

3 The Codeline

In this context, the codeline is the canonical set of source files required to produce your software. Typically codelines are branched, and the branches evolve into variant codelines embodying different releases. The best practices with regard to codelines are:

⟨ *Give each codeline a policy.* A codeline policy specifies the fair use and permissible check-ins for the codeline, and is the essential user's manual for codeline SCM. For example, the policy of a development codeline should state that it isn't for release; likewise, the policy of a release codeline should limit changes to approved bug fixes.[1] The policy can also describe how to document

---

[1] *Some sensible codeline policies:* **Development codeline**: interim code changes may be checked in; affected components must be buildable. **Release codeline**: software must build and pass regression tests before check-in; check-ins limited to bug fixes; no new features or functionality may be checked in; after check-in, branch is frozen until entire QA cycle is completed. **Mainline**: all components must compile and link, and pass regression tests; completed, tested new features may be checked in.

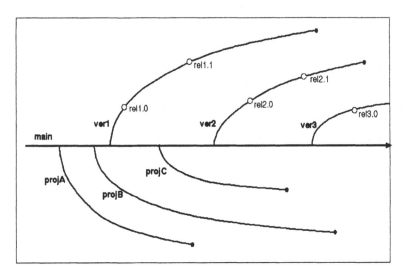

Fig.1 The Mainline Model

changes being checked in, what review is needed, what testing is required, and the expectations of codeline stability after check-ins. A policy is a critical component for a documented, enforceable software development process, and a codeline without a policy, from an SCM point of view, is out of control.

(*Give each codeline an owner.* Having defined a policy for a codeline, you'll soon encounter special cases where the policy is inapplicable or ambiguous. Developers facing these ambiguities will turn to the person in charge of the codeline for workarounds. When no one is in charge, developers tend to enact their own workarounds without documenting them. Or they simply procrastinate because they don't have enough information about the codeline to come up with a reasonable workaround. You can avoid this morass by appointing someone to own the codeline, and to shepherd it through its useful life. With this broader objective, the codeline owner can smooth the ride over rough spots in software development by advising developers on policy exceptions and documenting them.

(*Have a mainline.* A „mainline,„ or „trunk,„ is the branch of a codeline that evolves forever. A mainline provides an ultimate destination for almost all changes – both maintenance fixes and new features – and represents the primary, linear evolution of a software product. Release codelines and development codelines are branched from the mainline, and work that occurs in branches is propagated back to the mainline.

Figure 1 shows a mainline (called „main,„), from which several release lines („ver1,„ „ver2,„ and „ver3,„) and feature development lines („projA,„ „projb,„ and „projC,„) have been branched. Developers work in the mainline or in a feature development line. The release lines are reserved for testing and critical fixes, and are insulated

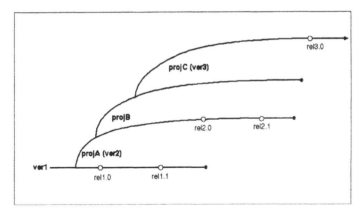

Fig. 2: The Promotion Model

from the hubbub of development. Eventually all changes submitted to the release lines and the feature development lines get merged into the mainline.

The adverse approach is to „promote‚‚ codelines; for example, to promote a development codeline to a release codeline, and branch off a new development codeline. For example, Figure 2 shows a development codeline promoted to a release codeline („ver1‚‚) and branched into another development codeline („projA‚‚). Each release codeline starts out as a development codeline, and development moves from codeline to codeline.

The promotion scheme suffers from two crippling drawbacks: (1) it requires the policy of a codeline to change, which is never easy to communicate to everyone; (2) it requires developers to relocate their work from one codeline to another, which is error-prone and time-consuming. *90% of SCM „process‚‚ is enforcing codeline promotion to compensate for the lack of a mainline.*

Process is streamlined and simplified when you use a mainline model. With a mainline, contributors' workspaces and environments are stable for the duration of their tasks at hand, and no additional administrative overhead is incurred as software products move forward to maturity.

4 Branching

Branching, the creation of variant codelines from other codelines, is the most problematic area of SCM. Different SCM tools support branching in markedly different ways, and different policies require that branching be used in still more different ways. We found the following guidelines helpful when branching (and sometimes when avoiding branching):

‹   *Branch only when necessary.* Every branch is more work – more builds, more changes to be propagated among codelines, more source file merges. If you keep this in mind every time you consider making a branch you may avoid sprouting unnecessary branches.

〈 *Don't copy when you mean to branch.* An alternative to using your SCM tool's branching mechanism is to copy a set of source files from one codeline and check them in to another as new files. Don't think that you can avoid the costs of branching by simply copying. Copying incurs all the headaches of branching – additional entities and increased complexity – but without the benefit of your SCM system's branching support. Don't be fooled: even „read-only„ copies shipped off to another development group „for reference only„ often return with changes made. Use your SCM system to make branches when you spin off parts or all of a codeline.

〈 *Branch on incompatible policy.* There is one simple rule to determine if a codeline should be branched: it should be branched when its users need different check-in policies. For example, a product release group may need a check-in policy that enforces rigorous testing, whereas a development team may need a policy that allows frequent check-ins of partially tested changes. This policy divergence calls for a codeline branch. When one development group doesn't wish to see another development group's changes, that is also a form of incompatible policy: each group should have its own branch.

〈 *Branch late.* To minimize the number of changes that need to be propagated from one branch to another, put off creating a branch as long as possible. For example, if the mainline branch contains all the new features ready for a release, do as much testing and bug fixing in it as you can before creating a release branch. Every bug fixed in the mainline before the release branch is created is one less change needing propagation between branches.

〈 *Branch instead of freeze.* On the other hand, if testing requires freezing a codeline, developers who have pending changes will have to sit on their changes until the testing is complete. If this is the case, branch the codeline early enough so that developers can check in and get on with their work.

5 Change Propagation

Once you have branched codelines, you face the chore of propagating file changes across branches. This is rarely a trivial task, but there are some things you can do to keep it manageable.

〈 *Make original changes in the branch that has evolved the least since branching.* It is much easier to merge a change from a file that is close to the common ancestor than it is to merge a change from a file that has diverged considerably. This is because the change in the file that has diverged may be built upon changes that are not being propagated, and those unwanted changes can confound the merge process. You can minimize the merge complexity by making original changes in the branch that is the most stable. For example, if a release codeline is branched from a mainline, make a bug fix first in the release line and then merge it into the mainline. If you make the bug fix in the mainline first, subsequently merging it into a release codeline may require you to *back out* other, incompatible changes that aren't meant to go into the release codeline.

⟨ *Propagate early and often.* When it's feasible to propagate a change from one branch to another (that is, if the change wouldn't violate the target branch's policy), do it sooner rather than later. Postponed and batched change propagations can result in stunningly complex file merges.

⟨ *Get the right person to do the merge.* The burden of change propagation can be lightened by assigning the responsibility to the engineer best prepared to resolve file conflicts. Changes can be propagated by (a) the owner of the target files, (b) the person who make the original changes, or (c) someone else. Either (a) or (b) will do a better job than (c).

6 Builds

A build is the business of constructing usable software from original source files. Builds are more manageable and less prone to problems when a few key practices are observed:

⟨ *Source + tools = product.* The only ingredients in a build should be source files and the tools to which they are input. Memorized procedures and yellow stickies have no place in this equation. Given the same source files and build tools, the resulting product should always be the same. If you have rote setup procedures, automate them in scripts. If you have manual setup steps, document them in build instructions. And document all tool specifications, including OS, compilers, include files, link libraries, make programs, and executable paths.

⟨ *Check in* all *original source.* When software can't be reliably reproduced from the same ingredients, chances are the ingredient list is incomplete. Frequently overlooked ingredients are makefiles, setup scripts, build scripts, build instructions, and tool specifications. All of these are the source you build with. Remember: *source + tools = product.*

⟨ *Segregate built objects from original source.* Organize your builds so that the directories containing original source files are not polluted by built objects. Original source files are those you create „from an original thought process„ with a text editor, an application generator, or any other interactive tool. Built objects are all the files that get created during your build process, including generated source files. Built objects should not go into your source code directories. Instead, build them into a directory tree of their own. This segregation allows you to limit the scope of SCM-managed directories to those that contain only source. It also corrals the files that tend to be large and/or expendable into one location, and simplifies disk space management for builds.

⟨ *Use common build tools.* Developers, test engineers, and release engineers should all use the same build tools. Much time is wasted when a developer cannot reproduce a problem found in testing, or when the released product varies from what was tested. Remember: *source + tools = product.*

⟨ *Build often.* Frequent, end-to-end builds with regression testing („sanity„ builds) have two benefits: (1) they reveal integration problems introduced by check-ins, and (2) they produce link libraries and other built objects that can be used by developers. In an ideal world, sanity builds would occur after every check-in, but in an active codeline it's more practical to do them at intervals, typically nightly. Every codeline branch should be subject to regular, frequent, and complete builds and regression testing, even when product release is in the distant future.

(*Keep build logs and build outputs.* For any built object you produce, you should be able to look up the exact operations (e.g., complete compiler flag and link command text) that produced the last known good version of it. Archive build outputs and logs, including source file versions (e.g., a label), tool and OS version info, compiler outputs, intermediate files, built objects, and test results, for future reference. As large software projects evolve, components are handed off from one group to another, and the receiving group may not be in a position to begin builds of new components immediately. When they do begin to build new components, they will need access to previous build logs in order to diagnose the integration problems they encounter.

7 Process

It would take an entire paper, or several papers, to explore the full scope of SCM process design and implementation, and many such papers have already been written. Furthermore, your shop has specific objectives and requirements that will be reflected in the process you implement, and we do not presume to know what those are. In our experience, however, some process concepts are key to any SCM implementation:

(*Track change packages.* Even though each file in a codeline has its revision history, each revision in its history is only useful in the context of a set of related files. The question „What other source files were changed along with this particular change to foo.c?„ can't be answered unless you track change *packages*, or sets of files related by a logical change. Change packages, not individual file changes, are the visible manifestation of software development. Some SCM systems track change packages for you; if yours doesn't, write an interface that does.

(*Track change package propagations.* One clear benefit of tracking change packages is that it becomes very easy propagate logical changes (e.g., bug fixes) from one codeline branch to another. However, it's not enough to simply propagate change packages across branches; you must keep track of which change packages have been propagated, which propagations are pending, and which codeline branches are likely donors or recipients of propagations. Otherwise you'll never be able to answer the question „Is the fix for bug X in the release Y codeline?„ Again, some SCM systems track change package propagations for you, whereas with others you'll have to write your own interface to do it. Ultimately, you should never have to resort to „diffing„ files to figure out if a change package has been propagated between codelines.

(*Distinguish change requests from change packages.* „What to do„ and „what was done„ are different data entities. For example, a bug report is a „what to do„

entity and a bug fix is a „what was done„ entity. Your SCM process should distinguish between the two, because in fact there can be a one-to-many relationship between change requests and change packages.

⟨   *Give everything an owner.* Every process, policy, document, product, component, codeline, branch, and task in your SCM system should have an owner. Owners give life to these entities by representing them; an entity with an owner can grow and mature. Ownerless entities are like obstacles in an ant trail – the ants simply march around them as if they weren't there.

⟨   *Use living documents.* The policies and procedures you implement should be described in living documents; that is, your process documentation should be as readily available and as subject to update as your managed source code. Documents that aren't accessible are useless; documents that aren't updateable are nearly so. Process documents should be accessible from all of your development environments: at your own workstation, at someone else's workstation, and from your machine at home. And process documents should be easily updateable, and updates should be immediately available.

8 Conclusion

Best practices in SCM, like best practices anywhere, always seem obvious once you've used them. The practices discussed in this paper have worked well for us, but we recognize that no single, short document can contain them all. So we have presented the practices that offer the greatest return and yet seem to be violated more often than not.

We welcome the opportunity to improve this document, and solicit both challenges to the above practices as well as the additions of new ones.

9 References

Berczuk, Steve. "Configuration Management Patterns", 1997. Available at http://www.bell-labs.com/cgiuser/OrgPatterns/ OrgPatterns?ConfigurationManagementPatterns.

Compton, Stephen B, *Configuration Management for Software*, VNR Computer Library, Van Nostrand Reinhold, 1993.

Continuus Software Corp., „Work Area Management„, *Continuus/CM: Change Management for Software Development.* Available at http://www.continuus.com/developers/developersACE.html.

Dart, Susan, "Spectrum of Functionality in Configuration Management Systems",

Software Engineering Institute, 1990. Available at http://www.sei.cmu.edu/ technology/case/scm/tech_rep/TR11_90/TOC_TR11_90.html

Jameson, Kevin, *Multi Platform Code Management*, O'Reilly & Associates, 1994

Linenbach, Terris, "Programmers' Canvas: A pattern for source code management" 1996. Available at http://www.rahul.net/terris/ProgrammersCanvas.htm.

Lyon, David D, *Practical CM*, Raven Publishing, 1997

McConnell, Steve, "Best Practices: Daily Build and Smoke Test", *EEE Software*, Vol. 13, No. 4, July 1996

van der Hoek, Andre, Hall, Richard S., Heimbigner, Dennis, and Wolf, Alexander L., "Software Release Management", *Proceedings of the 6th European Software Engineering Conference*, Zurich, Switzerland, 1997.

Experiences with Architectural Software Configuration Management in Ragnarok

Henrik Bærbak Christensen

Department of Computer Science
University of Aarhus
DK-8000 Århus C, Denmark
hbc@daimi.aau.dk

Abstract. This paper describes a model, denoted *architectural software configuration management*, that minimises the gap between software design and configuration management by allowing developers to do configuration- and version control of the abstractions and hierarchy in a software architecture. The model emphasises traceability and reproducibility by unifying the concepts version and bound configuration. Experiences with such a model, implemented in a prototype "Ragnarok", from three real-life, small- to medium-sized, software development projects are reported. The conclusion is that the presented model is viable and "feels natural" for software developers .

1 Introduction

The software configuration management community has developed a large number of powerful techniques, models, and systems for software configuration management (SCM) [20,18,15,35]. A less fortunate consequence seems to have been that often SCM has become complicated and burdensome for ordinary developers [2]. We believe this is partly because design/implementation on one hand and SCM on the other require different mental models [24,23,12] in many SCM systems.

This paper outlines an *architectural software configuration management* model where the logical software architecture [22,31] is used as basis for version and configuration control. Architecture is central as it forms the mental framework developers use to design, discuss, document and reuse software systems. Thereby, SCM is done in terms of concepts from a well-known domain, and less SCM specific concepts are introduced giving a shallower learning curve for developers. Furthermore, emphasis is put on traceability and reproducibility of configurations and architectural changes.

Essential features of the model have been implemented in a prototype, Ragnarok, that is currently used in three, real, software development projects.

B. Magnusson (Ed.): ECOOP 98, SCM-8, LNCS 1439, pp. 67–74, 1998.

2   Logical Versus Physical Structure

A sound, logical, software design is perhaps the most important aspect in successful software development, and *abstraction* and *hierarchy* are key concepts in a good design [6].

An abstraction is seldom an isolated entity but must be understood in its architectural context; abstractions are organised hierarchically by composition (aggregation/part-whole) and interrelated by dependencies (association/use).

As an example, in object-oriented architectures abstractions are typically classes and class-categories[1]. Composition groups classes (or class-categories) into class-categories, forming a hierarchy, while dependencies relate classes functionally (e.g. that a window class uses a general-purpose rectangle class.)

Abstractions usually have a physical implementation in a programming language. The coupling between logical and physical structure vary greatly in different programming languages and environments: Integrated environments for Smalltalk present the logical structure and hide the physical level; Java enforce a strict one-to-one mapping between (public) classes and files; BETA uses a special modularisation language; and in C++ the coupling is purely based on conventions. Though they all offer e.g. the class abstraction, their storage models vary greatly. Many SCM tools are based on the physical structure which is often too low level and generate an unfortunate gap between the mental model used for design/implementation on one hand and SCM on the other.

Our goal is to narrow this gap by allowing design, implementation, version control, and configuration management, to be done purely on a systems logical architecture at the user level and hide the concrete level of actual code fragment/file versioning.

Central to the architectural software configuration management model is the *software component*, which is an object representing an abstraction. The physical implementation (a set of code fragments) is stored in an attribute denoted the *substance* of the software component. *Relations* to other abstractions (composition and dependencies) are also stored as attributes. A software component is a flexible building block that may represent any granularity in a system from a simple method to a full system with a complicated substructure of components.

3   Architectural Versioning

The evolving item is the software component and each state is represented by a *software component version*—in essence reifying a version of an abstraction.

A software component version is an immutable, composite, object in a version database containing: A component identifier CID; a version identifier VID; a set S_{sub} of code fragment versions (substance snapshot); and two relation sets, S_{comp} and S_{dep}, each holding references to other software component versions (snapshots of the compositional relations and dependencies respectively). The

---

[1] A class-category is an aggregate of logically related classes (and/or class-categories) achieving a common goal [6].

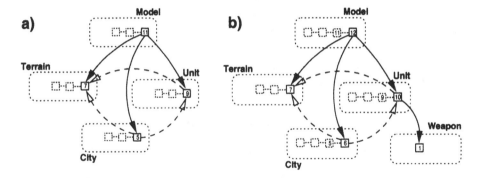

Fig. 1. Example of evolution of an abstraction representing a game model.

software component versions for a given component, CID, are arranged in a traditional version graph [33,14].

For the architecture to evolve, developers modify copies of component versions in a workspace (modifying substance and/or relations) before committing these to the version database.

An essential feature of the elements in the relation sets is that they are references to *specific* software component versions, not generic references.

3.1   Check-In and Check-Out

It is important to track milestones and releases of full systems as well as its parts; and on a smaller scale to enable developers to backtrack to known, stable, configurations.

The architectural model emphasises such bound configurations by means of a transitive closure check-in algorithm. When checking in a component version the algorithm recursively traverses all relation set references and creates new versions of all components along paths to modified components[2].

The check-out trivially reverses this process: The root component version is checked out, then the check-out is propagated recursively to all component versions referenced in the relation sets.

Example Consider a simple strategy game system where a class-category, Model, is composed of classes Terrain, City, and Unit, modelling fundamental game concepts. Figure 1a shows Model version 11: The version group for a component is depicted as a box with rounded corners containing the component versions (small quadrant with the version number inside) organised in a version graph. Solid lines going out of a component version represent composition relations, dashed lines dependencies.

---

[2] Compositional relations and dependencies are treated identically by the check-in, but the classification is important from a design and architectural perspective, exemplified in e.g. OMT and UML [30,29].

Consider a situation where an inner class, Weapon, is added to class Unit. After implementation and testing, a new version of Model is created in Fig. 1b. The check-in is propagated to component Weapon, it substance stored and a new version identity, 1, established. The same happens to Unit and City as they lie on a path from Model to Weapon. No new version of Terrain is necessary.

3.2   Versions are Configurations are Versions...

As visualised in Fig. 1 component versions and the relations between them can be viewed as directed graphs: Components versions are nodes and the references in the relation sets are arcs. Any component version is root in such a directed graph identifying a bound configuration of the abstraction and its context of relations and related abstractions at the time of check-in. Thus, the concepts version and bound configuration are unified. Even complex configurations are identified by a single component version, like e.g. "Model version 12" in Fig. 1.

It follows that not only are configurations first class objects—the evolution of configurations is also trivially recorded and accessible, in contrast to systems relying on labelling for bound configurations (e.g. ClearCase [2,11], CVS [4], etc.)

Another important consequence of having specific references to component versions in the relation sets is that the software architecture itself is under strict version control. An *architectural diff* algorithm can recursively compute differences in the relation sets between two versions of a component and report abstractions added, deleted, or moved, and changed dependencies. This provides better overview of architectural changes than a list of file contents differences.

3.3   Discussion

The emphasis on bound configurations does not prohibit using selection rules to create new configurations in workspace, but rule based selection plays a much lesser part. For instance Ragnarok provides the inevitable "get latest versions" rule as the only addition to the standard check-out procedure. Instead developers identify and communicate stabile libraries and subsystems through version identifications. Still our model arguably trades flexibility in version selection for the safety of traceable and reproducible configurations.

The architectural model avoids introducing concepts not found in the design domain like e.g. configuration languages, configuration items, labels, etc.

Space considerations prevent a full discussion of Ragnarok; a more detailed description discussing branch handling and cooperative- and parallel development can be found in [8]. A formal definition of model and algorithms is described in [10].

4   Experiences

A simple prototype implementation, Ragnarok, has been made of essential parts of the model to provide "proof-of-concept". To get fast feedback from users, some important design decisions were made to lower the implementation effort. Major decisions include:

- The physical level attribute (substance) of a component in workspace is implemented as a set of files in a directory. The drawback is that supporting fine-grained abstractions, like individual methods in a class, is infeasible. However, a file based approach allows Ragnarok to be used with existing tools and environments.
- File versioning handled by RCS [32].
- Copy scheme for workspaces like in CVS [4]. This scheme does not scale up, but the implementation is easy.

The Ragnarok prototype and documentation can be found on WWW [9].

4.1   User Groups

Currently the Ragnarok prototype is used daily in three real-life, on going, projects whose main characteristics are given below.

	ConSys	*BETA Compiler*	*Ragnarok*
Used since	Mar. 96	Feb. 97	Feb. 96
Data	C++, SQL, binary	BETA, C, html	BETA, LaTeX
Platform	NT	Unix, NT	Unix, NT
No. developers	3	4	1
No. components	110	36	36
No. files	1070	250	160
No. lines (KLOC)	185 + binary	110	40

The main source of data is guided, open-ended [28] interviews of the developers on the BETA compiler [5] and ConSys [21] projects. A secondary source of data is automatically generated usage logs from Ragnarok that have been analysed by simple statistical methods.

4.2   Results

The results can be summarised as follows:

Model "feels" natural: The user groups readily accept the software component to represent design entities and claim a close, if not one-to-one, mapping between their design and their software component structure. They "think" SCM in terms of components rather than files/directories. This claim is supported by the usage logs data where file related commands are seldom used.

Emphasis on bound configurations: While this is considered important for release and milestone management, the developers more emphasised the feeling of "security" in the daily development cycle as backtracking to working configurations is easy.

Traceable architectural evolution: The emphasis on tracing architectural change was valued; for instance the ConSys project has more than tripled its size in terms of number of components and files during the reported period.

5 Related Work

The underlying architectural version and configuration model in COOP/Orm [25,26,27] and POEM [24,23] has many similarities to this work. Both systems are focusing on supporting fine-grained abstractions but are not used in real-life projects. As such we feel that our work complements and adds credibility to COOP/Orm and POEM by reporting that architectural models are feasible in practice.

The concepts of module in Gandalf [19], family in Adele [3], and the configuration language PCL [34] also allow describing physical structure as attributes of the logical structure. In contrast to our model, these focus on generic configurations through intentional versioning [14] (Adele,PCL) or a dynamically bound "standard" version (Gandalf).

Some systems handle bound configurations by introducing special concepts like configuration items in e.g. Continuus/CM [7] or labels/tags in ClearCase [2,11], CVS [4], and others. Ragnarok avoids these concepts.

6 Conclusion

The architectural software configuration management model focuses on the logical software architecture that is then used to "drive" the version and configuration control process with emphasis on bound configurations. The benefit is that few SCM specific concepts are introduced, and the SCM concepts have a natural correspondence to concepts found in the design/development domain, thereby giving a shallow learning curve. Configurations equal versions, and therefore trivially first class objects and organised historically. The model provides strong traceability of architectural evolution. Experiences from real projects show that the model is viable, at least for small- to medium-sized projects.

Future directions of research include supporting fine-grained abstractions, improving the implementation to allow proof-of-concept experiments in large-scale projects, and improved support for cooperative and logical versioning [17]. It is the intention that the full Mjølner BETA system [1] is gradually put under Ragnarok SCM control.

References

1. P. Andersen, L. Bak, S. Brandt, J. L. Knudsen, O. L. Madsen, K. J. Møller, C. Nørgaard, and E. Sandvad. The Mjølner BETA System. In *Object-Oriented Environments - The Mjølner Approach*, pages 24–35. Prentice-Hall, 93.
2. U. Asklund and B. Magnusson. A Case-Study of Configuration Management with ClearCase in an Industrial Environment. In Conradi [13], pages 201–221.
3. N. Belkhatir and J. Estublier. Experience with a Database of Programs. In *Proceedings of the ACM SIGSOFT/SIGPLAN Software Engineering Symposium on Practical Software Development Environments*, volume 22, pages 84–91, jan 1987.
4. B. Berliner. CVS II: Parallelizing Software Development. In *USENIX*, Washington D.C., 1990.

5. http://www.daimi.aau.dk/~beta/.

6. G. Booch. *Object Oriented Design*. The Benjamin/Cummings Publishing Company, Inc., 1991.

7. M. Cagan. Untangling Configuration Management. In Estublier [16].

8. H. B. Christensen. Context-Preserving Software Configuration Management. In R. Conradi, editor, *Supplementary Proceedings: 7th International Workshop, SCM7*, pages 14–24, May 1997.

9. H. B. Christensen. *RCM 2.5 Quick Reference*. Department of Computer Science, University of Aarhus, 1997. http://www.daimi.aau.dk/~hbc/Ragnarok/rcm_quickref.html.

10. H. B. Christensen. A Formal Model for the Architectural Software Configuration Management Model. Technical report, Department of Computer Science, University of Aarhus, 1998. To appear in DAIMI PB series.

11. http://www.rational.com/products/clearcase/.

12. G. M. Clemm. Replacing Version Control with Job Control. In P. H. Feiler, editor, *Proceedings of the 2nd International Workshop on Software Configuration Management*, pages 162–169. ACM SIGSOFT, 1989.

13. R. Conradi, editor. *Software Configuration Management*, Lecture Notes in Computer Science 1235. ICSE'97 SCM-7 Workshop, Springer Verlag, 1997.

14. R. Conradi and B. Westfechtel. Towards a Uniform Version Model for Software Configuration Management. In Conradi [13].

15. S. Dart. Concepts in Configuration Management Systems. In P. H. Feiler, editor, *Proceedings of the 3rd International Workshop on Software Configuration Management*, pages 1–18. ACM Press, 1991.

16. J. Estublier, editor. *Software Configuration Management*, Lecture Notes in Computer Science 1005. ICSE SCM-4 and SCM-5 Workshops, Springer Verlag, 1995.

17. J. Estublier and R. Casallas. Three Dimensional Versioning. In Estublier [16], pages 118–135.

18. P. H. Feiler. Configuration Management Models in Commercial Environments. Technical Report CMU/SEI-91-TR-7, Software Engineering Institute, Carnegie-Mellon University, Pittsburgh, Pennsylvania 15213, Mar. 1991.

19. A. N. Habermann and D. Notkin. Gandalf: Software Development Environments. *IEEE Transactions on Software Engineering*, 12(12):1117–1127, dec 1986.

20. P. Ingram, C. Burrows, and I. Wesley. *Configuration Management Tools: a Detailed Evaluation*. Ovum Limited, 1993.

21. ISA. Consys. http://isals.dfi.aau.dk, 1996. ISA: Institute for Storage Ring Facilities, University of Aarhus.

22. D. A. Lamb. Introduction: Studies of Software Design. In D. A. Lamb, editor, *Studies of Software Design*, Lecture Notes in Computer Science 1078. ICSE'93 Workshop, Springer Verlag, 1996.

23. Y.-J. Lin and S. P. Reiss. Configuration Management in Terms of Modules. In Estublier [16].

24. Y.-J. Lin and S. P. Reiss. Configuration Management with Logical Structures. In *Proceedings of the 18th International Conference on Software Engineering*, pages 298–307. IEEE Computer Society Press, 1996.

25. B. Magnusson and U. Asklund. Fine Grained Version Control of Configurations in COOP/Orm. In I. Sommerville, editor, *Software Configuration Management*, Lecture Notes in Computer Science 1167, pages 31–48. ICSE'96 SCM-6 Workshop, Springer Verlag, 1996.

26. B. Magnusson, U. Asklund, and S. Minör. Fine Grained Revision Control for Collaborative Software Development. In *ACM SIGSOFT'93 - Symposium on the Foundations of Software Engineering*, Los Angeles, California, Dec. 1993.

27. S. Minör and B. Magnusson. A model for Semi-(a)Synchronous Collaborative Editing. In *Proceedings of Third European Conference on Computer-Supported Cooperative Work - ECSCW'93*, Milano, Italy, 1993. Kluwer Academic Press.

28. M. Q. Patton. *Qualitative Evaluation Methods*. Sage Publications, Beverly Hills, Calif., 1980.

29. Unified Modeling Language, version 1.0. Rational Software Corporation, Santa Clara/CA, Jan. 1997. URL:http://www.rational.com.

30. J. Rumbaugh, M. Blaha, W. Premerlani, F. Eddy, and W. Lorensen. *Object-Oriented Modeling and Design*. Prentice-Hall International Editions, 1991.

31. I. Sommerville. *Software Engineering*. Addison-Wesley Publishers Ltd., 4 edition, 1992.

32. W. F. Tichy. RCS – A System for Version Control. *Software – Practice & Experience*, 15(7):637–654, July 1985.

33. W. F. Tichy. Tools for Software Configuration Management. In J. F. H. Winkler, editor, *Proceedings of the International Workshop on Software Version and Configuration Control*. B. G. Teubner, Stuttgart, Jan. 1988.

34. E. Tryggeseth, B. Gulla, and R. Conradi. Modelling Systems with Variability using the PROTEUS Configuration Language. In Estublier [16].

35. A. van der Hoek. Configuration Management Yellow Pages. http://www.cs.colorado.edu/users/andre/configuration_management.html.

Toward SCM / PDM Integration?

Jacky Estublier, Jean-Marie Favre, Philippe Morat
Laboratoire L.S.R., University of Grenoble, IMAG Institute
Actimart, Bat 8, Av de Vignate, 38610 Gières, FRANCE
http://www-adele.imag.fr, {jacky|jmfavre|morat}@imag.fr

Abstract. Software Configuration Management (SCM) is the discipline of controlling the evolution of a software product. Product Data Management (PDM) is the disciple of designing and controlling the evolution of a product design. For a long time, these two domains have been disconnected, but they probably share common concepts and techniques. Furthermore, any large product development includes a substantial (and growing) part of software development. There is a need to control the evolution of both the product and its associated software. Thus we are faced with the question: are the involved concepts and techniques close enough to envision a common tool capable of supporting both domains. This paper tries to answer this question, through an analysis of the PDM standard STEP and tools characteristic of both domains: Metaphase for PDM; Clear Case and Adele for SCM.

"Those who know only England do not know England" (Rudyard Kipling). This paper is written by SCM experts, not PDM ones, and assumes that readers are more knowledgeable in SCM than PDM. The other objective of the paper is to make a critical assessment of SCM (and SE) in the light of another related domain PDM [9]

1 Introduction

The goal of engineering is to provide practical ways to build a product at a reasonable and predefined cost, quality and delay. This paper compares the state of art and practice between two disciplines: software engineering and most other engineering, focusing on computer-assisted product engineering.

For a long time, different engineering disciplines (civil, mechanical, electrical) have sought to control the way different physical products (buildings, planes, cars) can be designed and realized. Any complex product is built as an assembly of parts. The detail of each part exhibits internal characteristics related to the engineering involved (a surface, a room, an algorithm). But the large number of components, and their evolution, give rise to *product management* problems. To focus only on design data, the discipline is called *product data management* (PDM). Solutions to these problems, with concepts of versions and assembly, for example, have been provided long before the arrival of computers.

B. Magnusson (Ed.): ECOOP 98, SCM-8, LNCS 1439, pp. 75-94, 1998

Since the 70s, computers have been used to provide Computer Assistance (CAx) in two directions: Design (CAD) and Manufacturing (CAM). Simultaneously appears a new kind of engineering and associated products: software. Complete computer aided engineering environments (CAEE) have been built in most engineering domains.

These environments can be split in two parts: (1) domain *specific* tools (3D drawing, structure resistance computing, syntax directed programming editors and so on), whose goal is to define each piece of the product; (2) and tools related to the management of the product seen as an assembly of these pieces: storage (product model), assembly (composition), and evolution (versions and change control) of the pieces.

This paper focuses only on the second category of tools, called Software Configuration Management tools (SCM tools) in Software Engineering Environments, and Product Data Management tools (PDM tools) in Product Engineering Environments.

It is interesting to note that the distinction Programming in the Small and Programming in the Large is nothing else than the distinction Engineering *specific* vs. Engineering *generic*. PDM and SCM both deal with *generic* engineering issues thus with the same issues.

At that level of abstraction, SCM and PDM look identical. The goal of this paper is to go forward in the analysis of both classes of tools, trying to identify where the real differences are (if any), what know-how, conventions and standards have been developed in each domain, and to what extent these standards and conventions are arbitrary; to what extent the know-how developed in a domain can be applied in others. In conclusion, to what extent is it reasonable to envision a generic Computer Aided Engineering Environment (CAEE)?

The paper compares PDM and SCM characteristic tools. The selected tools are Metaphase because it is the leader in PDM. For SCM, we have selected ClearCase because it is a leader of the SCM market, and our system Adele, because, for almost 2 decades, it has been among the leaders of the SCM research field, and the product has currently more than 700 industrial licences inside major companies developing software.

It is an agreement in both SCM and PDM to distinguish between four major classes of services:

- The product model (model of the components and their relationships),
- The versioned product model (versioning, composition, selection),
- The relationship with the domain specific tools (work spaces, concurrent engineering)
- The process model (change control, activity control, organization control).

This paper is organized following this distinction. Chapter 2 looks at the standards, chapter 3 compares the data model; chapter 4 the evolution models; chapter 5 workspace control and chapter 6 process models.

2 The Standards

Before comparing the tools, it seems important to assess which are the standards, in each domain, that constrain tools concepts and mechanisms. As a matter of fact, in PDM, a tool designer is not free to propose mechanisms; the tool *must* support/enforce the STEP/EXPRESS standard.

2.1 PDM: The STEP Standard

STEP (STandard for the Exchange of Product model data) is an ISO standard (ISO DIS 10303). It is the result of industrial pressure coming from two concerns: (1) any large product artifact involves a large number of sub-contractors (the virtual enterprise problem), who must exchange requirements and designs; (2) the existence of very large libraries of standard components. The goal of STEP is to facilitate interoperability between different CAD environments by the exchange of standardized data product models.

It is very impressive (for a software engineer) to see the extent of that standard. It includes a language for product modeling (EXPRESS, Part 11). EXPRESS defines Generic Data Product Models (GDPM) and Integrated Resources (IR). Examples of such IRs are *Product Description and Support* or *Product Structure Configuration*, which are relevant for SCM, most others are domain specific like *lengh_unit* or *geometricaly_bounded_surface_shape_representation*.

On the basis of this set of standardized definitions, Application Protocols (AP) are defined. They describe a specific application domain. We are typically concerned with AP203 *Configuration Controlled 3D Designs of Mechanical Parts and Assemblies*, which was the first AP to reach the level of international standard, and it is effectively followed by professionals.

AP203 is very ambitious, and defines standard in very many directions, product models, configuration management, some process support (it defines concepts or people, organization, role, time, approvals), and gathers different engineering disciplines through the concept of contexts: *mechanical_context*, *product_definition_context*, *design_context*, *product_concept_context*.

Any tool supposed to assist professionals in these disciplines has to support, in one way or another the STEP standard. It is not our intention to describe the standard; the relevant aspects will be described through their instantiations in the Metaphase tool.

2.2 SCM: Is There a Standard?

When compared with STEP, it is clear that the software industry is not yet strong or mature enough to impose industry wide standards. The virtual enterprise is not yet a major concern (at least compared with the thousands of sub-contractors required for a plane or a car). Libraries or industry wide standard software components are still a dream. Only very coarse grain components (a database, a window manager...) are widely reused; replacing one component with another "similar" one is always problematic.

Software is a very young and, even if extremely successful, largely immature engineering. It is not surprising that nothing comparable to STEP has been realized so far. This make the SE field very active, dynamic and capable of fast adaptation. However, SE is rapidly maturing and the same type of evolution can be forecast. It corresponds to the well known "craft to engineering" evolution under way in our (SE) profession.

The consequence of such "unregulated" state is that each SCM tool is free to propose its own concepts and mechanisms. And, indeed, each SCM tool proposes something different, without any clear indication of why and how it is superior/different from other tool. It may be the case that, after some time, a standard will emerge from such competition. It would be a problem if such a standard is incompatible with those of PDM.

3 Product Modeling

PDM products can be made of millions of parts; software can also be complex. modeling such complex artifacts is an important issue. Product modeling must be explicit.

3.1 Data Models

A data model is a formalism making it possible to describe a product model. Relational data models or object-oriented data models are examples of such models. The data model determines the concepts on which the product model will be built. It has a major impact on the way products will be modelled, and even on the possibility of describing some kinds of assemblies. The availability of a data model offers many advantage over hard-wired tools.

PDM Data Models

In PDM, EXPRESS is the STEP data model. EXPRESS is an Object-Oriented modeling language dedicated to the static definition of structured artifacts verifying complex constraints.

Object classes define a set of attributes and a set of constraints. An attribute's value can be a reference to other objects (composition). EXPRESS proposes a rich type system based on traditional types like strings and integers but also on the availability of many type constructors: sets, lists, arrays, bags, tuples. For aggregates, ordering, cardinality (maximum and minimum), and unicity can be defined. Moreover attribute can be declared optional. For instance last_name in the example below can be undefined (noted?). The undefined value is allowed in an expression since its behaviour is explicitly described in the algebra. For instance the following expression holds:

FALSE AND ? = FALSE.

EXPRESS provides multiple inheritance and exhibits rare features like the possibility to express precise constraints on class extensions (e.g. the extension of classes A and B are disjoint). The following is a short piece of STEP Part 41.

```
SCHEMA person_organization_schema ; ........
ENTITY person ;
  id              : identifier ;
  last_name       : OPTIONAL label ;
  first_name      : OPTIONAL LIST [1, ?] OF label ;
  UNIQUE
  UR1 : id ;
  WHERE
  WR1: EXISTS (last_name) OR EXISTS (first_name) ;
  END_ENTITY ;
```

EXPRESS is designed to describes data structures and related invariants, not to describe dynamic aspects: data management or behaviour. It is striking to note that EXPRESS includes a complete algorithmic language aiming at expressing arbitrary complex constraints (e.g."all points are included in a concave surface") but not the behaviour of objects. EXPRESS does not provide methods.

In fact the EXPRESS language is used within the STEP standard, but each PDM tool proposes its own modeling language. In Metaphase, which is built on top of Oracle, a relationship may have attributes, but with very simple values. Conversely, until version 2, files were not handled: "Bulk data (i.e. files) should be handled in a separate manner,... including OS, third party tools, file systems archives" [11].

To sum up, PDM data models are usually rich enough to describe many kinds of data structures (so they could be used to describe software products) but the emphasis is usually on the definition of the static properties of complex objects, not on behaviour or technical issues like efficiency, file handling, and so on.

SCM Data Models

Traditionally, SCM systems have no explicit data model or when present, their data model is very weak. Most systems are based on hard-wired concepts like file and directory, making it impossible to use such tools to manage complex objects. Often the only attributes available are those supported by the file system.

Modern SCM systems are still weak. In ClearCase, only files and directories are known. There is no type system; all files have the same attribute. There are no real relationships (but hyperlinks); there is no concept of complex objects. Among commercial systems only Continuus has an O.O. model, but without relationships and a very basic language (script based).

Adele is a non-standard SCM system. It features a rich data model which is a combination of the Java syntax and execution model with the EXPRESS data model. Adele gathers the best of both fields: a rich data model known to be capable of representing any complex artifact, with an elegant and popular programming language known to be good at describing and executing algorithms. Moreover, Adele also includes advanced features like triggers to model dynamic behaviour and relationships to enhance data modeling facility. Due to its roots in SCM, Adele naturally supports efficient file handling.

To sum up, with a few exceptions, the emphasis in SCM is on file handling, not object modeling.

Summary

So, the questions are: could a data model be general enough to cover both PDM and SCM needs?. What should that data model contain?.

We believe that the answer to the first question is YES. A good data model candidate is object-oriented but extended with explicit relationships. In both fields, the need for explicit relationships has been clearly mentioned. The needs with respect to the description of dynamic behaviour is not so clear.

3.2 Product Models

Product models are data schemes expressed in terms of the data model. SCM product models typically contain definitions of classes such as Program, Module, Interface while PDM models define classes like GeometricObject, Assembly, or Part.

PDM Product Models

The term "Product Data" covers many kinds of information including shape, function, production cost, etc. but this information is centered around the structure of the product. Whatever the product, the basic concepts are parts and assemblies. Composition relationships are thus very important. For instance a bicycle is an assembly comprising two wheels, a frame and so on.

The backbone of a PDM model is the *composition relationship*.

Indeed, modeling and managing relationships is a key issue in PDM. Metaphase includes this concept in its data model. This is not true in the EXPRESS language: relationships are objects including two attributes 'related_object' and 'relating_object'. This kind of 'simulation' makes it possible to represent information without extending traditional object-oriented data-models, but high level concepts or constraints become difficult to express and it introduces performance issues. For instance, in EXPRESS, large portions of a product model are dedicated to enforce referential integrity or that composition relationships are acyclic. This contrasts with data models including such feature (e.g. DAG keyword in the Adele data model).

One of the particularities of the PDM product model, with respect to SCM, is that depending on the level of abstraction, it is possible to make the difference between different instances of the same model.

Consider for instance a bicycle model. A bicycle is made of two distinct occurrences (or instances) of a same wheel (a model). This kind of information is essential to compute production costs or bicycle weight, to draw physical representations, etc. Even if both wheels are identical (they have the same model), there is a need in some situations to distinguish the copies.

This introduces the notion of *part list* (Fig 1 a). This structure is a tree where each node corresponds to a physical occurrence of a component (each physical occurrence is included in a single physical assembly).).

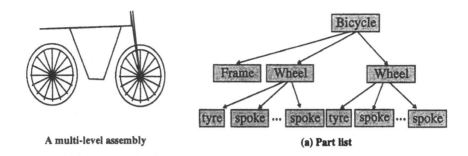

A multi-level assembly   **(a) Part list**

Figure 1: Composition modeling at the instance level(■)

The part list is inconvenient when the same part is used a large number of times (like rivets in a plane!). It is sometimes sufficient to think in term of models; it is the concept of *bill of materials (BOM)*, (Fig 2 b). Since a model can be used in different models, a node (which is a model) may have more than one parent, and its structure is a Direct Acyclic Graph.

Between the extremes, (nodes are models (a) or nodes are instances (b)), PDM tools offer the possibility to quantify the number of instances decorating the composition relationship with an attribute representing the number of occurrences (Fig 2 c)[1]. This kind of information is sufficient to compute costs, weight, etc. Sometimes it may be needed to distinguish an occurrence within a model with respect to models or to other occurrences possibly within higher level assemblies[2] (Fig 2 d).

Any mixture is legal inside the same model. It is thus possible to speak about "the first spoke of the front wheel of a bicycle", "the first spoke of a wheel", "the spokes of a wheel" or "the spokes".

The ability to manage this kind of representation is a major requirement in PDM. The STEP standard precisely defines product models using a set of data schemes expressed with the EXPRESS language (See Part 41 and 44 of the standard: *Fundamentals of product description*).

These product models are generic and shared by all application domains. AP203, the STEP standard for "3D designs of mechanical parts", refines these basic product models (shape, function, etc.). Indeed the standard is based on a layered architecture ranging from domain independent concepts to application specific ones.

---

[1] Note that this kind of representation requires attributes to be added to relationships. Indeed this is a fundamental requirement in PDM.

[2] Note that this kind of representation requires relationships to be drawn between other relationships. This facility is also required for representing substitute parts (section 4.2 on page 83).

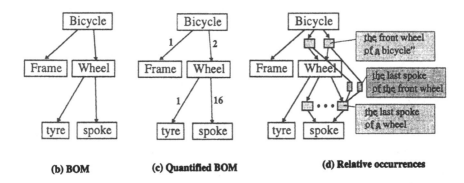

Figure 2: Composition modeling: from models(□) to instances(■)

In summary, PDM product models are based on sophisticated data models. The same set of core concepts is present in almost all PDM tools. Standardization efforts, like STEP, make the exchange of product data effective.

SCM Product Models

Many SCM tools consider that the structure of a software product model is a tree of files and directories. The data model is the file system data model, and the software structure is a simple tree. Most SCM tools have no more knowledge about the software they manage!

However, system models (i.e. the software product model) have been introduced, whose goal is to propose a more detailed product model. DSEE proposed system model concepts [22], but still based on the file product model. The earliest work was on Module Interconnection Languages, where each component made explicit its "require" and "provide" resources. The Gandalf environment [21], early versions of Adele [12] and more recently, in Proteus [33], more sophisticated system models were proposed, all based on a product model with predefined concepts like family, interface, realization and some predefined relationships.

In all cases, one of the goal is to make the software structure explicit, defining the relationships between components. It is interesting to note that the backbone of such models is the *dependency* relationship. These product models form graphs with nodes as components (attributed files).

One difficulty for SCM systems, comes from the fact that the dependency structure (a graph) does not replace but coexists with the file system structure (a tree), and they usually do not match. The management of both structures is not easy. This is why many SCM systems simply ignore the dependency structure. As a matter of fact, no major commercial SCM tool proposes a reasonable product model.

The problem of model vs. instance (duplicate instances) does not explicitly appear in SCM, even if INLINE directives (in C++) and some #Include are really performing duplications. Implicitly, SCM systems only consider the model concept.

In between the file structure and the dependency graph, Software Engineers often consider another tree structure based on concepts like module, subsystems, systems, which map better with the file structure. Configurations are another clustering mechanism, not used as they should be.

It is also interesting to note that a definition of standard product models, based on a standardized data model has been attempted a number of times in the Software Engineering field. The PCTE consortium was close to succeeding; based on the PCTE database data model (O.O. extended by explicit relationships and many other useful features), the consortium proposed a set of standardized schemes (SDS), very similar to what STEP has defined. Maybe because of the domain's lack of maturity, these de facto standards have not been accepted by professionals, and have been abandoned.

Summary

In PDM, the structure is not arbitrary; it does exist. The way an artifact is decomposed is constrained by reality (spacial and mechanical constraints). The fact a bicycle has two wheels is not an arbitrary decision taken by the designer.

Maybe for that reason, the structure is the natural way for designers to think about the product to build, and thus the way models are designed. PDM tools are based on elaborate data models, because their major task is to model the product structure; but not the functional structure. If PDM follows the same tracks as chip design, the emphasis on structure should move toward more functional and semantic relationships.

The way software is designed and decomposed is governed by trade-offs other than physical constraints involving functionality, ease of use, efficiency, generality, reliability, cost, and so on; but this is highly subjective and variable. The only objective reality is the file structure, which has little connection with the logical structure.

In SCM, the product structure is identified with the file system structure supporting the software. The real software structure is too often ignored. However the question is: what is the structure or architecture of software? What role should this play? What is the relationship between a system model, a design structure, an architecture model, a file system structure? What is the relationship between the design architecture and the product architecture at execution (why is the structure, in UML for example, lost)? All these questions are current research topics in Software Engineering. Anyway, a high level and unified formal modeling and support of software structure/architecture is under way, but probably not for tomorrow!

4 The Evolution Model

SCM as well as PDM can be defined as the control of the evolution of complex systems [35]. Thus, the core of such systems is their ability to model and control how complex artifacts evolve.

4.1 Versioned Data Model

The PDM data model, EXPRESS, does not include any versioning concept. All versioning is defined in the versioned product model.

This contrasts with SCM (and SE in general) approaches where versioning is always, in one way or another, embedded in the data model. There is an agreement to include at least the branch concept (a succession of revisions) in the data model. Many SCMs directly include an RCS like version model in their data model (and often rely on RCS to support it). ClearCase and Adele include versioning concepts in their data model (see 4.2).

It is also interesting to note that all work on Software Engineering Databases has identified that versioning in the data model is a need. PCTE, Orion, O2 and many other have proposed such mechanisms. The question that arises is why, in PDM, the data model is not versioned? What is the best approach? The answer is related to the efficiency vs. generality compromise. STEP is not designed for efficiency, while, in SCM, building file revisions involves delta techniques that are better handled efficiently at the lowest level. Most PDM tools, for efficiency reasons, have hard-wired the STEP versioning model, in which case it can be considered to be part of the data model.

4.2 Versioned Product Model

PDM Versioned Product Models

In PDM, again, the versioning concept comes from STEP. There are 3 versioning dimensions:

- **historical versioning** based on the *revision* concept,
- **logical versioning** based on *alternate*, *substitute* and *option* concepts,
- **domain versioning** based on *views*.

Historical Versioning, based on revision handling, is very similar to the revision concept found in SCM.

Logical Versioning. Each part of a mechanical product may exist in different versions. When an object X (a standard wheel) can be replaced in any assembly by another one Y (a carbon wheel), then an *alternate* relationship is established from X to Y. This relation is not symmetric; in a bicycle with a carbon wheel, its substitution by a standard wheel may not be legal.

Some substitutions are legal only in some assemblies. In a trail bicycle, the wheel can be a *RapidFixWheel*; this is modelled by a *Substitute* relationship linking the composition relationship and the *RapidFixWheel*.

The *option* concept allows to describe generic structures using quantifications. The product is defined with all its possible options. Then, depending on the option selection (see section 4.3 on page 86), the amount of instances can be changed, components added or removed. In the example, a standard bicycle has 2 mudguards; with the *trial* option, the number of mudguard becomes 0 i.e. we remove them.

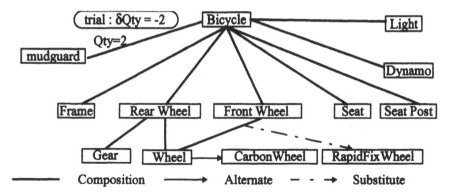

Figure 3: Alternate and substitute relationships

Domain Versioning.

PDM products are usually very complex and their engineering requires the collaboration of different specialists from various domains: mechanics, electrical,
aerodynamics, material, etc. Each specialist needs to see only what is required to do
his/her job: a *view* on the product. PDM tools implement this concept of view by a
label on composition relationships indicating in which views this decomposition is to
be visible. For instance, in Fig 4, the light pertains to the electrical view, the wheel to
the mechanical view, but the frame pertains to both. Views are also used to consider
different steps of the engineering process.

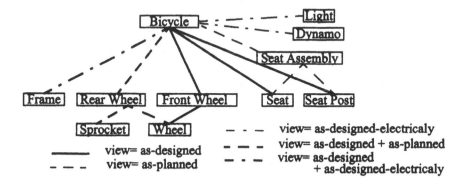

Figure 4: Views

Views are hierarchically structured. In the example, designed-electrically and as-
planned are derived from as-designed. This organization is useful to control change
propagation: a propagation is taken into account only if the modification is "view
dependent".

SCM Versioned Product Models

Versioning, in SCM, traditionally relies on SCCS/RCS like models. A file evolves in a sequence of revisions to form a branch. Different branches constitute variants. The semantics behind these concepts is weak: the last revisions are supposed to be the best and to be compatible with the previous ones, variants share similarities, have functional differences and coexist in parallel. In practice, in these systems, the only thing known about the similarities and differences between versions is that they share a large number of lines!

The revisions concept is shared, variants correspond to alternate and substitute. The alternate concept gives some more semantics to variants. In SCM, some tools also provide more semantics to branches.

In ClearCase, the semantics of branches is unclear. They may be logical variants or a local version in a workspace. The user has to deal explicitly with such low level concepts.

In older Adele versions, as well as in Gandalf, the set of variants implementing an interface constitutes an equivalence class (functional equivalence). The composition relationships only refer to the interface. It can be compared with the alternate concept, but alternate relationships do not build an equivalence class, since it is not symmetric. In Adele the concept of family gathers all the non functionally equivalent interfaces of the same object. It can be compared with the substitute relationship. This appealing solution was abandoned because it relied on a standardized product model, and no consensus has been reached yet on this topic (see section 3.2 on page 79).

A number of other versioning models have been proposed in SCM, most notably the change set paradigm, which has no equivalent in PDM. See [6] for a survey.

Adele versioning is based a three dimensional model: Historical, cooperative and logical. *Historical versioning* is applied to *objects* which evolve as a sequence of *states*. The model explicitly defines, for each object type, which attributes are duplicated in each state (state keyword), which ones are common (common keyword), which ones are immutable, which ones are such that a change implies the creation of a new state and so on.

Cooperative versioning is completely transparent for users, it is the consequence of a change in an isolated workspace; this is handled by the work space manager. *Logical versioning* is handled explicitly by users through specific semantic relationships. The previous Adele logical approach to versioning, based on interface/realization is nothing but one of the possible logical models supported by the system.

Summary

PDM propose (and impose) a complete and interesting variation model, which encompasses versioning with options and domain concepts. Options have a clear reality ground in PDM, not in SCM. The concept of option found in change set approaches [18] is rather different since it aims at subsuming all other versioning dimensions. Options, in SCM, are mostly found when installing a software, not during design.

Domain is a need in PDM since it involves different specialists, which is not the case in SCM. However the need for filtering information, not only based on version selection also applies to SCM.

When compared with PDM, SCM's most striking difference is that on the one hand, the state of practice relies on an old and basic mechanism (RCS like), and that, on the other hand, a large number of versioning models have been proposed, but very few of them have been really experimented, and almost none used in practice.

4.3 Selection

Clearly, variation and selection are closely connected; most often, to each level of variation corresponds a level of selection. It is very interesting to compare how the different systems have addressed this problem of selection.

In PDM, the STEP standard defines the concept of context. A *configuration context* then filters the pertinent information. A filter is applied to each variation dimension. Thus a context is the intersection of the filtering done by a view context (selecting the views), an effectivity context (selecting the revisions), an option context (selecting the options), an alternate and substitute context (selecting the variants) and a life cycle context.

In PDM, selection is understood as dynamic filtering of information, similar to views in databases.

In SCM, selection is better understood as "building a configuration", i.e. static computing aimed at building a complex object based on selected components; but most SCM systems do not support any selection. See [5] for a survey.

Adele is non-standard in that sophisticated selection mechanisms have been implemented since 1982. A selection is based on rules of three classes: constraints, preferences and defaults. The rule itself is a boolean expression like "[os = Unix] and [ws = SunView] and [DB = Oracle] or ...". The selection process exploits the semantics of the versioning relationships.

ClearCase is non standard in that it is the only (major?) system, in SCM, that does dynamic selection. Like in PDM, ClearCase rules filter dynamically the "right" branch which is visible provided a set of rules are satisfied. A rule can be like "*element /foo/ ..../Oracle*" which means that the"right" branch for file *foo* is the one with label *Oracle*.

5 Work Space Control

Work Space control can be defined as the way the product, or part of it, is provided in order to be manipulated by the domain specific tools. In SE, these tools are basically editors, compilers and linkers; in PDM they are specific editors (3D, structure, etc.) and various computations tools (resistance, flow, etc.).

In both cases 2 problems are to be solved:

- Presenting the pertinent part of the product in the convenient format and location,
- Concurrent engineering control (concurrent change control).

It is the role of the selection mechanisms, seen above to select the pertinent part of the product. The context concept, defined in STEP is defined for that purpose. The Selection rules of ClearCase (dynamic), and Adele (static) play the same role, but with a more limited ambition.

5.1 Representation

Metaphase is working directly on the underlying database. The representation is unique; it is the data model of the data base itself. A basic check-in/check-out protocol is added for files. There is no work space.

In SCM, representation control is a major topic. Software engineering tools require objects to be represented as files in a file system. The comfort, facility and efficiency of the workspace support is often considered as *the* key element of an SCM system (at least from a practitioner's point of view).

5.2 Concurrent Engineering

In PDM, due to the absence of a workspace, everybody shares the same data repository. The context concept allows to filter what is visible and what is not, but not to make data evolve in an isolated way, and reconcile changes later. Consequently, there is no concurrent engineering control. The transaction concept applies only to short (database) transactions.

In SCM, due to the nature of Workspace (often physically separate copies of the same files), concurrent engineering may lead to multiple concurrent changes over the same objects (files). From the beginning, different mechanisms have been proposed to avoid the anarchy of uncontrolled concurrent changes. The basic one is the locking mechanism traditionally associated with the check-in/check-out protocol, which simply avoids concurrent changes [SCCS 76]. Since then, different approaches have been proposed and experimented whose goal is to extend the transaction concept of databases to the so called long and cooperative transactions that takes place in the Workspace. The impossible challenge is to let each "transaction" change concurrently the same objects in an isolated way, and to find a way to compute what would have been the value of that objects if the transactions had been executed in sequence.

Currently, no system proposes a formal model of concurrent engineering strategies, at least at a high level. For example in ClearCase, there is no concept of concurrent engineering, but concepts of branch creation and selection in a large common repository; any strategy has to be built by hand from these basic elements, which proves to be tedious and confusing.

So, this aspect is rudimentary in today PDM tools, it is handled in SCM tools, even if still at the level of the basic mechanisms. In both cases progress is needed.

6 The Process Model

PDM

Process support, in the STEP standard, relies primarily on the approval concept. Approvals are required for many things in AP203: definition, effectivity, change_request, and so on. Each approval itself requires a *person* a *date* and an *organization*; it has a status with values *approved, not_yet_approved, disapproved* or *withdrawn*.

The STEP standard defines engineering release and change control processes. It defines the relationships between a *change_request* (versioned) and a *change* through concepts of *action_method*. It is the only place where the concept of activity appears. However nothing is said about these actions. It is only one possible change control process.

The STEP standard, has a rather static and product oriented view of processes. This is consistent with the goal of STEP, which is to exchange product data, with the proof that all important decisions have been consistently approved; it does not aim to support the actual process: "AP203 is a standard for all industry, as such, it represents data (your data) as an abstraction from the way in which your organization actually does business"[27].

Metaphase extends the STEP standard by defining *assignment* and *automatic* processes, *notifications* (e-mail or built-in notes) and defining a *state* for objects. Assignments only route objects to people for review or approval, while automatic processes simply launch an external program. It is a rather simple workflow system. To a more limited extent, Metaphase has the same characteristics and weaknesses as STEP; its process support is limited and focuses on products and approvals.

SCM

In SCM also, traditionally, process support is weak and focuses on product evolution. Many SCM systems predefined a number of processes with a few parameters for local adaptation; modern systems essentially propose State Transitions Diagrams (STD). The process is defined in terms of product STDs, most often using Unix script like formalisms. In SCM there is no standard process, no standard concept; each SCM system proposes different predefined process models.

ClearCase is non-standard in that its process support component, ClearGuide [4][24], is activity centered: the concept of STD applies to activities, not to products. ClearGuide proposes only sequential and parallel activities (i.e. no collaborative activities); the definition formalism is still script like; this makes process definition or adaptation rather tedious.

Adele is also non standard in that process support was for long a major research topic. Its basic process support mechanism (trigger based) is now completely hidden; process definition and customizing is realized through graphic interfaces proposing high-level concepts, including workflow and collaborative activities [7][14][2].

7 Conclusion

PDM tools are strong in product modeling. They have a long standing and now standardized product evolution control know how. But they are weak in concurrent engineering, work space control and process support. SCM tools are more recent; they are good at managing files and tools, but weak in product modeling, product evolution and process support. They have no consensus and no standards.

Not surprisingly, the gap between both classes of tools is narrowing. Further, since software is becoming a substantial and growing part of any complex product, and since consistent management of all engineering fields is needed; unification of both fields seems mandatory. However, concluding that integration is imminent is maybe too optimistic.

There are two fundamental differences between software engineering and other types of product engineering:

(1) In product engineering, there is a clear distinction between the design, called *product model* or *product data*, and the corresponding real artifact (a bicycle for example). In software engineering, the source code is the model but a compiler transforms at almost no cost the design into the product, which is also a (set of) files. The software is both the model and the product. (2) The structure of the product, the nature of each component, the way two components fit together are highly constrained by the reality in PDM (a bicycle has 2 wheels). In SE, all this almost arbitrary, a software is an intellectual construction. Worse, in SE, the technologies and methods are evolving very fast, no one of today standards will survive more than a few years.

On both classes of tool, usability, easy customizing and efficiency are critical aspects. We have consistent records of huge efforts in metaphase customizing and maintenance (in the range of a hundred man/years). To a more limited extent the same applies in SCM. In both domains practitioners complain severely about efficiency. There is very strong pressure, in both fields, to address usability and efficiency issues as a priority. A solution to these problems goes more in the direction of more specialized tools, rather than more general ones. Unification of fields is often not mentioned at all as a goal.

The fundamental differences between both fields are not that many, but do exist. Software is an abstraction, with almost no limitation in term of capabilities, structure, concepts, techniques and so on. Thus even if STEP models (data, versioning, evolution, selection) could be applied, it is unclear they are convenient for software Engineering[3].

SCM research topics include versioning models, data models, concurrent engineering models, system models, and there is no consensus yet on these topics, even if some deep controversies are vanishing. A consensus on a product model, as well as on a

---

[3] A specific work group inside STEP is working on a specific software standard

library of standard software components, does not seem likely to appear in the near future. Current concern is more with answering fundamental questions like: what is the structure/architecture of a (may be distributed) software? Fundamental work on software architecture is only starting. How to reuse components? New concepts and techniques for integration and interoperability are emerging (from Corba to Beans and ActiveX). It is unlikely solutions found in PDM apply as such to software.

Is it time to define standards in Software Engineering? The Software domain evolves at a very fast speed, much faster than mechanical or electrical engineering. New concepts and techniques are invented and applied very often, with clear impact on the services expected from an SCM tool. The SCM challenge is primarily to address this evolution, to propose new concepts and services matching the new needs, and to solve usability and efficiency issues. Fast adaptation and creativity seems more valued than standardisation. Field unification, especially if it requires standardisation, is not the priority. Software engineering is not yet ripe for standardization.

On the other hand, interoperability, reusability and the emergence of the software virtual enterprise are great incentives toward standardisation. The evolution of software engineering follows the evolution of any engineering, and standardization should occur. If such standardization occurs, it is critical that it be compatible with what has been defined in the other related engineering areas. Given the independence of both areas today, this is unlikely.

There is a fundamental effort to be undertaken to really understand the product structure, its architecture, the evolution and selections models required in software engineering and, if different from PDM, to find a way to deal with both models in a consistent way. Then a global solution that does not reduce efficiency, and makes the product easier to use, adapt and customize is to be found. This will require fundamental research and major experimentation.

		PDM	SCM
FUNDAM-ENTALS	Product	model ≠ product	model ≈ product
	Structure	constrained by reality	no real constraint
	Maturity	+	-
	Standard	e.g. STEP	no consensus
PRODUCT MODEL	Data model	Object oriented	Weak data models
	Main issue	Object modeling	File handling
	Components	parts / assemblies	modules, files
	Relation	composition relationship	dependence relationship + file hierarchy
	Models vs. instances	notion of occurrences and quantities	no duplication of components
	Standard	standardized product models (STEP's IR)	no standard

	versioned data model	No version concept in the EXPRESS data model	Versioning concept are included in the data model
VERSIONED PRODUCT MODEL	historical versioning	revision	revision
	logical versioning	alternate, substitute, option	variant or branch
	domain versioning	views (as-planned, as designed, ...)	--
	selection	context : view+effectivity +alternate+substitute+option	no, or attribute based
WORK SPACE	representation	data base	file system
	concurrent engineering	sharing	work space isolation
PM	process model	changes and approvals	tool specific

8 References

[1]   *"A Comprehensive Configuration Management Solution, Metaphase Product Structure Manager and Advanced Product Configurator"*, Metaphase Technology, MW00206-A.

[2]   M. Amiour. *A support for cooperation in Software Processes*. Doctoral Consortium of CAiSE'97. June 16-17. Barcelona, Spain. 1997.

[3]   Arbouy and al.; *"STEP : Concepts fondamentaux"*, Afnor, 1994, 188 pages.

[4]   *"ClearGuide: Product Overview"*. Technical report, Atria Software, Inc.

[5]   R. Conradi and B. Westfechtel. *"Configuring Versioned Software Product"*. In SCM-6 Workshop. pp. 88-109. Springer LNCS 1167. Berlin, March 1996.

[6]   R. Conradi and B. Westfechtel. *"Toward an Uniform Model for Software Configuration Management"*. In SCM-7 Workshop.pages 1-17. Springer LNCS 1235. May 1997.

[7]   S. Dami, J. Estublier and M. Amiour. *"APEL: a Graphical Yet Executable Formalism for Process Modeling"*. Automated Software Engineering journal, January 1998.

[8]   S. Dart. *"Concepts in Configuration Management Systems"*. *Proc. of the 3rd. Intl. Workshop on Software Configuration Management*. Trondheim, Norway, june, 1991.

[9]   Christof Ebert. *The Road to Maturity : Navigating Between Craft and Science*. IEEE Software. November/December 1997, page 77-82

[10]   *"Discipline in Software Development"*, White Paper, Sherpa Corporation document WPCC001, Janvier 1995, 11 pages.

[11]   *"EDL/Metaphase, Overview"*, Metaphase Technology, MW00200-A, 29 pages.

[12]   J. Estublier. A configuration manager: *The Adele Database of Programs*. In Proceedings of the workshop on Software Environments for Programming-in-the-Large. Pages 140-147. Harwichport, Massachussets, June 1985.

[13]   J. Estublier. *"Workspace Management in Software Engineering Environments"*. in SCM-6 Workshop. Springer LNCS 1167. Berlin, Germany, March 1996.

[14]   J. Estublier and S. Dami and M. Amiour. *High Level Process Modeling for SCM Systems*. SCM 7, LNCS 1235. pages=81--98, May, Boston, USA, 1997

[15]   J. Estublier and R. Casallas. *"Three Dimensional Versioning"*. In SCM-4 and SCM-5 Workshops. J. Estublier editor, September, 1995. Springer LNCS 1005.

[16]   J. Estublier and R. Casallas. *"The Adele Software Configuration Manager"*. Configuration Management, Edited by W. Tichy; J. Wiley and Sons. 1994. Trends in software.

[17]   C. Fernstrom. *Process Weaver: adding process support to Unix.*, In *Proc. of the 2nd Intl Conf. on the Software Process,* Berlin, Germany, 25-26 February, 1993.

[18]   B. Gulla, E.A. Carlson, D. Yeh. *Change-Oriented version description in EPOS.* Software Engineering Journal, 6(6):378-386, Nov 1991.

[19]   M. Hardwick, B.R. Dowine, M. Kutcher, D.L. Spooner, *"Concurrent Engineering with Delta Files'*, IEEE Computer Graphics and Applications, January 1995, pp. 62-68.

[20]   *"Product Data Representation and Exchange, Part 21: Clear text encoding of the exchange structure"*, ISO-DISO-10303-21, 1992, 72 pages.

[21]   G. E. Kaiser and N. Haberman. *An environment for system version control*. In digest of papers of Spring CompCon 83. Pages 415, 420. IEEE computer society press., Feb 1983.

[22]   D. B. Leblang. and G.D. McLean. *Configuration Management for large-scale software development efforts*. In Proceedings of the workshop on Software Environments for Programming-in-the-Large. Pages 122-127. Harwichport, Massachussets, June 1985.

[23]   D. B. Leblang. *"The CM Challenge: Configuration Management that Works"*. Configuration Management, Edited by W. Tichy; J. Wiley and Sons. 1994. Trends in software.

[24]   D.B. Leblang. *Managing the Software Development Process with ClearGuide*. SCM 7, LNCS 1235. pages=66, 80, May, Boston, USA, 1997

[25]   J. Micallef and G. M. Clemm. *"The Asgard System: Activity-Based Configuration Management"*. In ICSE'96 and SCM-6 Workshop, Berlin, Germany, March, 1996.

[26]   *"Product Data Representation and Exchange - Part 11: The EXPRESS Language Reference Manual"*, ISO-DIS-10303-11, ISO, Agust 1992, 138 pages.

[27]   *"Recommended Practices for AP 203"*, PDES Inc., june 1995, 81 pages.

[28]   Schemas Express Part 22 - ISO-10303, 26 pages.

[29]   Schemas Express 41-46, ISO-10303, 41 pages.

[30]   Schema Part 203 - ISO-10303, 19 pages.

[31]   *"STEP Part 1: Overview and fundamental principles"*, ISO TC184/SC4/WG5, November 1991, 9 pages.

[32]   *"STEP Part 12: Express-I Language Reference Manual"*, ISO TC184/SC4, Norme ISO, June 1993, 102 pages.

[33]   E. Triggeseth, B. Gullsw, R. Conradi. *Modelling systems with variability Using the PROTEUS Configuration Language*. In SCM 7, LNCS 1005. pp. 216-240, Seattle. May 1995.

[34]   Walter F Tichy. *Design implementation and evaluation of a revision control system.* In *Proc.6th Int. Conf. Software Eng., Tokyo,* September 1982.

[35]   Walter F. Tichy. *Tools for software configuration management*. In *Proc. of the Int. Workshop on Software Version and Configuration Control*, pp. 1–20, Grassau, January 1988.

[36]   *"Working Smarter with Objects: Metaphase Object Management Framework"*, Metaphase Technology, MW00202-A, Control Data Systems, 22 pages.

[37]   P. Wilson, *"Express Tools and Services (1990-1995)"*, Catholic University of America, NIST, September 1995, 154 pages.

Software Configuration Management and Engineering Data Management: Differences and Similarities

Bernhard Westfechtel[1] and Reidar Conradi[2]

[1] Lehrstuhl für Informatik III, RWTH Aachen
Ahornstrasse 55, D-52074 Aachen
bernhard@i3.informatik.rwth-aachen.de
[2] Norwegian University of Science and Technology (NTNU)
N-7034 Trondheim, Norway
conradi@idi.ntnu.no

Abstract. Engineering data management and software configuration management have been evolving fairly independently. On the other hand, it has been observed earlier that many parallels exist [10]. In this paper, we examine the similarities of and differences between EDM and SCM. Many concepts are similar, but there are some differences concerning the objects to be managed. As a consequence, some sophisticated features of modern SCM systems are not applicable in the EDM domain because they are based on assumptions which do not hold there (objects represented as text files, tools operating towards the file system). Some suggestions for further work on version models and on the architecture of version support systems are outlined.

1 Introduction

Engineering data management [29] — frequently also called product data management [19] — is concerned with the management of design data in engineering disciplines such as mechanical (CAE/CIM), electrical (VLSI), or chemical engineering. That is, it is concerned with managing machine-readable data about physical objects, not the objects itself. Since the term "software engineering" was coined in the late 60s [34], many people believe that software construction is — or should be — an engineering discipline as well. As a consequence, we would expect software configuration management (SCM) to be a part of engineering data management (EDM).

Indeed, software engineering support tools and EDM tools have much in common: design philosophies and methods (e.g., object-orientation), complex and versioned data structures, storage and exchange of parts of such data, an associated tool architecture, flexible user interfaces, etc. However, the EDM and SCM community have been evolving fairly independently. On the other hand, the parallels were recognized some time ago. In 1990, Randy Katz published a paper on version models for engineering data [23]. Only recently, we surveyed the

B. Magnusson (Ed.): ECOOP 98, SCM-8, LNCS 1439, pp. 95–106, 1998.
© Springer-Verlag Berlin Heidelberg 1998

state-of-the-art in SCM in the same journal [9]. Although both papers introduce different terminologies and taxonomies, the similarities are still striking.

The ongoing series of SCM workshops provides an important forum for presenting theoretical and practical work in this field [7]. This year, "S" stands for "System" rather than "Software", encouraging a more global perspective concerning the objects to be managed. What does this mean to SCM? This paper contributes a partial answer by comparing SCM and EDM, mainly focusing on version models, or how to structure the version space.

Our comparison is mainly based on an analysis of approaches presented in the scientific literature. We cover both research prototypes and commercial systems. Our expertise refers primarily to the SCM domain, but we have also gathered some experience in EDM [43].

Section 2 illustrates the parallels between EDM and SCM by a couple of examples. Section 3 compares both domains more systematically with respect to the product space (the objects to be managed) and the version space (the concepts for maintaining versions of evolving objects). Looking at EDM and SCM more closely, we identify some important differences which have had a major impact on the development of EDM and SCM systems. Section 4 summarizes our findings.

2   Similarities Between EDM and SCM

Comparing EDM and SCM, we observed that virtually every concept occurring in one domain is also present in the other. Moreover, there are several systems with striking similarities which their authors were not aware of. Below, we give some examples to support this claim.

Object and version plane. In several systems, objects and relationships are arranged into planes which are related by version refinement. For example, this holds for OVM [22], which has been developed for VLSI design, and CoMa [42], which has been applied to both software engineering and mechanical engineering. In both systems, the object plane contains versioned objects (with object identifiers) and their relationships. The version plane refines the object plane, so that each versioned object is refined into a set of versions (with version identifiers) standing in a version graph. Similarly, relationships between versioned objects are refined into more detailed relationships between their versions. We may try to split the version plane further in an "upper" variant layer, and a "lower" revision layer, but these layers are intertwined multi-layers – corresponding to branching in the version graph. The object plane may be used in the following ways: As a view, it provides an abstraction of the bulk of information in the version plane. As a set of constraints, it describes which elements may or must be created in the version plane.

Design and module hierarchies. EDM systems support hierarchies of versioned design objects. This can be done in different ways. Here, we discuss only one of these. The Version Server [6] represents versions of VLSI design objects as follows: Each version has both a contents and a (potentially) empty set of composition relationships pointing to versions of nested design objects. Thus, the version of some composite object uniquely determines the versions of its components ("version first" selection). POEM [28] applies the same modeling approach to software engineering, relying on module hierarchies where modules are connected by (acyclic) dependencies. A module version references versions of those modules on which it depends.

Product versioning. Several SCM systems, including EPOS [27] and Voodoo [35], apply repositories to manage versions of software objects and to combine these into whole configurations. We first specify a version description, serving as a filter against the repository and defining a uni-version "product view" (i.e., version-first selection). Later, during tool-initiated queries against the selected and available product view, we are not concerned with versioning (product-last selection).

Product versioning also appeared "outside" SCM. For example, the database version approach [5] was developed for the object-oriented DBMS O_2 [2]. Here, database versions are organized into a tree, so that versioning of objects is completely transparent once a database version has been selected.

Attribute-based versioning. Attribute-based versioning is a technique to integrate versioning into the data model. When we define a version model on top of some data model (e.g., OO or ER), we must declare pairs of types: one type for a versioned object and one type for its versions, respectively. In the SCM system Adele [13], we can define one versioned object type instead. The type definition distinguishes between versioned attributes (e.g., textual contents) whose values are specific to each version, and unversioned attributes (e.g., change logs) whose values are shared by all versions and are thus properties of the versioned object as a whole. Again, this approach is not constrained to SCM. For example, attribute-based versioning was also proposed for the object-oriented DBMS EXTRA [37].

Interfaces and realizations. Several SCM systems have been designed for configuring modular programs. For example, in Gandalf [18] a module has a unique interface and potentially multiple realization variants. For each variant, there is a sequence of revisions. Adele generalizes this approach by its family concept: each family may have multiple variants or views of an interface, e.g., subsets of signatures of exported functions or header-files expressed in different programming languages.

Similar models were developed for EDM. For example, the CADLAB system [3] configures versions of VLSI design objects and makes a distinction between interfaces and realizations as well. In contrast to Gandalf and Adele, CADLAB permits different versions of one design object to co-exist in one configuration. However, such co-existence is intentionally supported by a few SCM systems as well. For example, the Cedar System Modeler [24] allows that different clients select different implementations of the same interface. This is particularly important in distributed systems, where heterogeneous processing nodes often run slightly different variants of the "same" software, e.g., Unix vs. NT, or Intel-80x86 vs. SPARC.

3   Differences Between EDM and SCM

Despite these similarities, some crucial differences exist between EDM and SCM systems. These concern both the product space, i.e., the objects to be managed and their relationships, and the version space, i.e., the way how versions of these objects and relationships are organized.

3.1   Product Space

Objects. SCM systems deal with general software objects in machine-readable form, so-called software configuration items. These objects comprise requirements specifications, software architecture designs, module interfaces, module bodies, test cases, test logs, various documentation, project plans, etc. Much of SCM functionality concerns management of human-produced source programs, represented as text files and manipulated with development tools such as editors, compilers, linkers, and debuggers. A classical SCM system therefore provides a central repository (database) for efficient storing of versioned text files. Further, it offers merge tools for combining versions based on an analysis of textual differences. It usually includes a Make tool [14] to reliably and efficiently regenerate an executable software system, based on compile and link steps.

Several software objects encompass "structured" (non-textual) information, such as diagrams and tables in e.g., requirements specifications, architectural designs or project plans (as Gannt diagrams or spread sheets). Indeed, CASE tools for software specification and design may employ very complex data structures [16]. (Compilers and debuggers do likewise, but their data structures are considered intermediate and not permanent, or can be regenerated automatically from source texts.) However, instead of storing data structures in a DBMS, most CASE tools use textual representations to store and exchange data – cf. the discussion on object-oriented databases [1]. Typical textual formats are the ones used e.g., by SDL editors. Of more standard exchange formats, we can mention CDIF [12] for software engineering and IDL [38,11] for compiling interchange. Since these data representations are tool-produced and tool-consumed, they may not be easily readable or maintainable by human developers.

As an assessment of the software tool situation, we can say that modern CASE tools are not much in use. Text-based software development, mainly centered around programming-related activities, is still dominant. However, this situation is expected to change, especially in the light of the upcoming portfolio of UML tools. So, in the long term, the Integrated Programming Environments [33] from the 80s may become a future reality. We then need to permanently store and interchange more complex data structures, such as abstract syntax trees or graphs.

So, for the time being, we can conclude that SCM is considered a more important step towards process maturity than tool support for requirements engineering and design. This is reflected in the recommendations from ISO-9001 and CMM-level2, both emphasizing product management. So far, many SCM systems mainly focus on the management of text files. Although the designers of SCM systems have recognized the needs for managing structured objects, they have not gone far in this respect for several reasons. First, the marketplace demands SCM support for programming with classical tools such as text editors, compilers, and debuggers. Second, management of structured objects is hard to support and requires sophisticated object management techniques. Third, there is little agreement on common data models for structured objects, and implementing special solutions for specific customers does not pay off.

In EDM, today's situation is different. In typical engineering applications, text files play only a minor role. For example, this applies to the VLSI domain, where we have e.g. functional, logic and layout descriptions of designs. In CAE/CIM, there are also a vast number of types of design objects, since the corresponding physical product has a complex and diverse breakdown, e.g. sub-objects such as cranes, walls, floors, windows, pipes, valves, pumps, wires etc. Furthermore, PPC (production planning and control) systems frequently store their data in relational databases. Thus, the domain-specific tools which are integrated with an EDM system, often store their data in (potentially home-grown) databases and frequently use their private data representations.

The services provided by SCM systems may be inadequate or insufficient in EDM applications. Let us give two examples:

- In SCM, a *Check-out command* extracts a version from a central repository into a local, file-based workspace. Internally, this may involve a conversion from the internal data format (for efficiently storing multiple versions using deltas) into a plain text file. However, conceptually no conversion takes place: we simple retrieve the file which we stored into the repository earlier. This may not be sufficient in EDM, where we have heterogeneous data representations. Thus, a more sophisticated conversion may have to be carried out between the data format used in the repository and the data format requested by the tool in its workspace, and vice versa.
- Recently, *virtual file systems* have become popular in SCM. Clearcase [25], ICE [44], and n-DFS [15] are some examples of SCM systems which provide the tools with a virtual workspace. E.g., Clearcase allows Unix and NT users to transparently access the repository through their native file systems. In many EDM settings, however, such facilities are not offered. For instance, the informatics and mechanical engineering department in Aachen jointly performed the SUKITS project [43], where we had to integrate tools running under MS-DOS, VMS, and different Unix versions. Many of these tools were also based on proprietary data formats and home-grown database systems.

As a consequence, a virtual file system was simply not viable, at least on present operating systems.

Since integration of heterogeneous tools is difficult to perform, several efforts have been launched to standardize the data representations. Most notably, the STEP initiative (Standard for the Exchange of Product Model Data [21]) defines a data model (EXPRESS) for product data and so-called partial models for certain subdomains (e.g., CAD or manufacturing planning), i.e., schemas described in EXPRESS. These schemas are remarkably rich and cover several thousands of pages, defining e.g. the representation of geometric data at a very fine-grained level. There is no counterpart to STEP in software engineering since there is little agreement on software life cycle models and notations for software objects (note the upcoming UML, however). On the other hand, STEP addresses the management of engineering data throughout the whole product life cycle, i.e., it does not prescribe the way an EDM system organizes design objects. Part 41 of the STEP standard (Product Structure Configuration Management) covers only the composition of the final product (usually maintained by PPC systems), but not the organization of all the design objects which describe it.

STEP also defines a textual data format for the exchange of product data between heterogeneous tools. STEP-compatible tools are required to import and export these textual STEP files without loss of information. In the case of STEP-compatible tools, the EDM system can provide a repository of versioned text files in a quite similar way as in the SCM domain. In the long run, this solution is not satisfactory because design objects stored in STEP are still considered individually, ignoring coarse- and fine-grained relationships.

Relationships. SCM often utilizes "horizontal" dependencies between software objects, usually traceability dependencies or import/include dependencies. These dependencies are often used for change propagation, e.g., for build processes. Many of these are inferred from the source code by parsers, e.g., the MakeDepend utility in the Make tool, which have limited knowledge of the syntax of the underlying programming language.

At first glance, EDM differs from SCM in that hierarchies, or "vertical" composition relationships (Part-Of relation), are considered the most important relationships in EDM. However, a closer look reveals that certain kinds of composition relationships in EDM correspond to dependency relationships in SCM. For example, the Version Server manages a hierarchy of VLSI design objects. But the design hierarchy is different from the part hierarchy. The latter refers to the physical parts the final product is composed of. For example, a processor consists of a set of registers, an arithmetic-logic unit (ALU), etc. The part hierarchy models physical composition[1]. In contrast, the design hierarchy models relationships between design objects. The design of a processor does not physically contain the design of the ALU (which can be used for many processors).

---

[1] In fact, there are different kinds of part hierarchies, e.g., folded and unfolded ones, but this is irrelevant to the point we want to make here.

Rather, the processor design *references* the ALU design (relationship between applied occurrence and definition). Thus, in the case of design hierarchies we actually deal with dependencies (see also the discussion of design and module hierarchies in Section 2) as they appear in software engineering (e.g., include dependencies between modules in C)[2].

3.2 Version Space

Version space representations. Virtually all SCM systems can be traced back to either SCCS [36] / RCS [39] and conditional compilation. In the former case, the version space of a software object is represented by a version graph. In the latter case, the version space is defined by attributes and their combination constraints (so-called version rules). Thus, an n-dimensional grid is appropriate to represent the version space (with each axis corresponding to one attribute). Examples of SCM systems based on SCCS/RCS are DSEE [26] and its successor Clearcase [25], while EPOS [32] and ICE [44] have their roots in conditional compilation.

Virtually all EDM systems are based on version graphs. Remarkably, alternatives to version graphs are not mentioned in Katz's paper at all. Both revisions and variants of individual components can be represented in version graphs. However, multi-dimensional variation does cause problems because of the combinatorial explosion of the required number of branches.

State-based and change-based versioning. The mainstream of SCM systems relies on state-based versioning, i.e., a version is described by the properties of the evolution state it represents. For example, this can be done by identifying some revision (by a revision-attribute holding a time stamp or revision number) and some variant (by variant-attributes holding enumerated or string values). However, a small number of SCM systems are founded on change-based versioning, i.e., a version is described by the functional changes performed relative to some baseline. Recently, state-based and change-based approaches have started to converge [8]. For example, Asgard [30] implements change-based on top of state-based versioning. The opposite solution (state-based on top of change-based) is also viable, in e.g., EPOS [31] and ICE.

However, change-based versioning until now seems to have been ignored by the EDM community. At least, we are not aware of any change-based EDM system. The only exception is the Version Server [6] which adopts the PIE [17] approach by collecting logically related changes in layers. However, even in this case it seems as if the concept of change-based versioning has not been fully recognized. We do believe that there is no fundamental reason for this. Indeed, change-based versioning can be applied to EDM as well. The concept of change is equally useful for organizing work in this domain as in SCM.

---

[2] This is still a bit simplified because design hierarchies are always acyclic, while dependencies may sometimes contain cycles (e.g., class references in Eiffel).

Extensional and intensional versioning. Extensional versioning means that the members of the version set (i.e., all versions) of a versioned object are defined by explicit enumeration. Each of these members has been created previously by Check-in. Thus, extensional versioning is concerned with the reconstruction of existing versions.

In the case of intensional versioning, the version set is defined implicitly by the properties of its members. Any version may be constructed which satisfies these properties — regardless of whether it has ever been constructed before. Intensional versioning implies flexibility: any requested version can be constructed on demand. On the other hand, we have to take care of consistency: the outcome must be correct with respect to version constraints (e.g., consistent selection of the same variant) and product constraints (e.g., syntactic and semantic consistency with respect to the rules of a programming language). Thus, inconsistent combinations have to be detected and excluded.

Note, however, that a configuration, being a selected set of individual versions, seldom has been "Checked-in" as a whole, even if each component individually was explicitly Checked-in. Indeed, we can compose previously unseen and thus "new" configurations, even if their components are not new. Here, we may consider each component as a "delta" of the encompassing configuration.

All SCM systems support extensional versioning, most of them provide support for intensional versioning as well. Different architectures are employed for the combination. The classical solution is to realize intensional versioning on top of extensional versioning, as in Adele or Clearcase. To this end, a configuration is described by an expression referring to versions of components which are selected from version graphs. The inverse approach takes intensional versioning as the base on top of which we can implement extensional versioning. EPOS and ICE demonstrate that version graphs can be simulated on top of (a derivative of) conditional compilation. Please note that both EPOS and ICE offer a basic, uniform version model, i.e., a framework on top of which different version models can be implemented. Compared to conditional compilation, the strength of these systems lies in their deductive database capabilities, in particular concerning consistency constraints.

By and large, intensional versioning has attracted little attention in EDM systems. Again, there is no fundamental reason for this. As in SCM, design objects may evolve into a large number of revisions and variants, and many changes are applied over their lifetime. Versions of design objects have to be combined in a consistent way in EDM as well. However, support is limited e.g. to SQL-like database queries.

Could SCM systems such as EPOS and ICE be applied successfully to EDM? The answer is probably "no". The point is that intensional versioning is deeply built into the SCM system (extensional versioning being realized on top rather than below intensional versioning). EPOS and ICE perform intensional versioning at the fine-grained level ("fine-grained merges"). Both systems handle software objects represented as text files. In addition, EPOS supports arbitrary versioned attributes in a crude way – but the OID and TYPEID attributes are not versionable! In both systems, fragments (attributes) are tagged with visibility expressions, being boolean expression over a set of global versioning-attributes, and updated upon Check-in.

This approach does not carry well over to design objects. In this case, we have to cope with a variety of native data formats. If the contents of design objects cannot be interpreted by the EDM system, we cannot do more than just store the contents "as-is". Perhaps, we can do this efficiently by a built-in Diff on binary files, but certainly we could do better if we knew the logical structure. Even if we can store the data in textual form (e.g., as a STEP file), a textual *merge*[3] is usually not sufficient. In particular, textual merging of STEP files may produce syntactically inconsistent results. This applies to textual merging of programs as well. But the difference is that programs are edited by the user. Therefore, we may expect that the user is capable of fixing an erroneous merge. We cannot make this assumption when merging STEP files, since these are not meant to be human-readable and -editable.

These difficulties may explain that conditional compilation has not played any significant role in EDM. Indeed, conditional compilation requires adequate support for fine-grained configuration of the contents of design objects. This requirement is rarely met, see next section.

Different versioning characteristics. We might expect different versioning characteristics in the SCM and EDM domain. For example, a classical argument is given by Tichy in [40]. Since software may be changed more easily than hardware, SCM has to cope with significantly more revisions and variants than CM for hardware. Even if we accept that claim to hold, we have to keep in mind that EDM does not deal with physical parts. Rather, it is concerned with the descriptions of these. Thus, we have to compare the product development process in engineering disciplines against the software development process. Prior to production, design objects may change very rapidly and frequently. Development methods such as simultaneous and concurrent engineering [4] take this into account (e.g., by encouraging pre-releases of intermediate versions of design objects so that design errors can be detected much earlier). It is by no means evident that software objects evolve more dynamically than design objects in EDM. So far, there is very little published data from either of these domains. We must only conclude that all this needs further exploration.

4   Conclusion

From our investigations, we draw the following conclusions:

- The concepts underlying SCM and EDM systems are very similar. For virtually every concept in one of these domains, we can also find an occurrence in the other.

---

[3] Below, we use the term "merge" loosely to denote any kind of intensional versioning, including both conditional compilation and 3-way merging.

- There are some differences which are merely terminological. For example, we have shown that the so-called design hierarchies are actually built from dependencies.
- Other differences are accidental. For example, change-based versioning could be applied in EDM as well. The idea has simply not been taken up so far.
- A fundamental difference exists with respect to the kinds of objects to be managed. Up to now, SCM mainly focuses on the management of software objects (mainly programs) represented as text files (as mentioned earlier, this will change when CASE tools are going to be used more widely). Tool integration primarily refers to compilers, editors and debuggers. Virtual file systems are seen as the ideal workspace support.

  In contrast, the most important objects in engineering application are non-textual (e.g., designs or production plans). Applications store their data in a variety of formats, and they frequently do not execute in the file system.
- Many SCM systems support intensional versioning, while only a few EDM systems address this to a limited extent. In particular, systems which provide fine-grained, built-in support for intensional versioning are expected to fail in EDM because of the large variety of data formats involved.
- The ability to allow multiple variants or representations of the "same" object in a configuration becomes increasingly more relevant in federated and/or distributed systems.

By and large, SCM and EDM are related fairly closely. As a consequence, experts from both domains should cooperate more intensively than they used to do. In particular, cooperation is required to support the development of hybrid products consisting of both hardware and software components in a uniform way.

Acknowledgements

Many thanks go to the EPOS group in Trondheim and the IPSEN group in Aachen. The comments of the unknown reviewers are also gratefully acknowledged.

References

1. M. Atkinson, F. Bançilhon, D. DeWitt, K. Dittrich, D. Maier, and S. Zdonik. The object-oriented database system manifesto. In *Proc. DOOD'89, Kyoto, Japan*, pages 40–57, Dec. 1989.
2. F. Bançilhon, C. Delobel, and P. Kannelakis, editors. *Building an Object-Oriented Database System: The Story of O_2*. Morgan Kaufmann, 1992.
3. M. Brielmann, E. Kupitz, D. Mallon, et al. A Common Data Schema for Tool Integration. In *Proceedings CAD'92*, pages 127–140. Springer Verlag, 1992.
4. H.-J. Bullinger and J. Warschat, editors. *Concurrent Simultaneous Engineering Systems*. Springer-Verlag, 1996.
5. W. Cellary and G. Jomier. Consistency of Versions in Object-Oriented Databases. In Bançilhon et al. [2], pages 447–462.

6. E. E. Chang, D. Gedye, and R. H. Katz. The Design and Implementation of a Version Server for Computer-Aided Design Data. *Software — Practice and Experience*, 19(3):199–222, Mar. 1989.

7. R. Conradi, editor. *Software Configuration Management: Proceedings from SCM7 Workshop*, Boston, USA, 18–19 May 1997. Springer Verlag LNCS 1235, 234 p.

8. R. Conradi and B. Westfechtel. Towards a Uniform Version Model for Software Configuration Management. In Conradi [7], pages 1–17.

9. R. Conradi and B. Westfechtel. Version Models for Software Configuration Management, 59 p. *ACM Computing Surveys*, 1998. (Accepted August 1997).

10. S. A. Dart. Parallels in Computer-Aided Design Frameworks and Software Development Environments Efforts. *IFIP Transactions A*, 16:175–189, 1992.

11. T. Didriksen, A. Lie, and R. Conradi. IDL as a Data Description Language for a Programming Environment Database. *ACM SIGPLAN Notices*, pages 71–78, Nov. 1987. (Special issue on IDL, ed. C. Robert Morgan).

12. Electronic Industries Associates, Engineering Department, Arlington, VA. *CDIF CASE Data Interchange Format EIA/IS-106/107*.

13. J. Estublier and R. Casallas. The Adele Software Configuration Manager. In Tichy [41], pages 2–11.

14. S. I. Feldman. Make — a Program for Maintaining Computer Programs. *Software — Practice and Experience*, 9(3):255–265, Mar. 1979.

15. G. Fowler, D. Korn, and H. Rao. n-DFS: The Multiple Dimensional File System. In Tichy [41], pages 135–154.

16. A. Fuggetta. A Classification of CASE Technology. *IEEE Computer*, pages 25–38, Dec. 1993.

17. I. P. Goldstein and D. G. Bobrow. A Layered Approach to Software Design. Technical Report CSL-80-5, XEROX PARC, Palo Alto, California, 1980.

18. A. N. Habermann and D. Notkin. Gandalf: Software Development Environments. *IEEE Trans. on Software Engineering*, SE-12(12):1117–1127, Dec. 1986. (Special issue on GANDALF).

19. S. B. Harris. Business Strategy and the Role of Engineering Product Data Management: A Literature Review and Summary of the Emerging Research Questions. *Proceedings of the Institution of Mechanical Engineers, Part B (Journal of Engineering Manufacture)*, 210(B3):207–220, 1996.

20. P. B. Henderson, editor. *Proc. 1st ACM SIGSOFT/SIGPLAN Software Engineering Symposium on Practical Software Development Environments* (Pittsburgh), Apr. 1984. In ACM SIGPLAN Notices 19(5), May 1984.

21. ISO. *ISO 10303: Product Data Representation and Exchange (the STEP Standard)*.

22. W. Käfer and H. Schöning. Mapping a Version Model to a Complex-Object Data Model. In *Proceedings 8th International Conference on Data Engineering*, pages 348–357, Tempe, Arizona, 1992. IEEE Computer Society Press.

23. R. H. Katz. Toward a Unified Framework for Version Modeling in Engineering Databases. *ACM Computing Surveys*, 22(4):375–408, Dec. 1990.

24. B. W. Lampson and E. E. Schmidt. Practical Use of a Polymorphic Applicative Language. In *Proc. 10th ACM SIGACT/SIGPLAN Symposium on Principles of Programming Languages*, pages 237–255, Austin, Texas, USA, Jan. 1983.

25. D. Leblang. The CM Challenge: Configuration Management that Works. In Tichy [41], pages 1–38.

26. D. B. Leblang and R. P. Chase, Jr. Computer-aided Software Engineering in a Distributed Workstation Environment. In Henderson [20], pages 104–112. In ACM SIGPLAN Notices 19(5), May 1984.

27. A. Lie, R. Conradi, T. Didriksen, E. Karlsson, S. O. Hallsteinsen, and P. Holager. Change Oriented Versioning. In C. Ghezzi and J. A. McDermid, editors, *Proceedings of the 2nd European Software Engineering Conference*, LNCS 387, pages 191–202, Coventry, UK, Sept. 1989. Springer Verlag.

28. Y.-J. Lin and S. P. Reiss. Configuration Management with Logical Structures. In *Proc. of the 18th International Conference on Software Engineering*, pages 298–307, Berlin, Mar. 1996. IEEE Computer Society Press.

29. K. G. McIntosh. *Engineering Data Management — A Guide to Successful Implementation*. McGraw-Hill, Maidenhead, England, 1995.

30. J. Micallef and G. Clemm. The Asgard System: Activity-Based Configuration Management. In I. Sommerville, editor, *Software Configuration Management: ICSE'96 SCM-6 Workshop*, LNCS 1167, pages 175–186, Berlin, Germany, Mar. 1996. Springer-Verlag.

31. B. Munch. HiCOV: Managing the Version Space. In I. Sommerville, editor, *Software Configuration Management: ICSE'96 SCM-6 Workshop*, LNCS 1167, pages 110–126, Berlin, Germany, Mar. 1996. Springer-Verlag.

32. B. P. Munch, R. Conradi, J.-O. Larsen, M. N. Nguyen, and P. H. Westby. Integrated Product and Process Management in EPOS. *Journal of Integrated CAE*, 1995. (Special issue on Integrated Product and Process Modeling), 30 p.

33. M. Nagl, editor. *Building Tightly-Integrated Software Development Environments: The IPSEN Approach*. LNCS 1170, 709 p. Springer Verlag, Berlin, 1996.

34. P. Naur and B. Randell, editors. *Software Engineering - Proc. NATO Conference in* Garmisch-Partenkirchen, *1968*. NATO Science Committee, Scientific Affairs Division, NATO, Brussels, Jan. 1969.

35. C. Reichenberger. Concepts and Techniques for Software Version Control. *Software — Concepts and Tools*, 15(3):97–104, July 1994.

36. M. J. Rochkind. The Source Code Control System. *IEEE Trans. on Software Engineering*, SE-1(4):364–370, 1975.

37. E. Sciore. Version and Configuration Management in an Object-Oriented Data Model. *VLDB Journal*, 3(1):77–106, Jan. 1994.

38. R. Snodgrass. *The IDL Description Language: Definition and Use*. Computer Science Press, Rockville, MD 20850, USA, 1989.

39. W. F. Tichy. RCS — A System for Version Control. *Software — Practice and Experience*, 15(7):637–654, 1985.

40. W. F. Tichy. Tools for Software Configuration Management. In J. F. H. Winkler, editor, *Proceedings of the International Workshop on Software Version and Configuration Control*, pages 1–20, Grassau, Germany, 1988. Teubner Verlag.

41. W. F. Tichy, editor. *Configuration Management*, volume 2 of *Trends in Software*. John Wiley and Sons, New York, 1994.

42. B. Westfechtel. A Graph-Based System for Managing Configurations of Engineering Design Documents. *International Journal of Software Engineering and Knowledge Engineering*, 6(4):549–583, Dec. 1996.

43. B. Westfechtel. Integrated Product and Process Management for Engineering Design Applications. *Integrated Computer-Aided Engineering*, 3(1):20–35, Jan. 1996.

44. A. Zeller and G. Snelting. Unified Versioning through Feature Logic. *ACM Transactions on Software Engineering and Methodology*, 6(4):397–440, Oct. 1997.

Product Configuration Using Object Oriented Grammars

Görel Hedin[1], Lennart Ohlsson[2], and John McKenna[3]

[1] Dept of Computer Science, Lund University, Sweden. Gorel.Hedin@dna.lth.se
[2] Utilia Consult, Malmö, Sweden. lennart@utilia.se
[3] Alfa Laval Thermal AB, Lund, Sweden. djohn.mckenna@alfalaval.com

Abstract. This paper presents a technique for product configuration modelling based on object-orientation and attribute grammars. The technique allows efficient interactive configurator tools to be generated for specified product families. Additional benefits include a high degree of checkability, early validation, readability, and reusability. The technique is particularly aimed at mass-customization products and an example concerning the mechanical configuration of plate heat exchangers is used to demonstrate its benefits.

1   Introduction

Complex products are often designed as product families where each customized product is a configuration of interrelated components. A *product configurator* is a tool which supports the product configuration process so that all the design and configuration rules which are expressed in a product configuration model are guaranteed to be satisfied. The configurator simplifies the manufacturing process by assuring that all orders received are possible to build. Interactive configurator tools can support quick and flexible customization by giving immediate and accurate information about the available combinations of options.

Ideally, the product configuration model should be written in a form which captures the design intent in a direct way, allowing the model to be easily read and changed by the domain engineers themselves, without involving expert programmers. It should be possible to generate computer-aided configuration tools automatically from the model. In this scenario, the software cost for a product change can be easily predicted, and changes can be introduced within days.

As a step towards this ideal scenario, we have developed OPG (Object-Oriented Product Grammar) - a configuration model description language which is based on object-oriented programming and attribute grammars. Object-orientation provides suitable modelling support and attribute grammars forms a suitable base for expressing configuration rules. Attribute grammars furthermore provide a well-established and efficient technology for the generation of interactive tools [16, 10].

The OPG work has grown out of an effort to formally describe the mechanical configuration of plate heat exchangers in a cooperation project between Lund University and Alfa Laval Thermal, the world leading supplier of plate and spiral heat exchangers. Alfa Laval Thermal has developed an interactive configuration tool called CAS 2000 (Computer Aided Sales) [1] which is used at market companies around the world. The tool allows customized design of plate heat exchangers. The user can interactively enter requirements on e.g. pressures and temperatures, and select a number of different options according to engineering rules. The tool

B. Magnusson (Ed.): ECOOP 98, SCM-8, LNCS 1439, pp. 107-126, 1998
© Springer-Verlag Berlin Heidelberg 1998

automatically presents valid alternatives for selection, and also checks that the designed plate heat exchanger is internally consistent, i.e., that it is possible to build. When a design is complete, the tool can prepare quotations for customers and send electronic orders to the appropriate manufacturing unit.

The immediate goal of the OPG work is to be able to replace the hand implemented configurator in CAS 2000 with a configurator generated automatically from declarative descriptions, thereby allowing the tool to be updated quickly to incorporate new product developments, eliminating the need for programming.

The rest of this paper is organized as follows. Section 2 gives an overview of our running example: plate heat exchangers, and the configuration problems involved for this product. Section 3 explains the architecture we propose for product configuration, and section 4 discusses key elements in the OPG formalism. A discussion is given in section 5 where we also give an outlook on future work. Section 6 discusses related work and section 7 concludes the paper.

2   Plate Heat Exchangers

A heat exchanger is a device for heating or cooling a fluid by exchanging heat with another fluid. Examples of use are in chemical processing, dairy processing, air conditioning, etc. A plate heat exchanger (PHE) consists of a pack of metal plates and the fluids are directed into alternate channels between the plates so that a large area for heat exchange is obtained without letting the fluids mix. Fig. 1 shows the basic structure of a PHE.

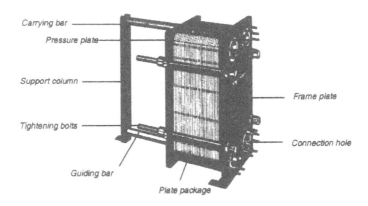

Fig. 1. Mechanical configuration of plate heat exchanger

Our example concerns the *mechanical configuration* of the PHE, i.e. how a plate package is configured with frame plate, pressure plate, carrying bar, support column, tightening bolts, etc. Each frame plate and pressure plate has four holes which can be used in different ways. Four of the holes are used for connecting the incoming and outgoing two fluids. Other holes can be covered with inspection covers (to allow inspection of a fluid). Some holes will not be in contact with any fluid, because the plate package does not have a hole in the corresponding position. In that case, the hole is simply covered by a blind cover. Examples of configuration options include how to place the connections and covers, how to select components of matching sizes and of appropriate material so that adjacent materials do not corrode and so that the components will stand the pressure requirements. When different configurations are possible, the cheapest one is usually preferable.

What is interesting about this example is that PHEs as such are not mass produced. Rather, the individual components, such as plates, carrying bars, support columns, etc., come in many different variants (each of which is mass produced), but each individual sold PHE usually represents a unique configuration of components. The components come in many different sizes and material in order to fit different plate package configurations and to cater for the customer requirements on for example pressure and corrosion properties.

Alfa Laval Thermal has for more than two decades applied leading edge production principles such as process oriented organization and build-to-order manufacturing, or what is now known as mass-customization. The product model used is known as a building block system. From a manufacturing perspective a block is a named assembly with a fixed set of components, i.e. it identifies a particular bill-of-material. For example, a given "tightening bolts block" identifies a certain set of actual nuts and bolts. From a sales perspective, however, a block appears as a component in the sense that blocks are the atomic elements which can be configured into a customer specific product.

3   The OPG Configuration Model

Taking a general perspective, we can view a product configuration as a set of connected *components*, each with a number of *properties*. A number of *rules* over the components and properties define the validity of the configuration: A *valid product configuration* is a configuration where all rules are satisfied. This general view is common in product configuration, see e.g. [19, 17]. An interactive product configurator tool, like CAS 2000 discussed above, allows the user to interactively edit a product configuration by adding, removing, or changing components. The tool constantly checks if the current configuration is valid and also helps the user to select components which will result in a valid configuration.

OPG (Object-Oriented Product Grammar) is a formal product configuration model based on object-orientation and attribute grammars. This model allows specification on three levels:

Type level: Specification of product types and their principle components, e.g. plate heat·exchangers and their principle components such as frame plate, pressure plate, carrying bar, etc.

Prototype level: Specification of the mass-produced components which can be used in product configuration. E.g., specification of different mass-produced frame plates.

Configuration level: Specification of individual customized configurations. E.g., a milk cooler configured from instances of specific mass-produced components.

Our work aims at the possibility to automatically generate product-specific configurator tools like CAS 2000 by giving the product type specification as input to a tool generator and using the description of the mass-produced components as a database of the configurator tool. Fig. 2 outlines this approach. The main reason to support the generation of the configurator tool is to be able to quickly incorporate changes to the configurator as the product type evolves. In addition, it is important to support a high degree of consistency checking at all three levels, and that the specifications are highly readable and reusable to support evolution.

3.1   The Component Hierarchy

As mentioned, a product configuration is a set of connected components with properties and rules. In OPG, the components are connected in a hierarchy. In section 5 we will discuss the possibilities of generalizing this to a graph. A very simplified component hierarchy for a plate heat exchanger is shown in Fig. 3. The top component represents the complete PHE consisting of a PlatePackage and a Frame. The Frame in turn consists of a FramePlate, a PressurePlate, and TighteningBolts. This PHE does not have any CarryingBar or SupportColumn - these components are in general optional, but may be required in specific configurations. All four Holes on the FramePlate have contact with fluid (FluidContact) and are fitted with Linings. On the PressurePlate, three of the Holes are not in contact with fluid (NoFluidContact) and are covered with BlindCovers, whereas the fourth hole is in contact with fluid (FluidContact) and is fitted with a Lining and an InspectionCover. The PlatePackage has, in principle, an internal configuration of different kinds of plates, but since we are dealing with mechanical configuration only, we simply view it as a black box here.

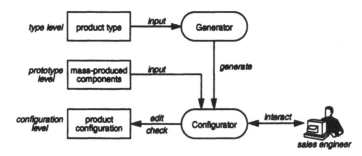

Fig. 2. Specification levels and tools

Some of the components, e.g. FramePlate, correspond to physical mass-produced components, and we call these *prototypical components*. These components will typically have a bill-of-material associated with them. Other components do not have a physical correspondence and are called *configuration components*. These components may have the role of grouping prototypical components, e.g. Frame, indicating a configuration choice, e.g. FluidContact and NoFluidContact, or modelling customer requirements, e.g. PHE.

A component *c* on the path towards the root from a component *s* is said to be *enclosing s*. Inversely, the *s* component is said to be a *subcomponent* of *c*. For example, the InspectionCover component in Fig. 3 has the following enclosing components: FluidContact, Hole, PressurePlate, Frame, PHE.

3.2   The Specification Levels

Different aspects of the components, connections, properties, and rules, are specified at different specification levels:

Type level: At this level component types are declared to model the types of components which occur in configurations. The types are arranged in an inheritance hierarchy of more general and more specific types (supertypes and subtypes). For each component type, its connections (in the component hierarchy) are declared, indicating mandatory and optional subcomponents, and arrays of subcomponents. Each component type also contains declarations of properties and rules.

Fig. 3. A component hierarchy

Prototype level: At this level *prototypes*, i.e. instances of the prototypical component types, are specified, to model the components that are mass produced. Each prototype is given explicit values for some or all of the connections and properties declared in its type. Usually, all of the properties of a prototype are given values at this level, but the possibility to leave out some of the property values allows the specification of *parameterized* components. For example, an insulation board may be manufactured as piece goods, sold by the metre, and its property *length* may be given a value at the configuration level rather than at the prototype level.

Configuration level: At this level instances of configuration component types and copies of prototypes are specified and the (remaining) connections and properties are given values.

Fig. 4 shows an example of types, prototypes, and a partial configuration. The type level specifies prototypical types like FramePlate, Hole, and Lining, and configuration types like HoleContact and its two subtypes FluidContact and NoFluidContact. At the prototype level, different prototypes for FramePlate (FP1, FP2, ...) and Lining (L1, L2, ...) are specified with differing property values. The example also shows the possibility for prototypes to specify subcomponents, by specifying the different Holes for a FramePlate. At the configuration level, instances of FluidContact are specified and connected with copies of the FP1 and L1 prototypes.

The model is clearly heavily inspired by object-orientation. The component types correspond to classes, the prototypes to prototype instances of the classes, and the instances at the configuration level to instances of classes or copies of prototypes. The object-oriented concept of prototypes and copies [13] has also been used in the area of product configuration by e.g. Peltonen et al. [15]. Our use of prototypes is, however, a direct application of the Prototype design pattern [7] rather than the use of prototype or delegation-based programming as in [13, 15].

The model is also heavily inspired by attribute grammars. An attribute grammar is an extension of a context-free grammar with attributes and semantic rules [12]. OPG component types with its connections correspond to the nonterminals and productions of the context-free part of the grammar, and the OPG properties and rules to the attributes and semantic rules of the grammar. Some of our previous work [8] shows the benefits of using object-oriented notations for attribute grammars, similar to how it is done here. The configuration, i.e. the component hierarchy, corresponds to an attributed syntax tree, and the notion of valid product configuration is directly analogous to the notion of a syntax tree with a valid attribution. Attribute grammars have proven especially suitable for generating interactive language-based editors [16], and our earlier work shows how to use object-oriented attribute grammar techniques to obtain very efficient incremental evaluators [10]. Such evaluators can incrementally check the attribution validity as the user edits the syntax tree, and the technique is directly applicable to product configurator tools where an automated mechanism can check the validity of a configuration as it is edited.

An important aspect of product configurator tools is that they should support the user not only with checking validity, but with selecting valid components. To provide attribute-grammar based support for this is an area for future work, but we have developed fragments of such techniques in the area of language-based editing, where e.g. semantic editing can be used to provide a user with menus of visible and type-correct identifiers [9].

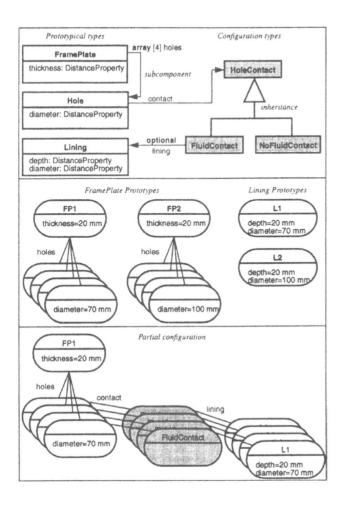

Fig. 4. Examples of types, prototypes, and instances in a partial configuration

4   Elements in OPG

4.1   Properties

All properties are declared at the type level, but may be given values at the prototype or configuration level. There are three different modes for properties depending on how they are given values: prototype properties, configuration properties, and derived properties.

Prototype Properties. These are properties which are given values at the prototype level. A prototype property typically reflects some physical characteristic of the component, e.g. thickness or diameter as in the example above, or some imposed characteristic such as a price.

Configuration Properties. These are properties which are given values at the configuration level, either by the user explicitly or computed by some external tool. A configuration property set by the user typically reflects a customer requirement. For example, the Frame type has several configuration properties such as operatingPressure, upperTemperature, and lowerTemperature. External tools may also set configuration properties, allowing these tools to be interfaced to the main configurator. For example, an external tool computing the plate package configuration could set the properties of the PlatePackage component, e.g. length, plateMaterial, and gasketMaterial. These properties can then be used by the main configurator to check the validity of the mechanical configuration.

Derived Properties. The value of a derived property is computed by a rule, making use of other property values or constants. Typically, derived properties are introduced in order to make other rules simpler to express. We will see examples of this later. There are two principle ways of defining the value of a derived property: by a rule in the component holding the derived property, or by a rule in the immediately enclosing component. This can be used to propagate property values up or down a component hierarchy in order to make them easily accessible at different locations. A derived property does not have to be explicitly stored, but can be computed whenever its value is needed. It can thus be implemented as a function.

The prototype and configuration properties correspond to lexemes in a context free grammar (e.g. identifiers, integer constants, boolean constants, string constants, etc.). Derived properties, defined upwards or downwards, correspond exactly to the synthesized and inherited attributes in an attribute grammar. As discussed in [8], it is particularly simple to implement the attributes (derived properties) as functions by using the virtual function construct in object-oriented languages.

4.2   Rules

Rules in OPG are placed in the component types and are specified at the type level. A rule is local in the sense that it can refer to the properties of *self* (an instance of the component type) and also to other components accessible in certain ways from *self*. There are two kinds of rules: defining rules and validity rules:

Defining rules: A defining rule is a rule defining the value of a derived property. It corresponds to a semantic rule of an attribute grammar.

Validity rules: A validity rule is a boolean expression over properties. A configuration is said to be valid if all the validity rules in the configuration are satisfied. A validity rule corresponds to a semantic condition in an attribute grammar.

OPG offers two ways of accessing properties in other components than *self*:

Subcomponent reference: A rule may access or define properties of immediate subcomponents of *self*.

Enclosing reference: A rule may access a property of an enclosing component quali-
fied by a given type.

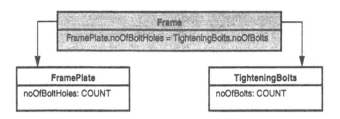

Fig. 5. Rule accessing subcomponent properties

Fig. 5 shows an example of accessing subcomponent properties: A validity rule in
Frame checks that the FramePlate subcomponent has the same number of bolt holes
as there are bolts in the TighteningBolts subcomponent.[1]

The possibility to access and define properties in *self* and in immediate
subcomponents corresponds directly to the mechanism for defining and accessing
attributes in classical attribute grammars. In principle, this possibility is sufficient for
expressing arbitrary rules, because it is always possible to introduce derived
properties which copy the information from one point in the configuration hierarchy
to another. However, this introduction of derived copy properties can be cumbersome
and lead to a cluttered specification. This problem is well known in attribute
grammars and many attribute grammar notation languages therefore introduce various
shortcut notations to avoid having to introduce such copy properties, see e.g. [11].
The *enclosing* mechanism mentioned above is one such shortcut notation (called
"including" in [11]). By letting a component c directly access a property p in an
enclosing component e, we can avoid introducing a number of derived properties
which copy the value of p from e down to c. Besides cutting down on the number of
properties and rules, this shortcut notation is very important for reusability reasons
because it very effectively reduces the dependencies between different component
types. In the next section we will see how the *enclosing* mechanism can be used very
effectively in combination with mixin types.

In general, if a rule needs to refer to properties in two components c_1 and c_2, there
are different alternatives for where to place the rule. By using a combination of
derived properties and the *enclosing* mechanism, the rule could be placed in any of
the components on the path from c_1 to c_2. Which placement is chosen can greatly
affect the size, readability, and reusability of the specification.

---

[1] In case a component has only one subcomponent of a particular type, the type name (e.g.
FramePlate) can be used to access the subcomponent. It is also possible to give
subcomponents explicit names as was done in Fig. 4.

As an example: consider checking that the depth of a Lining is the same as the depth of the Hole in which it is placed. In our example, Hole has no explicit property *depth*, but if the Hole is in a FramePlate, the depth of the Hole is of course the same as the thickness of the FramePlate. Fig. 6 shows a solution which combines the use of derived properties and the *enclosing* mechanism.

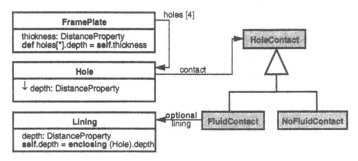

Fig. 6. Combined use of derived properties and the *enclosing* mechanism

In this example, *depth* is defined as a (downwards) derived property (indicated by "↓"). The FramePlate has a defining rule which defines the value of *depth* of the Hole subcomponents. The Lining has a validation rule which uses the *enclosing* mechanism to access the *depth* property and compare it with its own *depth* property. It would be possible to obtain a slightly smaller specification by letting the Lining refer directly to the thickness property of FramePlate, thus making the depth property and its defining rule unnecessary. However, that would make the specification less reusable because it would not work for Holes in other components like, for example, PressurePlate. This could be fixed by refactoring the type hierarchy, introducing a supertype for Frame-Plate and PressurePlate where the thickness property would be declared, but this would on the other hand make the specification bigger. We also find the solution in Fig. 6 more readable: the two rules express closely our explanation of the problem in informal english.

4.3   Main Types and Mixins

The component types we have seen so far model prototypical components and config-uration components. We call these *main types* because the type captures the main aspect of the component. Main types can be organized in a single inheritance hierarchy to model different levels of generality. For example, (see fig. 7) BlindCover models blind covers at a general level, whereas its subtypes LargeBlindCover and SmallBlindCover are specialized alternatives: a LargeBlindCover must stand the pressure imposed from the plate package and is therefore bolted to the FramePlate or PressurePlate, whereas a SmallBlindCover is attached by a simple snap mechanism. This is modelled by specifying different properties and rules in LargeBlindCover and SmallBlindCover.

It is often the case that component types which are unrelated in the main type hierarchy, nevertheless share some properties and rules. In this case, one would like to express the shared behavior in a separate type and reuse it by inheriting that type to the appropriate main types (by multiple inheritance). Such types are called *mixins*, see e.g. [4]. OPG mixin and main types differ in the following ways:

- Whereas a main type models the main aspect of a component, a mixin type models only a partial behavior which may be common to several unrelated main types.

- A main type may inherit from at most one other main type (single inheritance), but from any number of mixin types (multiple inheritance).

- Inheritance of mixin types is done in order to obtain specification reuse whereas inheritance of main types is done to model specialized alternatives in a configuration.

- A subcomponent must be declared to be of a main type. Mixin types may not be used.

- A mixin type may not contain declarations of subcomponents, only property declarations and rules.

- A mixin type is always abstract, i.e. it cannot be instantiated on its own.

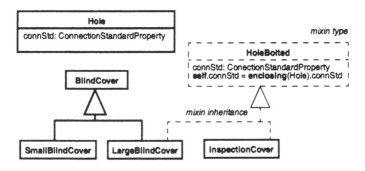

Fig. 7. Use of mixin types

The separation of types into two kinds: a full kind (main types) which can be arranged using single inheritance, and a partial kind (mixin types) which can be arranged using multiple inheritance is often recommended in object-oriented programming, see e.g. [20]. This substantially improves readability and reusability over general multiple inheritance, while retaining most advantages. A similar technique is also used in Java with its separation into class types and interface types [2]. The combination of mixins with shortcut notations like "enclosing" is very powerful. In attribute grammars this technique has been used very effectively to define e.g. reusable scope rules [11] (the use of mixins is there called "symbol inheritance").

Fig. 7 shows an example of main and mixin inheritance. LargeBlindCover and InspectionCover are unrelated in the main type hierarchy, but nevertheless have a common characteristic: they are components which are bolted to a hole in a

FramePlate or PressurePlate, and they need to use the same connection standard as is used for the hole in the plate they are bolted to. To avoid repeating the specification of this characteristic we specify it in a mixin type HoleBolted which is inherited by both LargeBlindCover and InspectionCover.

Pairs of Mixin Types

The use of the *enclosing* construct makes a component dependent on some type in its context. If not used with care, this may lead to reduced reusability, in case it is meaningful to use the component in some other context. Therefore, when a component type C refers to an enclosing type E, the following question should be posed: would it be meaningful to have a C component in some other context which does not contain an E component? If the answer is "yes", the reusability of C is unnecessarily limited because of its dependency on E. In our examples of *enclosing* above, the enclosing type is Hole. It seems reasonable to argue that the accessing types Lining, Inspection-Cover, and LargeBlindCover are meaningful only in the context of a Hole, and there is thus no problem with reusability.

In other cases, when the answer is "yes", one may consider introducing a mixin type also for the enclosing component. This introduces a pair of mixins which are designed to work together: the "upper" mixin declares some properties which are accessed using the *enclosing* mechanism in the "lower" mixin. This solves the reusability problem because it makes the mixin types independent of the actual components where they are mixed in, allowing the behavior to be mixed in for different components and different contexts.

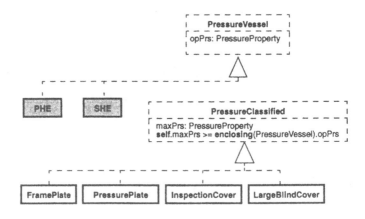

Fig. 8. Use of mixin pairs

Consider the following example. In an operating PHE, the fluids have a certain pressure, and many of the components like FramePlates, PressurePlates, Inspection-Covers, and LargeBlindCovers must stand at least this pressure. A first solution to this problem would be to introduce a mixin type PressureClassified which declares a property maxPressure and uses the *enclosing* mechanism to compared it with the operatingPressure property of PHE. However, it is quite possible that we would like to reuse the InspectionCover and LargeBlindCover types when modelling another product, for example a spiral heat exchanger (SHE). In that case, these types would appear in the context of a SHE component, and the maxPressure should instead be compared with the operatingPressure property of SHE. The solution is to introduce a mixin PressureVessel which is inherited by both PHE and SHE as shown in Fig. 8. The mixins PressureVessel and PressureClassified operate as a pair. They model the general behavior of having a pressure vessel with an operating pressure, and components attached to it are classified to stand at least that pressure. The mixin pair can then be reused for any product exhibiting this general behavior.

5   Discussion

OPG is aimed at obtaining descriptions which are small, highly readable, and easy to evolve and reuse; to obtain a high degree of checkability; and to allow automatic generation of efficient interactive configuration tools. We will now discuss different aspects of OPG and how it contributes to these goals.

Architecture. The proposed architecture which is divided into the three levels of types, prototypes, and configuration, supports the different phases in the design and configuration process. Product designers define a family of related products by working at the type level. The prototype level describes the different mass-produced components. The type level serves as an interface for defining new prototypes, placing requirements on what physical and other external characteristics the new prototype must possess. If values can be set for these properties, it will be possible to define the prototype and use it in future configurations. Typically, these prototypical properties will serve as requirements on subcontractors manufacturing the mass-produced parts. Sales engineers work at the configuration level, defining how actual customized products are configured from mass-fabricated parts. This architecture fits mass-customization problems like e.g. plate heat exchangers. For other kinds of products the design may be more intertwined with configuration, e.g. as indicated in [15].

Checkability. The three-level architecture allows a clear definition of what kinds of validity can be checked at each level. At the type level, the type system itself allows a basic validity check, similar to the compile-time checking of strongly typed programming languages like Pascal and Java, e.g. making sure that all accessed properties actually exist (i.e. that they are declared). The AG-inspired use of derived properties furthermore allows checking if the derived properties are well-defined, i.e., that for any possible configuration, there will be exactly one defining rule for each derived property, thus avoiding under- or overdetermination with regards to derived properties. This is an important aspect because it supports early error checking and can make designers more confident they have designed a consistent model.

At the prototype level, it is possible to check if the prototype is complete, i.e. if all prototypical properties are given values. It is also possible to do a partial check on the validity of the prototype, by checking validity rules which use only prototypical prop erties of the (compound) prototype. At the configuration level, it is possible to do full validity checking by checking if all validity rules are satisfied.

Interactive Configurator Tools. As described earlier, the AG technology allows efficient interactive configurator tools to be generated from the type-level specification. Such tools can support structure-oriented editing of configurations (using graphical or textual editing techniques) and can check the validity as the configuration is edited, using incremental attribute evaluation techniques. The validity checking can be done very efficiently by AG evaluation techniques, making use of statically computed evaluation plans (tables computed at tool generation time). It is important that the incremental evaluation is efficient in order to allow an interactive construction of the configuration, giving immediate feedback on possible rule violations.

Readability and Reusability. All rules in OPG are local to a component and may access properties of other components relative to that component. This is in contrast to the global "for all" rules which often are used in knowledge-based systems. Because of the implicit identification of the component itself, subcomponents, and components in its context, local rules are usually much easier to understand. As discussed in section 4.3, a high degree of reusability is obtained through the combined use of mixins and the *enclosing* mechanism.

5.1   Future Work

We have used OPG successfully to model the mechanical configuration of plate heat exchangers, resulting in a specification of 26 main types, 7 mixins, and 32 rules. Some aspects which are not supported currently in OPG, but which are interesting topics for future research include the following:

Support for Valid Choices. The AG-based model immediately supports only *checking* the validity of a configuration. It is also desirable to support the user in *constructing* a valid configuration. The user builds a configuration by successively adding components, and at any time, the current partial configuration will limit the valid choices for remaining components. The configurator should have support for constructing valid configurations by presenting only the valid choices, and for automatically adding components when there is only one valid choice. It is also possible to automatically complete a partial configuration using default components and configuration properties. We plan to add such support by formalizing the choice-generation framework used in CAS 2000 and integrate it into the OPG model.

Support for Graphs. OPG supports only configurations organized as a tree of components. In general, one would like to support also graphs. We plan to support this in a similar way as is done in Door attribute grammars [10], i.e., by introducing reference-valued derived properties. This allows an arbitrary connection between two of the components in a tree to be set up using derived properties, thus in effect turning the tree into a graph. Rules can then access properties directly along such a connection.

Support for Versioning. A product family is usually not constant, but evolves over time and the descriptions should be subject to revision control. It is very important that existing type-instance and prototype-copy relations are not made inconsistent when the types and prototypes evolve. These problems are similar to schema evolution problems in object-oriented data bases, see e.g. [21], and similar techniques will probably be useful for product models.

6   Related Work

6.1   Product Configurator Tools

Table-Based Tools. Many simpler hand-coded configurator tools use a table-based approach. In these systems, each base product has a table which lists its available features. A product is specified by choosing a base product and then adding a number of features. When two features are not allowed to be combined for some base product, this combination is listed in another table, a conflict table. This approach is based on the assumption that features are highly independent of one another so that conflicts are rare. At Alfa Laval Thermal, this technique was used in the first version of CAS (CAS 1), developed in 1988. A drawback with the table based approach is that it can handle only quite simple dependencies between product components. To allow more complex dependencies it is necessary to have some kind of rule concept which allows configuration rules to be expressed over the components and their properties.

Framework-Based Tools. Another approach to configuration systems is the *object-oriented framework* approach. Here the components of a configuration are modelled in an object-oriented manner. All configuration rules are described as matching conditions between attributes of the objects, and the logic is implemented by change propagation rules. By ensuring that these rules define uni-directional chains, a highly efficient change propagation mechanism can be implemented in the generic framework. The actual rules for a specific product are then expressed by extending the framework with hand-written code. As a result the model is fairly maintainable although there is a translation step from domain experts to programmers which limits verifiability. This approach is used in Alfa Laval's current CAS 2000 system developed in 1992 [1].

Knowledge-Based Tools. We differ between simpler *rule-based* systems and more advanced *constraint-based* systems. *Rule-based* configuration systems are based on logic programming and use a technology similar to expert systems. The formalism allows all the relevant rules to be stated explicitly, and the order of evaluation is decided by a general purpose inference engine which thereby determines the execution logic. Rule-based systems are declarative, but they often have only limited support for modularization. Typically, they work in a non-interactive mode, computing a complete configuration from user requirements. An example of a rule based configuration system is the seminal XCON (or R1) system for configuration of computer systems [14].

An evolution of the rule-based systems are the *constraint-based* systems. Constraint-based systems typically have two major advantages over conventional rule-
based systems. Firstly, different kinds of resolution strategies can be applied to different kinds of constraints which can give significant improvements in execution efficiency. Secondly, constraints are usually defined in some kind of object-oriented
model of the product. The classes in an object-oriented model gives a natural basis for
modularization so that large models can be structured in a way that make them locally
understandable. Constraint-based configurators thereby achieve both declarative
expression of configuration logic and a natural modularization of the model. Recent
constraint-based tools such as OBELICS [3] also support interactive configuration,
allowing the user to interactively select key components.

Comparison. A weakness of knowledge-based systems is that they are based on a
dynamically determined execution order. For hard configuration problems, i.e., when
the configurator has to optimize over a large space of possible configurations, the
flexibility and possibilities for global optimizations outweighs the drawbacks. Many
configuration problems, however, are not hard. What is important is instead that the
tool can be highly interactive and give immediate feedback on what the user selects.
In other words, the system should be highly supportive of running "what-if"
scenarios.

OPG's attribute grammar approach presented in this paper combines the advantages of declarative statement of optimized execution efficiency and highly
responsive interactive support. As the user changes the configuration, dependent rules
can be re-evaluated incrementally according to a statically determined execution
order, giving immediate feedback on the validity of the configuration.

OPG is also focused on providing early error detection in the product model. This
is supported by the strong type system and in the possibility to check that all attributes
are uniquely defined by the rules. This is in contrast to the tradition in knowledge-
based systems which are usually based on dynamic checking only.

6.2   Product Data Management

Product configuration modelling is one aspect in the larger context of Product Data
Management (PDM) which covers all information related to product design and
manufacturing. Most PDM system in industrial use today have little functionality that
is specific to product data. Their main emphasis is versioning of files (typically for
CAD-programs and word-processors) combined with work flow support and change
management. Usually some form of support for the bill-of-material concept,
i.e.hierarchical configurations, is also included.

PDM is slowly evolving away from this document-centric view towards more
explicit product models. In a product model, information is structured so that it can be
easily processed by different kinds of software tools, for example product configurators. When needed, various kinds of documents can be derived automatically from the
model.

Product modelling technology is often based on some kind of object-oriented formalism with mechanisms for describing properties and rules. The most notable example here is the EXPRESS language [17] created by the STEP initiative which is an

ongoing effort to create an international standard for the exchange of product model data.

On the surface, OPG is similar to EXPRESS because they are both product modelling languages with constructs like classes, properties, and rules (called entities, attributes, and rules in EXPRESS). However, there are many differences, the main one being that OPG explicitly supports an attribute grammar model with a component hierarchy (abstract syntax tree) and upwards and downwards derived properties. EXPRESS supports upwards derived properties, but downwards derived properties and the use of properties in enclosing classes would have to be simulated by using validity rules and explicit specification of enclosing components, leading to complex specifications not suited for AG processing and less suited for reuse and early error-detection. Furthermore, OPG has explicit support for prototypes whereas in EXPRESS these would have to be simulated by subclasses. To summarize, OPG is a product modelling language suitable for mass-customization products and for the generation of interactive configuration tools. It would, however, be possible to translate OPG to EXPRESS in order to make OPG specifications available to EXPRESS-based tools.

6.3   Software Configuration Management

Configuration management techniques have been developed independently for mechanical products and software products, and it may be interesting to compare these different problems and techniques.

In both cases, there is a configuration problem, i.e. a problem of selecting specific components to form a complete product which is internally consistent in some way. An overview of Software Configuration Management (SCM) systems is given in [5]. Most SCM systems are *version-oriented*, where each component exists in several versions organized as *variants* (alternative versions) and *revisions* (consecutive versions). Often, the component set making up the product is predefined, e.g. in a makefile, and the central configuration problem is to select a suitable version for each of the components, typically in order to configurate a product suitable for a given execution platform. In OPG, the central configuration problem is instead to select which components make up the product.

A fundamental difference is that a component in OPG may occur in several instances in the product, e.g. the PHE configuration in Fig. 3 contains 4 instances of Lining. In SCM, on the other hand, a component appears at most once in the configuration. In some SCM systems, the definition of the component set is intertwined with version selection, resulting in a configuration process more similar to OPG. However, the fundamental difference concerning multiple/single component instances remains.

The types and prototypes in OPG may be compared with components and variants in SCM: prototypes may be seen as different variants of their type. In OPG, the prototypes of a type differ in their property values. Similarly, the variants of a component in SCM are often characterized by attributes or features [6, 22]. However, the selection rules work quite differently. In OPG, the rules are localized to the components and check consistency between a component and its enclosing components and subcomponents, e.g. checking that a Lining has the same diameter as its enclosing Hole. In SCM, the rules are usually global and used to select component variants regardless of their context, e.g., selecting the Unix variant of all source module components in the system. One SCM system which does make use of local rules is DCDL [18] where rules are part of class definitions and can check consistency between a component and its subcomponents.

Revision control is central in SCM: within a component variant, there may be several consecutive revisions which can be attributed with date, release number, etc. In contrast, each OPG variant (prototype) exists in only one version. The reason is that the physical components modelled by prototypes are not seen as being in a revision relation: either they are completely interchangeable, in which case they are modelled by the same prototype; or they differ in some property values, in which case they are modelled by different prototypes. Typically, different physical components are modelled by the same prototype if they are manufactured by different subcontractors, but have the same function in the product, and which actual component is selected at manufacturing is irrelevant to the customer. Revision control is, however, highly relevant to OPG at its *meta level*, i.e. when specifying OPG types and prototypes in order to generate a configuration tool. These specifications are evolving software which can be placed under revision control, as noted in section 5.1.

The current trends in software architecture of using component technology will give rise to new configuration problems in software which have similarities to the mass-customization problems treated by OPG. As interconnection standards like COM, CORBA, and Java Beans are coming into wide use, the granularity of the units of deployment is decreasing. Monolithic applications are giving way to a larger number of more or less independent components, moving the main configuration problem from build-time to install-time, or even to launch- or run-time. The responsibility for building correct configurations is thereby separated from component development. This separation must then be compensated by the components being more self-contained. When delivered, they must contain sufficiently rich meta-data to enable automatic generation and/or validation of correct configurations. The problem is similar to that of product mass-customization, and it is possible that product configuration formalisms like OPG can play a role here. The SCM system DCDL [18] is aimed at run-time configuration problems, and as noted above it has some similarity to OPG in that it also supports local rules.

7   Conclusions

OPG is a product modelling language which is primarily aimed at configuration of highly customized products built from mass-produced components. We believe it shows the benefits of basing configuration technology on object-orientation and attribute grammars. This combination gives strong modelling capabilities, allowing configuration constraints to be expressed and understood locally. The *enclosing* mechanism and the use of mixin pairs in particular allows the model to be highly factorized so that redundant information is avoided. The type-prototype-copy architecture is introduced to match the different levels of product component type, mass-produced component, and actual component. The use of attribute grammars gives OPG both a theoretical basis for early validation and techniques for the automatic generation of efficient interactive configurator tools.

References

1. Alfa Laval Thermal AB. *CAS 2000. User's Manual*. Lund, Sweden, 1993.
2. K. Arnold and J. Gosling. *The Java Programming Language*. Addison-Wesley. 1996.
3. T. Axling and S. Haridi. A tool for developing interactive configuration applications. *Journal of Logic Programming* 26(2): 147-168 (1996).
4. G. Bracha and W. Cook. Mixin-Based Inheritance. OOPSLA/ECOOP'90. *ACM SIGPLAN Notices*, Vol. 25, No 10, pp. 303-311. 1990.
5. R. Conradi and B. Westfechtel. Configuring Versioned Software Products. In *Software Configuration Management, ICSE'96 SCM-6 Workshop*. pp 88-109. LNCS 1167, Springer-Verlag. 1996.
6. J. Estublier and R. Casallas. The Adele Configuration Manager. In Tichy (Ed.) *Configuration Management*, Wiley, 1994.
7. E. Gamma, R. Helm, R. Johnson, J. Vlissides. *Design Patterns. Elements of Reusable Object-Oriented Software*. Addison-Wesley. 1995.
8. G. Hedin. An object-oriented notation for attribute grammars. *ECOOP'89*. BCS Workshop Series, pp 329-345, Cambridge University Press. 1989.
9. G. Hedin. Context-sensitive editing in Orm. Proceedings of the *Nordic Workshop on Programming Environment Research*. Tampere University of Technology, Finland. Software Syst. Lab. TR 14. 1992.
10. G. Hedin. An overview of Door attribute grammars. *International Conference on Compiler Construction (CC'94)*. LNCS 786, Springer Verlag. 1994.
11. U. Kastens and W. M. Waite. Modularity and Reusability in Attribute Grammars. *Acta Informatica*, 31:601-627, 1994.
12. D. E. Knuth. Semantics of context-free languages. *Mathematical Systems Theory*, 2(2):127-145, June 1968.
13. H. Lieberman. Using prototype objects to implement shared behavior in object oriented systems. In OOPSLA'86, pp 214-223. *ACM SIGPLAN Notices,* Vol. 21, No. 11, September 1986.
14. J. McDermott. R1: A Rule-Based Configurer of Computer Systems. *Artificial Intelligence*, Vol. 19, 1 (Sept 1982):39-88.
15. H. Peltonen, T. Männistö, K. Alho, R. Sulonen. Product Configurations - An Application for Prototype Object Approach. In *ECOOP'94*, pp 513-534. LNCS 821, Springer Verlag. 1994.
16. T. W. Reps and T. Teitelbaum. *The Synthesizer Generator. A system for constructing language-based editors*. Springer Verlag. 1989.
17. D. Schenck and P. Wilson. *Information Modeling the EXPRESS Way*. Oxford University Press. 1994.

18. B. R. Schmerl and C. D. Marlin. Versioning and consistency for dynamically composed configurations. In *Software Configuration Management, ICSE'97 SCM-7 Workshop.* pp 49-65. LNCS 1235, Springer-Verlag. 1997.

19. J. J. Shah and M. Mäntylä. *Parametric and Feature-Based CAD/CAM.* Wiley. 1995.

20. Taligent Inc. *Taligent's guide to designing programs - well-mannered object-oriented design in C++.* Addison-Wesley. 1994.

21. A. H. Skarra and S. B. Zdonik. The management of changing types in an object-oriented database. In OOPSLA'86, pp 483-495. *ACM SIGPLAN Notices,* Vol. 21, No. 11, September 1986.

22. A. Zeller and G. Snelting. Handling Version Sets Through Feature Logic. In *Software Engineering - ESEC'95.* pp 191-204. LNCS 989. Springer-Verlag. 1995.

Versioning System Models
Through Description Logic

Andreas Zeller

Technische Universität Braunschweig, Abteilung Softwaretechnologie
Bültenweg 88, D-38092 Braunschweig, Germany
zeller@acm.org

Abstract. In software configuration management, little attention has been paid to the evolution of *system models*, that is, the description of the components that make up a system, and the *relationships* between them. We present an extension to the version set model based on description logic, where *roles*, set-valued features, model relationships between version sets. Relationships are versioned with their components; features are propagated and unified along component relationships, ensuring configuration completeness and consistency. The integrated version set model has been realized in ICE MAKE, a MAKE clone dealing with versioned system models. ICE MAKE constructs arbitrary version sets according to their respective dependencies and deduces features and dependencies as imposed by the propagated configuration constraints.

Key words: Software configuration management, Version control, Software architecture, Deduction and theorem proving, Knowledge representation formalisms and methods

1 Introduction

Maintaining a multitude of configurations is a software configuration management (SCM) task. However, the vast majority of SCM systems are "one-of-many" systems – one specific configuration must be chosen before performing any action. This is only natural, since the vast majority of programming tools do not know about versioning and operate on one specific item. But it is also unfortunate, since the SCM maintainer has a different "many-of-many" perspective, reflecting on the common and differing features of several possible configurations.

In the *version set model* [13], we already have demonstrated how a SCM system can support the "many-of-many" perspective by treating *version sets* (rather than individual items) as subjects of SCM tasks and procedures. Version sets are denoted using *feature logic*, identifying sets of software components by their common features. Our prototype implementation ICE (incremental configuration environment) [10] provides a virtual file system that allows read and write access to arbitrary version sets represented using CPP #ifdef...#endif directives, such that the maintainer can view and change arbitrary version sets.

In this paper, we show how to realize the "many-of-many" perspective in *system modeling* and *system construction*. For this purpose, we need a versioned

B. Magnusson (Ed.): ECOOP 98, SCM-8, LNCS 1439, pp. 127–132, 1998.

representation of system models—a versioned description of the components that make up a system, and the relationships between them. Such relationships cannot be expressed in feature logic. But there is an extension, *description logic*, that provides versioned relationships while guaranteeing completeness and consistency of derived configurations.

2   From Features to Roles

Feature logic [7] is a formal base for describing *version sets* [13,11] by their *features*—functional properties of items with a specific value. The basic operation is *selection* ("*:*")–the feature term *feature: value* denotes the set of all objects whose *feature* is *value*. For instance, two printer device driver variants may be distinguished by the values of their *print-language* and *bitmaps* features:

$$driver_1 = [print\text{-}language: postscript, bitmaps: yes] \tag{1}$$
$$driver_2 = [print\text{-}language: text, bitmaps: no] \ . \tag{2}$$

Union ("⊔" or "[...]") unites version sets—e.g. to give the set of all variants:

$$driver = driver_1 \sqcup driver_2$$
$$= \left\{ \begin{array}{l} [print\text{-}language: postscript, bitmaps: yes], \\ [print\text{-}language: text, bitmaps: no] \end{array} \right\}$$

Intersection ("⊓" or "{...}") selects version subsets according to their features:

$$driver \sqcap [bitmaps: yes] = driver_1 \ .$$

This intersection works because features are *functional*—they can have only one value. Hence, the selection [*bitmaps: yes*] excludes all other values of the *bitmaps* feature. Set complements ("~") and implications ("→") are also provided.

Description logic now extends feature logic with *roles* [7]. Naturally speaking, a role is a non-functional feature—that is, it can have arbitrary sets of values. This is useful for non-functional properties such as *authorship*—a software component may have multiple authors, which is clearly a non-functional property.

The set of possible role values is restrained by *existential quantification*, written *role* ∋ *value*, which says "at least one of the values of *role* is member of *value*", or shorter, "*role* has *value*". (Contrast this "has" or "∋" to the "is" or "*:*" of selection).[1]

Using the quantification operator, we can extend the definition of *driver_1* (1) to identify the author (*author*) and the set of contained objects (*object*):

$$driver_1 = \begin{bmatrix} author \ni lisa, object \ni driver, \\ print\text{-}language: postscript, bitmaps: yes \end{bmatrix}$$

stating that the set of authors includes Lisa, and that the set of objects includes the *driver* object.

---

[1] Smolka [7] uses the prefix operators $\exists r(S) \equiv r \ni S$ and $\forall r(S) \equiv \sim\!\exists r(\sim\!S)$ instead.

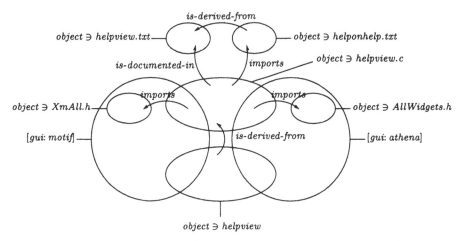

Fig. 1. *imports, is-derived-from,* and *is-documented-in* relationships in `helpview`

3   Modeling Versioned Systems

Our basic idea is now to *model versioned relationships as* roles *of versioned components,* that is, version sets. The values of such roles are no longer simply atoms, but *version sets* as well: Each relationship between two version sets S and S' is modeled by assigning S a role r whose value includes S', written as $r \ni S'$. The version set S' again may be related to other version sets.

As an example, consider a program `helpview`, an interactive program to browse help texts. `helpview` comes in two versions, identified as `helpview[gui: motif]`, which uses the MOTIF widget set for its graphical user interface (GUI); and the alternate version `helpview[gui: athena]`, which uses an ATHENA widget set. (In ICE, $F[S]$ identifies the version S of a file F). The C source file, `helpview.c` also comes in a MOTIF version, importing the `XmAll.h` header file, and an ATHENA version, importing its declarations from `AllWidgets.h`. Both versions of the `helpview.c` source also import a text document `helponhelp.txt` derived from the overall documentation `helpview.txt`.

In figure 1, we have illustrated the dependencies between the various components of the `helpview` system. Neither relationship is functional, the concept description modeling *helpview.c* thus uses roles to represent its relationships; note how the *gui* feature implies the *imports* relationship.

$$
T = \begin{bmatrix}
object \ni (helpview.c), \\
gui: \{motif, athena\}, \\
is\text{-}documented\text{-}in \ni (object \ni helpview.txt), \\
imports \ni [object \ni helponhelp.txt, is\text{-}derived\text{-}from \ni (object \ni helpview.txt)], \\
[gui: motif] \rightarrow imports \ni (object \ni XmAll.h), \\
[gui: athena] \rightarrow imports \ni (object \ni AllWidgets.h)
\end{bmatrix}
$$

$$(3)$$

Individual variants of the *helpview* system are obtained by intersecting T with a selection term. For instance, the MOTIF variant is obtained through $T \sqcap$

[*gui: motif*], which excludes all subsets of [*gui: athena*]. Another possibility is to select a version using relationships—if we want a version that does *not* import the *XmAll.h* header file, we can select $T \sqcap \sim imports \ni (object \ni XmAll.h)$ and obtain the ATHENA version.

In all version set operations, relationships (i.e. roles) are tightly coupled to both the originating and the referenced version sets—that is, they cannot be versioned independently of the related items. We may now enforce that the features of related version sets be *unified*—that is, any configuration composed from related version sets must have identical feature values. This is most useful in composing consistent configurations, shown in the next section.

4   Intensional System Construction

In practice, actual users do not see concept descriptions, nor do they ever perform set operations on them. These are implemented by specialized tools. As an example, we have tuned up a classical MAKE implementation to be aware of versioned relationships—that is, versioned MAKE dependencies. The desired system is specified by its features, realizing *intensional system construction* as in EPOS [5] or ADELE [4].

Consider the `helpview` system, as stated above. In a classical MAKE, we would have to enumerate each version with its individual dependencies and commands—that is, one rule for each `helpview` executable, and one rule for each `helpview.c` source variant. Let us further assume our system comes in two different dates. This approach is feasible, as shown in the following MAKE file:

```
helpview-gui-motif-1997: helpview.c-gui-motif-1997 XmAll.h ...
    $(COMPILE) helpview.c-gui-motif
helpview-gui-motif-1998: helpview.c-gui-motif-1998 XmAll.h ...
    $(COMPILE) helpview.c-gui-motif
helpview-gui-athena-1997: helpview.c-gui-athena-1997 AllWidgets.h ...
    $(COMPILE) helpview.c-gui-athena
helpview-gui-athena-1998: helpview.c-gui-athena-1998 AllWidgets.h ...
    $(COMPILE) helpview.c-gui-athena
... and so on for each configuration ...
```

Obviously, this scheme cannot be scaled up indefinitely: each new configuration dimension besides `gui` and `date` multiplies the number of configurations, resulting an a combinatorical explosion. In practice, we would instantiate a generic MAKE template instead and revert to the "one-of-many" perspective.

As stated above, we prefer the "many-of-many" perspective and implemented an alternate MAKE on top of the ICE system, called ICE MAKE [2]. Like SHAPE [6] and PCL [9], ICE MAKE supports explicit variance in system models, and like the CAPITL system [1], it uses feature terms to identify versions and derived components. The novel aspect is that ICE MAKE integrates versioning of components, systems, and system models into a simple, unified approach.

In ICE MAKE, a MAKE target file may exist in multiple versions, each with a different set of dependencies and construction commands. The features of each target (such as [gui: motif]) are *unified* with the features of each source, along the (versioned) *is-derived-from* dependencies as modeled through appropriate concept descriptions, as shown in section 3.

In our case, this means that a [gui: athena] target can only have a [gui: athena] source. A source with unspecified gui is also acceptable, but gui can never have an alternate value—gui is a feature. This simple rule suffices for writing the ICE MAKE file as:

```
helpview: helpview.c helponhelp.txt
    $(COMPILE) helpview.c
helpview[gui: motif]: XmAll.h
helpview[gui: athena]: AllWidgets.h
```

We see that only the [gui: motif] version of helpview depends on XmAll.h: we have a *conditional dependency*: helpview depends on XmAll.h only if its GUI is MOTIF. This gives us a *versioned system model*: depending on the GUI setting, different relationships apply. The MAKE file is just an alternate representation of the versioned *is-derived-from* dependencies as shown in (3).

But what happened to the date feature? Since any target inherits the features of the sources it depends upon, the, say, [date: 1998] version of helpview cannot depend on a component with a differing date feature. Hence, ICE MAKE can automatically exclude the 1997 versions. Although the date feature is not mentioned in the MAKE file, ICE MAKE will automatically determine the appropriate dependencies and exclude inconsistent configurations.

A side effect of all this feature propagation and unification is the automatic identification of derived components. All targets can be uniquely identified by the features inherited from their sources—for instance, as helpview[gui: athena, date: 1997]. If a desired target T has the same sources as an existing derived component T', ICE MAKE can simply copy T' to T rather than constructing T.

To sum up, rather than manually searching or generating the appropriate MAKE file from a variety of possible versions, we simply specify the desired features—regardless of whether variants, revisions, or workspaces are considered:

```
$ make helpview[date:1998-04-16,user:lisa]
```

And if Lisa's colleague Tom, by chance, already built the same configuration, ICE MAKE will simply make Tom's configuration available in Lisa's workspace.

5 Conclusion

To capture the semantics of SCM objects and operations, one single formalism suffices: *description logic*. Using description logic, we can

- integrate versioning of components, systems, and system models,
- maintain consistency when composing and constructing configurations
- keeping the benefits of feature logic, especially the unified versioning model.

ICE MAKE demonstrates these benefits—the benefits of a sound theory when used in software engineering practice.

Acknowledgements. Michael Brandes did a great job in implementing ICE MAKE. Set-valued features and versioned relationships came into life after fruitful discussions with Geoffrey Clemm, Susan Dart, and Bernhard Westfechtel. Kerstin Reese and Gregor Snelting provided valuable comments on earlier revisions of this paper.

References

1. ADAMS, P., AND SOLOMON, M. An overview of the CAPITL software development environment. In Estublier [3], pp. 1–34.
2. BRANDES, M. Deduktive Programmkonstruktion auf Basis von MAKE. Master's thesis, Technical University of Braunschweig, Germany, Dec. 1996. In German.
3. ESTUBLIER, J., Ed. *Software Configuration Management: selected papers / ICSE SCM-4 and SCM-5 workshops* (Seattle, Washington, Oct. 1995), vol. 1005 of *Lecture Notes in Computer Science*, Springer-Verlag.
4. ESTUBLIER, J., AND CASALLAS, R. The Adele configuration manager. In Tichy [8], ch. 4, pp. 99–133.
5. GULLA, B., KARLSSON, E.-A., AND YEH, D. Change-oriented version descriptions in EPOS. *Software Engineering Journal 6*, 6 (Nov. 1991), 378–386.
6. MAHLER, A. Variants: Keeping things together and telling them apart. In Tichy [8], ch. 3, pp. 39–69.
7. SMOLKA, G. Feature-constrained logics for unification grammars. *Journal of Logic Programming 12* (1992), 51–87.
8. TICHY, W. F., Ed. *Configuration Management*, vol. 2 of *Trends in Software*. John Wiley & Sons, Chichester, UK, 1994.
9. TRYGGESETH, E., GULLA, B., AND CONRADI, R. Modelling systems with variability using the PROTEUS configuration language. In Estublier [3], pp. 216–240.
10. ZELLER, A. Smooth operations with square operators—The version set model in ICE. In *Proc. 6th International Workshop on Software Configuration Management* (Berlin, Germany, Mar. 1996), I. Sommerville, Ed., vol. 1167 of *Lecture Notes in Computer Science*, Springer-Verlag, pp. 8–30.
11. ZELLER, A. *Configuration Management with Version Sets*. PhD thesis, Technical University of Braunschweig, Germany, Apr. 1997.
12. ZELLER, A. Versioning software systems through concept descriptions. Computer Science Report 97-01, Technical University of Braunschweig, Germany, Jan. 1997.
13. ZELLER, A., AND SNELTING, G. Unified versioning through feature logic. *ACM Transactions on Software Engineering and Methodology 6*, 4 (Oct. 1997), 398–441.

Current snapshots of ICE MAKE can be accessed through the ICE WWW page, http://www.cs.tu-bs.de/softech/ice/; further material on description logic and its use in system modeling is available in a technical report [12].

Supporting Fine-Grained Traceability in Software Development Environments

Peter Lindsay and Owen Traynor

Software Verification Research Centre,
The University of Queensland,
Queensland 4072, Australia

Abstract. This paper describes the facilities currently available to support auditing and traceability within a system which provides fine-grained configuration and version management. We contend that the relationship between the configuration management system and the underlying version control system is a critical factor which governs many aspects of the facilities supporting traceability. The model of traceability is formally specified relative to our configuration and versioning models.

1 Introduction

Managing and controlling change is a critical part of software engineering. Software components typically pass through many different versions during both the initial development of a system and the ongoing maintenance of the system once deployed. The facilities that are available in such systems for tracing the evolution of requirements through the design, coding, validation and verification stages are especially critical.

The history that documents the evolution of a software system is, in essence, the embodiment of that system. We believe that an accurate account of that history is critical in assessing the worth of the deployed system and in ensuring that subsequent developments of that system are made in a coherent and consistent fashion. The history of a system also provides a wealth of information regarding design decisions and implementation choices [6, 8].

We believe that traceability facilities that allow the documentation of a system at a finer level of granularity than the tradition build, or baseline models, provide access to essential information that is often lost in these traditional approaches. Such facilities also provide the information needed to reduce the effort required to rework or redevelop systems in the context of changes to requirements.

1.1 Configuration Management(CM) for Formal Methods

Formal Methods of software development have particular needs in relation to CM. Formal Methods are based on the use of mathematically precise definitions of development components and their relationships, together with the use of

B. Magnusson (Ed.): ECOOP 98, SCM-8, LNCS 1439, pp. 133–139, 1998.

mathematical analysis techniques – including theorem proving – for establishing correctness. The fact that individual development components have mathematical meaning makes it possible to formally verify that desired relationships hold within and between development components. In contrast to traditional development methods, cross-development configuration consistency can be defined precisely and at fine levels of granularity [7].

Consistent with this observation is our view of traceability. Our traceability model allows us to track, at fine levels of granularity, the changes that a system has undergone that moves the system through its evolving, consistent, versions. Since we are working in a context where relationship and dependencies are formally modelled, we can use this as a basis for defining formal models of traceability. Such an approach offers a great deal in the context of high integrity system development. In critical system development it is important to be able to trace the evolution of individual safety requirements right through the design to final implementation [5].

Our approach has been to define configuration consistency models (or *configuration models*, for short) which define the key configuration items, the relationships between them, and the consistency and completeness conditions required for the configuration. In our approach, configuration models form the core part a formal software development environment (FSDE), with development processes defined relative to the core models. This means that the consistency and completeness of a development can be established largely independently of the development process applied, giving flexibility and trustworthiness in the one framework [2, 3, 1].

In the spirit of these configuration models, we take a similar approach when defining the notions of traceability. Out trace models are defined relative to the core configuration models. Again, the form of this definition allows us to establish consistency criteria for our framework. Ensuring that such consistency criteria are met, is an important issue, especially in the context of high-integrity development.

2   The Case Study

2.1   Documents and Dependency Relations

We start by felling some trees to better see the forest. We shall consider part of a development consisting simply of two documents – called A and B here, for short – which consist of sets of requirements and which are expected to conform with one another in some way. For example, A might be a Software Requirements Specification (SRS) and B an Architectural Requirements Specification, describing a module structure and how the requirements from the SRS are allocated to modules.

The dependency relation to be managed is the relationship which describes how requirements in B address requirements in A. In general, such a relationship is many-to-many: e.g. a single SRS requirement may be addressed in different places in the architecture document, and a single architectural requirement may address multiple SRS requirements. The *addresses* relation is analogous in some ways to the 'is up to date with respect to' notion for traditional SCM systems, as used by the Unix MAKE facility for example. Note however that for informal objects such as requirements, the relation is user-determined and cannot be automated.

A **conformance matrix** (or traceability table) is a common means of indicating the relationship between two development documents. For each item in one of the development documents, the matrix lists the corresponding items in the other document, typically by paragraph or section number.

2.2   Version, Configuration Management and Change Tracking

For simplicity, we use a simple "version tree" model as the basis for version control, for objects of all granularities: paragraphs, documents, matrics, etc.

The configuration management problem is to manage the "configuration" consisting of the two documents and their conformance matrix. We say the conformance matrix is *complete* if each of A's requirements are addressed somewhere in B. As part of the case study, we shall assume that at any time the conformance matrix may be incomplete, but it is always *correct*: i.e., that if the matrix says that r addresses t, then this relationship was determined by a user and the requirements have not changed in the interim.

We shall track changes to paragraphs that either directly affect the meaning of the paragraph or the document in which it is included. Requirements engineering experience has shown that most changes can be factored into components of the following types:

add: creates a new paragraph with no prior history
split: creates a number of new paragraphs by splitting an existing paragraph
combine: creates a new paragraph by combing existing paragraphs
delete: deletes a paragraph
replace: replaces existing paragraphs by a new paragraph
modify: modify the paragraph without changing its meaning

2.3   Requirements Tracing

The ability to track dependencies is an important part of high integrity development, and is one of the main mechanisms required in development audit and evaluation. For space reasons we consider one form of tracing only here: requirement evolution. The problem is, given a specific version of a requirement, report how the requirement changed subsequently (see Fig. 1). However, our model supports many other forms of traceability check, including finding which A requirements have not yet been addressed, and finding which B requirements are extraneous (i.e., do not address an A requirement).

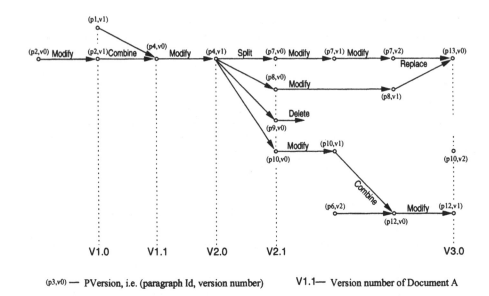

(p3,v0) — PVersion, i.e. (paragraph Id, version number)   V1.1— Version number of Document A

Fig. 1. Tracing the evolution of a given paragraph version

3   Formal Specification

This section outlines the data model on which our fine-grained configuration management is based. More complete definitions, including the important data invariants and policy information, are given in [4].

3.1   Version Control

Our simple model for version control is based on *forests* of version trees and parameterised over the type *Type* of objects being placed under version control:

$$
\begin{array}{l}
\rule{4cm}{0.4pt}\ VForest[\,Type\,] \rule{4cm}{0.4pt} \\
nodes : \mathbb{P}\ VLabel \\
deref : VLabel \nrightarrow Type \\
parent : VLabel \nrightarrow VLabel \\
roots : \mathbb{P}\ VLabel \\
\end{array}
$$

In the above, *VLabel* represents version labels, the mapping *deref* "dereferences" version labels, and the mapping *parent* returns the parent of non-root nodes in the forest.

3.2   Versions of Paragraphs

Paragraphs will be identified by a label from the type *PId*. A specific *paragraph version* consists of the paragraph's identifier and a specific version label:

$$PVersion \qquad PId \times VLabel$$

A collection of *specific paragraph versions* (in which each paragraph is represented at most once) is thus modelled by the type $PId \nrightarrow VLabel$.

The collection of *paragraph changes* is modelled as follows:

$$
\begin{aligned}
PChange \; ::= \; & add\langle\!\langle PVersion \rangle\!\rangle \\
| \; & delete\langle\!\langle PVersion \rangle\!\rangle \\
| \; & split\langle\!\langle PVersion \times PVersion^+ \rangle\!\rangle \\
| \; & combine\langle\!\langle PVersion^+ \times PVersion \rangle\!\rangle \\
| \; & derive\langle\!\langle PVersion^+ \times PVersion \rangle\!\rangle \\
| \; & replace\langle\!\langle PVersion^+ \times PVersion \rangle\!\rangle \\
| \; & modify\langle\!\langle PId \times VLabel \times VLabel \rangle\!\rangle
\end{aligned}
$$

The following defines a predicate for checking whether a change affects a given paragraph version:

$$isChangedBy : PVersion \leftrightarrow PChange$$

$$
\begin{aligned}
& \neg\; isChangedBy(pv', add(pv)) \\
& isChangedBy(pv', delete(pv)) \Leftrightarrow pv' = pv \\
& isChangedBy(pv', split(pv, pvs)) \Leftrightarrow pv' = pv \\
& isChangedBy(pv', combine(pvs, pv)) \Leftrightarrow pv' \in \mathrm{ran}\,pvs \\
& \neg\; isChangedBy(pv', derive(pvs, pv)) \\
& isChangedBy(pv', replace(pvs, pv)) \Leftrightarrow pv' \in \mathrm{ran}\,pvs \\
& isChangedBy(pv', modify(a, u, v)) \Leftrightarrow pv' = (a, u)
\end{aligned}
$$

3.3   Documents

For the purposes of this paper, documents are modelled as unstructured collections of paragraph versions. Each document version is modelled as a collection of specific paragraph versions and a *delta set* of the paragraph changes that have been made since the document was last frozen:

Document

$sparas : PId \nrightarrow VLabel$
$delta : \mathbb{P}\, PChange$

The *complete history of a document* is modelled here as a pair consisting of a paragraph collection (a mapping from paragraph identifiers to paragraph version forests), and a collection of document versions:

DocHistory

$paras : PId \nrightarrow VForest[Text]$
$docs : VForest[Document]$

3.4 Tracing Evolution of Paragraphs

This section shows that the above model is rich enough to allow the evolution of individual paragraphs to be traced forwards through a document's history.

The following function defines the set of paragraphs which result from a change to a given paragraph:

$$givesRiseTo : PVersion \times PChange \nrightarrow \mathbb{P} \, PVersion$$

$$\text{dom } givesRiseTo = isChangedBy$$
$$givesRiseTo(pv, delete(pv)) = \varnothing$$
$$givesRiseTo(pv, split(pv, pvs)) = \text{ran } pvs$$
$$i \in 1 \mathinner{.\,.} n \Rightarrow givesRiseTo(pvs(i), combine(pvs, pv)) = \{pv\}$$
$$i \in 1 \mathinner{.\,.} n \Rightarrow givesRiseTo(pvs(i), replace(pvs, pv)) = \{pv\}$$
$$givesRiseTo((a, u), modify(a, u, v)) = \{(a, v)\}$$

Finally, the following function extracts the changes which occur "downstream" in a given paragraph's evolution:

$$forwardsTrace : PVersion \times DocHistory \nrightarrow \mathbb{P} \, PChange$$

$$forwardsTrace(pv, docs) =$$
$$\quad \text{if } \exists \, V \in docs.nodes; \ c \in docs.deref(V).delta \bullet isChangedBy(pv, c)$$
$$\quad \text{then } \{c\} \cup \bigcup\{pv' : givesRiseTo(pv, c) \bullet forwardsTrace(pv', docs)\}$$
$$\quad \text{else } \varnothing$$

3.5 Document Conformance

The case study is completed by demonstrating how conformance between pairs of documents can be modelled. First, the conformance matrix is modelled as a relation between individual paragraphs in two documents:

$$CMatrix \qquad PId \leftrightarrow PId$$

Finally, the whole configuration is modelled as a pair of document histories, a forest of conformance matrix versions, and a relation which records which versions of the three objects make up legitimate configurations:

$$\_\_DocPair\_\_$$
$$A, B : DocHistory$$
$$cmatrix : VForest[CMatrix]$$
$$corres : \mathbb{P}(VLabel \times VLabel \times VLabel)$$

4 Conclusions

There are two dimensions to the benefits accrued by the use of fine-grained versioning models in our case study. The first is due to the fact that we consider the individual components of our systems as first class citizens in the context of configurations. This allows substantial flexibility in the way in which consistency of an overall system is determined, as well as focusing attention on the specific objects undergoing change.

The second benefit comes from the actual versioning of the system components themselves. It allows us to define consistency criteria in terms of the conditions that must be satisfied by the individual components. We can then show that the chosen versioning model actually meets the criteria.

Acknowledgements The authors gratefully acknowledge the useful contributions of Yaowei Liu and Sabine Sachweh to the work presented here.

References

1. Song C. Choi and Walt Scacchi. Assuring the correctness of configured software descriptions. In *Proc 2nd Intl Workshop on Software Configuration Management, ACM SIGSOFT Software Engineering Notes*, volume 14, pages 66–75. ACM Press, 1989.

2. P.A. Lindsay, Y. Liu, and O. Traynor. Managing document conformance: a case study in fine-grained configuration management. In *Aust Comp Sci Communications.*, volume 19(1), pages 373–382, 1997.

3. P.A. Lindsay and O. Traynor. Version and configuration management of formal theories. In *Proc. Formal Methods Pacific (FMP'97)*. Springer Verlag, 1997.

4. P.A. Lindsay and O. Traynor. A formal model of fine grained traceability in software development environments. Technical Report 98-10, Software Verification Research Centre, School of Information Technology, The University of Queensland, St. Lucia, QLD 4072, Australia, 1998.

5. U.K. Ministry of Defence. Safety Management Requirements for Defence Systems Containing Programmable Electronics. Second Draft Defence Standard 00-56, August 1996.

6. F.A.C. Pinheiro and J.G. Goguen. An object-oriented tool for tracing requirements. *IEEE Software*, pages 52–64, 1996.

7. K.J. Ross and P.A. Lindsay. Maintaining consistency under changes to formal specifications. In *FME'93: Industrial Strength Formal Methods*. Springer Verlag, 1993. Proc. First Internat. Symp. of Formal Methods Europe, Odense, Denmark, April 1993.

8. S. Sachweh and W. Schäfer. Version management for tightly integrated software engineering environments. In *Proc. 7th Int. Conf. on Software Eng Environments*, pages 21–31, The Netherlands, 1995. IEEE Computer Society Press.

System Modeling Resurrected*

André van der Hoek, Dennis Heimbigner, and Alexander L. Wolf

Software Engineering Research Laboratory
Department of Computer Science
University of Colorado
Boulder, CO 80309 USA
{andre,dennis,alw}@cs.colorado.edu

Abstract. Over the past few years, research into system modeling has
dwindled in favor of other interests in the field of configuration management. Outside influence, in the form of the emergence of the discipline
of software architecture, demands that renewed attention is paid to system modeling because it places new requirements on, and offers new
opportunities to, system modeling. In this paper we investigate these
requirements and opportunities in more detail.

1 Introduction

Version models, system construction, and system modeling have historically been
the main issues for configuration management. A large amount of research has
been carried out in these areas [1, 3, 5, 8, 10], of which a significant portion
has made the transition into commercial configuration management systems.
The focus of research has now shifted towards other interests. The introduction
of software process support in configuration management systems [4, 7], the
development of distributed configuration management systems [6, 14], and the
creation of unified version models [2, 17] are currently among the more prominent
concerns.

Despite the change in focus, research to develop new version models and provide better system construction tools certainly has continued [15, 16]. However,
the lost issue in this transition seems to be *system modeling*. System modeling
is the activity of describing the structure of a system in terms of its components and the relationships among them. Virtually no attention has been paid
to system modeling since the development of DCDL [11] and PCL [13].

The goal of this paper is to resurrect system modeling. We advocate that it
should, once again, be one of the primary research areas in configuration management. This resurrection is warranted by the recent emergence of a new research discipline, software architecture. In particular, the discipline of software

* This work was supported in part by the Air Force Material Command, Rome Laboratory, and the Defense Advanced Research Projects Agency under Contract Number
F30602-94-C-0253. The content of the information does not necessarily reflect the
position or the policy of the Government and no official endorsement should be
inferred.

B. Magnusson (Ed.): ECOOP 98, SCM-8, LNCS 1439, pp. 140–145, 1998.
© Springer-Verlag Berlin Heidelberg 1998

architecture has been developing advanced, high-level architecture description languages that could be used by configuration management systems to advance their system modeling capabilities. These languages provide new opportunities and requirements for system modeling that were previously unrecognized, but which should now be addressed by the configuration management community. The experience base that has accumulated can be leveraged towards the development of new, integrated system models.

2   Software Architecture

System models in software architecture are often encapsulated in an architecture description language (ADL). In a typical ADL, a system is modeled as a set of primary, course grain components. These components are then combined into a complete system by explicitly modeled connections. To illustrate this mechanism, Figure 1 presents a simple client-server system that is modeled in Rapide [9], an ADL that is fairly representative of the other ADLs that have been developed to date. Shown are two components, a Client and a Server component. Each component is modeled with an interface that specifies both the functionality that is provided by the component and the functionality that the component expects to be provided by other components. In Rapide, these functionalities are specified using events. The Server component, for example, is capable of receiving and processing two events: Initialize and Compute. In turn, it produces one other event, Result. These events are used at the architectural level to connect components. In our client-server system, the Calculate functionality that is required by the Client component is attached to the functionality Compute that is provided by the Server component. This implies that whenever the Client component generates a Calculate event it is received by the Server component as a Compute event.

Most ADLs not only model components and connections, but they also explicitly model the interaction behavior of a component. In Rapide, this is done by specifying the relationship between the events that a component receives and the events that it produces. The behavior of the Server component, for example, is such that it produces a single event, Result, for each Compute event that it receives. Also, from the specification it should be clear that the Initialize event is simply consumed by the Server component; no events are produced by the Server component as a direct result of receiving an Initialize event.

The last aspect to be discussed about components is that they can contain constraints. These constraints specify the order in which a component can process events. The Server component, for example, requires that it receives a single Initialize event before it can process any number of Compute events. Such constraints can be used by analyzers to verify the consistency of a system by determining whether any of the constraints are violated.

It is now time to consider what type of contributions ADLs can make to system modeling as it has been known in configuration management. We do

```
type Server is interface
action in   Initialize();
        in   Compute(Value: Float);
        out Result(Value: Float);
constraint
    match Start -> Initialize'Call -> (Compute'Call *);
behavior
    NewValue : var Float;
begin
    (?x in Float) Compute(?x) => Result($NewValue);;
end Server;

type Client is interface
action in   Result(Value: Float);
        out Initialize();
        out Calculate(Value: Float);
behavior
    InitialValue : var Float := 0.0;
begin
    Start => Initialize;
            Calculate($InitialValue);;
end Client;

architecture ClientServer() return root is
    C : Client;
    S : Server;
connect
    (?x in Float) C.Calculate(?x) => S.Compute(?x);
    (?y in Float) S.Result(?y)    => C.Result(?y);
end ClientServer;
```

Fig. 1. Example of an Architectural System Model in Rapide.

so by investigating the applicability of the individual parts of ADLs to system modeling.

Components Traditional system models have equated components to the physical parts of a system. In PCL [13], for example, components are the result of a hierarchical breakdown of a system into its constituent subsystems. Typical usage of a configuration management system implies that a breakdown into logical components is desired, even though it is not directly supported. For example, in a compiler logical components such as "lexer" and "parser" are typically the entities that developers manipulate. These are not necessarily the physical components that are present in the system model; those correspond to such entities as "abstract syntax tree" and "file i/o".

ADLs model the logical components of a system. The inclusion in system models of architectural component modeling techniques therefore improves system modeling, because developers are able to manipulate a system from the desired, logical viewpoint.

Connectors Connectors advance the state of the art of system modeling in more than one way. First, the combination of components and connectors presents an accurate architectural view of a system. Traditional system models only modeled a hierarchical decomposition of a system without modeling the relationships among the resulting components. This omission causes many problems, such as the inadvertent removal of existing relationships or the erroneous introduction of new ones. Currently, it is hard to discover or avoid such mistakes. Since connectors model the relationships among components, they provide users with explicit information to guide them in the development process, thereby avoiding some of the mistakes that would have been made otherwise.

A second advantage of connectors is the simplification of change impact analysis. The impact of changes does not have to be deduced solely by analyzing source code, but can instead be derived from the system model using architectural dependence analysis techniques [12]. This in turn simplifies build management, as less recompilation can be achieved as well. As an example, consider a connector that is implemented as a global variable. This variable is declared in a header file that is included by many source files. Normally, all source files that depend on the header file are recompiled if the global variable is changed. If the system model instead indicates that the global variable is a connector between just two components, only the source files of those components need to be recompiled.

Behavior The inclusion of behavior has an important affect on system modeling. In the past the consistency of a system could only be verified by compiling, executing, and testing the system. Behavior modeling allows for verification that is based on the system model. As a particular version of a system is selected, it can be verified by analyzers for behavioral consistency. Of course, such verification does not guarantee correctness of the eventual system, but it does avoid a certain number of mistakes in the selection process, especially when change set technology is used or if a large version space exists. As an example, consider two change sets that can be applied to our client-server system of Figure 1. The first change set removes the Initialize event from the Server component as the component now initializes itself; the second change set removes the Initialize event from the Client component. This is modeled as two change sets since other variants of the Server component exist that still require to be initialized. If we only apply the first change set to the architecture, a system model analyzer can detect that the Client component still produces an Initialize event that should be consumed by the Server component; both change sets should be included. Such types of selection mistakes can thus be avoided even before the system is compiled and executed.

Constraints Constraints serve a similar role in system modeling as behavior; they assist in the verification of a system in much the same way. After a particular selection of a system version has been made, analyzers can verify whether any constraints are violated, and therefore guarantee correctness of a system at the system model level. For example, suppose the architecture of our client-server system incorporates two `Client` components as opposed to just one. A system model analyzer can detect that the `Initialize` event is received twice by the `Server` component because it is generated by both `Client` components. The constraint set by the `Server` component is therefore violated and the system is incorrect. These types of problems are normally only discovered when a system is tested.

3   Conclusions

The research that is presented in this paper is part of a larger effort that we are undertaking to advance the state of the art in system modeling. It is our belief that a common system model can be developed that combines the strengths of the models in both the areas of software architecture and configuration management. Moreover, we believe that it is best to take a configuration management centric view in this unification process. Because system models have been in existence in this discipline for many years, a significant experience base has been accumulated that can be leveraged. More importantly, existing configuration management systems provide an operating environment that already contains system modeling techniques to which new capabilities can be attached. Therefore, we argue that system modeling should be resurrected to once again as a primary research area in configuration management.

References

[1] V. Ambriola and L. Bendix. Object-oriented Configuration Control. In *Proceedings of the Second International Workshop on Software Configuration Management*, pages 133–136. ACM SIGSOFT, 1989.

[2] R. Conradi and B. Westfechtel. Towards a Uniform Version Model for Software Configuration Management. In *Proceedings of the Seventh International Workshop on Software Configuration Management*, number 1235 in Lecture Notes in Computer Science, pages 1–17, New York, New York, 1997. Springer-Verlag.

[3] J. Estublier and R. Casallas. The Adele Configuration Manager. In W. Tichy, editor, *Configuration Management*, number 2 in Trends in Software, pages 99–134. Wiley, London, Great Britain, 1994.

[4] J. Estublier, S. Dami, and M. Amiour. High Level Process Modeling for SCM Systems. In *Proceedings of the Seventh International Workshop on Software Configuration Management*, number 1235 in Lecture Notes in Computer Science, pages 81–97, New York, New York, 1997. Springer-Verlag.

[5] S.I. Feldman. MAKE — A Program for Maintaining Computer Programs. *Software—Practice and Experience*, (9):252–265, April 1979.

[6] J.J. Hunt, F. Lamers, J. Reuter, and W.F. Tichy. Distributed Configuration Management via Java and the World Wide Web. In *Proceedings of the Seventh International Workshop on Software Configuration Management*, number 1235 in Lecture Notes in Computer Science, pages 161–174, New York, New York, 1997. Springer-Verlag.

[7] D.B. Leblang. Managing the Software Development Process with ClearGuide. In *Proceedings of the Seventh International Workshop on Software Configuration Management*, number 1235 in Lecture Notes in Computer Science, pages 66–80, New York, New York, 1997. Springer-Verlag.

[8] D.B. Leblang, R.P. Chase, Jr., and H. Spilke. Increasing Productivity with a Parallel Configuration Manager. In *Proceedings of the International Workshop on Software Versioning and Configuration Control*, pages 144–158, 1988.

[9] D.C. Luckham and J. Vera. An Event-Based Architecture Definition Language. *IEEE Transactions on Software Engineering*, 21(9):717–734, September 1995.

[10] K. Marzullo and D. Wiebe. A Software System Modelling Facility. In *Proceedings of the ACM SIGSOFT/SIGPLAN Software Engineering Symposium on Practical Software Development Environments*. ACM SIGSOFT, April 1984.

[11] B.R. Schmerl and C.D. Marlin. Versioning and Consistency for Dynamically Composed Configurations. In *Proceedings of the Seventh International Workshop on Software Configuration Management*, number 1235 in Lecture Notes in Computer Science, pages 49–65, New York, New York, 1997. Springer-Verlag.

[12] J.A. Stafford, D.J. Richardson, and A.L. Wolf. Chaining: A Software Architecture Dependence Analysis Technique. Technical Report CU–CS–845–97, Department of Computer Science, University of Colorado, Boulder, Colorado, September 1997.

[13] E. Tryggeseth, B. Gulla, and R. Conradi. Modelling Systems with Variability using the PROTEUS Configuration Language. In *Software Configuration Management: ICSE SCM-4 and SCM-5 Workshops Selected Papers*, number 1005 in Lecture Notes in Computer Science, pages 216–240, New York, New York, 1995. Springer-Verlag.

[14] A. van der Hoek, D.M. Heimbigner, and A.L. Wolf. A Generic, Peer-to-Peer Repository for Distributed Configuration Management. In *Proceedings of the 18th International Conference on Software Engineering*, pages 308–317. Association for Computer Machinery, March 1996.

[15] D. Wiborg Weber. Change Sets Versus Change Packages: Comparing Implementations of Change-Based SCM. In *Proceedings of the Seventh International Workshop on Software Configuration Management*, number 1235 in Lecture Notes in Computer Science, pages 25–35, New York, New York, 1997. Springer-Verlag.

[16] L. Wingerd and C. Seiwald. Constructing a Large Product with Jam. In *Proceedings of the Seventh International Workshop on Software Configuration Management*, number 1235 in Lecture Notes in Computer Science, pages 36–48, New York, New York, 1997. Springer-Verlag.

[17] A. Zeller and G. Snelting. Unified Versioning through Feature Logic. *ACM Transactions on Software Engineering and Methodology*, 6(4):398–441, October 1997.

Version Sensitive Editing: Change History as a Programming Tool

David L. Atkins

Bell Laboratories, Naperville, IL 60566, USA,
datkins@bell-labs.com
http://www.bell-labs.com/~datkins

Abstract. Software Version Control Systems (VCSs) are used to store the versions of program source code created throughout the software development cycle. The traditional purpose of such systems has been mostly administrative, providing the safe storage of source code and the ability to recreate earlier versions, as well as tracking the progress of new feature development and problem resolution. Software developers often regard the VCS as a necessary but unpleasant encumbrance to the software design and coding process. However, when the change history data gathered by the VCS is easily available to the programmer in the context of an editor, the programming process is enhanced. Faults introduced by earlier changes can be more rapidly located, dependencies on other changes can be avoided, and the version history provides valuable hindsight that can help to guide future development.

1 Introduction

Software development projects typically use a Version Control System (VCS) to store program source code and maintain the history of changes. Although the main purpose of the VCS is to provide administrative control over the code modifications and assure the reproducibility of past versions of the source code, the VCS is a rich repository of historical change information. Tools provided by the VCS may provide some access to this data, but usually the information is in the form of reports tracking the progress of feature development or problem resolution and does not show the details of the source code revisions. Recently more attention has been paid to visualizing software version history [Bal96] and interpreting source change patterns.[Bal97] These approaches mine the change history data for a great deal of information about the system as a whole and can be very useful as discovery and analysis tools. Using the revision history to perform a static postmortem of what has taken place during development can provide valuable insights into the software design and indicate areas for improvement.

We believe that an awareness of the software's origin at a detailed level can significantly improve the coding process. For example, knowing that the original code author regarded certain lines of change as a "quick and dirty fix" is an important factor in deciding how it should be changed. Or, knowing that some

B. Magnusson (Ed.): ECOOP 98, SCM-8, LNCS 1439, pp. 146–157, 1998.

lines of code have been untouched for several years while some other lines have changed in the past week certainly helps to locate a problem that has appeared in the last week. Being able to associate lines of code with their reasons for existence is almost like having the authors available to provide commentary on the software design.

The revision history is a valuable knowledge base and many of the questions about the code's vintage are most likely to occur as new changes are being made, i.e., while editing the program source. For example, to understand the past revisions to a file being edited with existing tools, the programmer first extracts two versions of the file from the VCS as plain text files, and then uses a tool such as Unix *diff* to compare the extracted files and reconstruct the change history. Such a procedure is inconvenient, requires the programmer to know which versions to extract, and only indirectly accesses information stored in the VCS. However, tight integration of the revision history and the editor could make the version data directly available at the right time in the right context, with an ease of access that encourages its use.

In the next section we discuss how a typical VCS stores version information and how that information relates to the coding activity. Section 3 describes the Version Editor, a tool that integrates editing with access to the VCS data. Section 4 illustrates the use of this tool in several scenarios. Finally, the last sections comment on the interface and implementation of the Version Editor and suggest areas for further investigation.

2   Version Control Data and the Coding Environment

Typical Version Control Systems require the programmer to retrieve (check out) a source file for editing. The programmer then modifies the file and returns (checks in) the revised file to the VCS, creating a delta to the file. The delta encapsulates the modification made to the file: the change itself (as the lines inserted and deleted), who made the change, and when. The VCS usually requires some sort of description of the change and may associate many deltas to one or more files with the same change description; tools are provided to extract versions of the source with a particular set of deltas applied to each file. The development process will often provide a mechanism for maintaining and updating the status of the modification as it moves through testing, final approval, and incorporation into a product. In this type of system, there is much information stored about each change.

At the file level, each line of a source file could be associated with the programmer who created the line, the date and time that the line was created, the description of the reason for the change, and the status of the change. Most of this information is buried deeply in the implementation of the VCS. For example, a VCS that uses the Source Code Control System (SCCS)[Roc75] or Revision Control System (RCS)[Tic85] for storage will have delta information about each file that could be used to determine who inserted and deleted each line, and when the delta was made. Figure 1 shows the three views of a file as it changes

over time and how the corresponding version history is stored by SCCS. In such
a system, the deleted lines (i.e., those lines that no longer appear in the most
current version of the file) are also stored. Although this information exists in
the VCS, and is used to construct past versions of the program source, the information is not readily available to the programmer working on a current version
of a file.

```
#include <stdio.h>
main() {
   printf("Hello,world");
}



#include <stdio.h>
main() {
   printf("Hello,world\n");
}



#include <stdio.h>
main() {
   printf("Hello,world\n");
   exit(0);
}
```

```
@d Delta 1.3 by dla 97/10/13   3 2
@c Added graceful exit
@d Delta 1.2 by tball 97/9/18   2 1
@c Fixed missing newline
@d Delta 1.1 by dla 97/9/16   1 0
@c created 97/9/16 13:56:19 by dla
@I 1
#include <stdio.h>
main() {
@D 2
   printf("Hello,world");
@E 2
@I 2
   printf("Hello,world\n");
@E 2
@I 3
   exit(0);
@E 3
}
@E 1
```

Fig. 1. Seqence of revisions and corresponding SCCS storage.

The typical coding process consists of iterations through a checkout-edit-
checkin cycle, using any text editor to modify the source code retrieved from
the VCS. The view of the code in the editor ignores change history information.
That is, the working version of the source code contains no version information,
it is simply text. In this environment, the programmer has no way of knowing
if the lines of code being viewed were part of a bug fix or feature development,
whether the lines were changed last week or two years ago, or in which versions
of the product the code will appear.

However, knowing the origin and status of the source can be an essential
factor in understanding the code and how it should be modified. Programmers
often resort to comparing file versions with *diff* in order to understand what
has changed recently and the development methodology may even require code
inspections using listings that mark the code that has been changed. Many VCSs
provide tools to annotate a version of a file with change data or perform a comparison between two versions. However, such tools are external to the actual
editing activity and require the programmer to invoke the tool each time some

contextual version information is needed. The information must then be correlated manually to the lines of code being viewed in the text editor. Comparison tools also require that the programmer know which versions to compare, and that may not be readily apparent.

To be most useful to the programmer, the change history data must be easily accessible at the time it is most needed — while the programmer is looking at the code and deciding how to modify it. In addition to ease of access, the programmer should be able to view past versions of the code in the context of the current working version in order to fully comprehend the evolution of the program source.

An ideal software development environment would be able to provide the programmer with immediate answers to the following questions while the programmer is looking at existing lines of code and attempting to change them:

- What changes have I made so far?
- When was this line created?
- Why was this line created?
- Who created this line?
- What other lines were created for the same change?
- What lines were deleted by this change?
- What is the status of this change?
- What is the status of other lines surrounding my change?

Moreover, the answers should be available in the context in which they are asked. That is, answering the questions should not require a context shift to a separate tool from where the code is being edited. And, it should be possible to ask the questions easily with minimal training in the use of a new environment.

3   The Version Editor

The Version Editor (VE) is our implementation of such a version sensitive programming environment. VE is a replacement for a standard text editor but also has access to the version data stored by the VCS and can use that data to answer questions and control editing. This tool has been used over the last decade by many software developers in small to very large projects within Lucent Technologies. VE works with several SCCS-based VCSs used at Lucent, including SABLIME and the Extended Change Management System (ECMS)[Mid97] , as well as working with plain SCCS files. Since VE duplicates the interfaces of Vi and Emacs (the two most widely used screen editors in the Lucent development community), programmers are able to use the tool with little or no training. The rest of this section describes how VE integrates the VCS information into editing.

VE makes the change information about each line easily available. For a plain SCCS file, the delta information consists of the login of the user inserting the line, the date the line was inserted, the SCCS delta number, and the description of the delta if there is one. SABLIME and ECMS systems extend the version information by using Modification Requests (MRs) to group together one or more deltas to one or more files with a brief description (abstract), a long description, and status (e.g., in-progress, submitted for testing, approved). For SABLIME and ECMS files, VE can display the MR associated with a line, the status of the MR, the date of the delta, who made the delta, and the abstract of the MR. VE displays this information about the current line in a status area of the display, either continuously, or on demand. Thus, for each line the programmer can instantly know the when, who, and why of the line's origin.

In its default configuration, VE provides the programmer with immediate visual feedback about the current delta. Lines that have been touched in the current editing session (since the file was checked out from the VCS) are highlighted (e.g., by bold face type or reverse video), allowing the user to always know what they have changed so far. This is particularly valuable when iterating over an edit-compile-test cycle since the programmer can see at a glance where the original version has been modified and the size of the change.

For example, Figure 2 shows how the example file looks in VE after the function main has been changed to return an integer value. VE highlights the second and fourth lines in bold since those are the lines touched by the change. The original second line was changed by adding "int" as a return type for the main function and the fourth line is a new line added to the original version. As the editing takes place, VE highlights the line to show visually that it has been changed in this editing cycle. Note also that the editor's cursor is sitting on line three and VE shows the version history for that line.

```
#include <stdio.h>
int main() {
▯ printf(" Hello,world\n" );
   return(0);
}


SID 1.2 by tball,97/9/18 [Fixed missing newline]
"main.c" [modified] line 3 of 5
```

Fig. 2. VE view with changed lines in bold

Not only does VE keep track of changed lines, but VE also remembers the original lines. Usually the programmer is most interested in the way the file looks now, with the revisions just made. However, in some cases, it helps to see the current changes in the context of the way the file looked before those changes. VE allows the editing view to be adjusted so that deleted lines can be seen along with the newly inserted lines, where the deleted lines are distinguished by display attributes, e.g., underlining. In such a view, VE is careful to prohibit the deleted lines from being edited since they no longer exist in the checked out version of the file, and are only shown by VE for informational purposes. However, deleted lines may be copied, which is especially handy when portions of "old" code need to be resurrected.

The ability to display deleted lines is not restricted to the current delta, but can be controlled by a variety of version attributes stored by the VCS. In the extreme, all deleted lines could be made visible in VE, permitting a view of the complete evolution of the file.

VE also has a command to "un-delete" a line that has been deleted in the current session. This allows fine control over the editing activity and preserves the importance of the current delta highlighting. Note that un-deleting is different from the standard undo feature of many editors since any deletion of a line in the current session may be undone regardless of any editing activity that has taken place since the deletion.

The version attributes for each line are used for several purposes in VE. As noted above, lines deleted by the current delta can be made visible. In general, the visibility and visual presentation (bold, underline, color, etc.) of a line is determined by its version attributes. Although the default view corresponds to the checked out version of the file with the current edits highlighted, the programmer can adjust the visibility and display criteria to produce a variety of views. For example, highlighting could be used to attract attention to all lines inserted after a particular date, or all lines whose change status is not yet approved by testers, or all lines touched by a particular set of changes. The view can be adjusted while the programmer is editing in VE to dynamically alter the viewing context as questions arise. The same criteria can be used to view multiple files, or each file may have its own interesting view, and the view can be toggled easily to allow comparison of versions.

In addition to affecting the display, version attributes can be used to perform searches in VE. For example, when the cursor is sitting on a line, a simple editor command can advance the cursor to the next line with the same version attributes, i.e., the next line inserted by the same delta. In general, version attributes can be used to perform searches much as an ordinary editor allows pattern searches. The programmer could search to the next line inserted after a certain date, by a specific programmer, associated with a particular MR, or any Boolean combination of these and other attributes. Thus the file may be navigated on the basis of its change history.

4   Example Coding Scenarios

In this section we present two simple examples of using the Version Editor to improve the code editing process. These examples were extrapolated from real coding experiences using VE.

In the first scenario, assume that we have a large program that performs many file manipulations. The program has been working well, but has recently developed a problem with too many files being left open. To track down this problem, all sections of the code that open files must be checked to make sure that the open files are eventually closed. Various code browsing tools can be used to locate the relevant areas of the program source, but careful code examination is required to identify the problem. Figure 3 shows a normal editing view of one of many instances in the program where files are opened and closed. At first glance, the code looks to be correct, with the directory opened and then closed.

```
String FindSource(String base, String dir) {
    DIR * dirp = opendir(dir);
    for (int i = 0; i < NS; ++i) {      // Loop over suffix list
        String tmp = base + suffix[i];   // Target name to find
        for (dirent *de = readdir(dirp); de != NULL; de = readdir(dirp))
            if (tmp == de->d_name) {   // We found it, stop looking
                return tmp;
            }
        rewinddir(dirp);
    }
    closedir(dirp);
    return "";    // No match was found
}

"findsource.c", line 13 of 19
```

Fig. 3. Plain vi view of possible problem code

However, knowing that the problem has appeared recently is a valuable clue. By using VE to highlight the recent changes as in Figure 4, the problem area can be identified much more quickly. In this view, the lines deleted in the last month are made visible and are underlined, and the lines added in the last month display in boldface. When we examine the function that is opening a directory and traversing it in this view, we immediately see that a recent change causes the function to return from a loop, where it had previously broken out of the loop with control flow progressing to the normal function return at the end. Since the open directory is only closed outside of the loop, the change from "break" to "return" means that the directory is never closed.

It is certainly possible that by studying the code carefully, we would eventually notice this control flow problem. However, given that we may have dozens of such code fragments to examine, finding the problem would take much longer. VE's highlighting shows us instantly that there has been a recent change to this code, so it warrants closer scrutiny. The in-context display of the actual change facilitates an understanding of the effect of the change relative to the problem we are investigating, permitting the error to be quickly recognized and fixed.

```
String FindSource(String base, String dir) {
    DIR * dirp = opendir(dir);
    String result;    // The filename, if found
    for (int i = 0; i < NS; ++i) {     // Loop over suffix list
        String tmp = base + suffix[i];    // Target name to find
        for (dirent *de = readdir(dirp); de != NULL; de = readdir(dirp))
            if (tmp == de->d_name) {     // We found it, stop looking
                result = tmp;
                break;
                return tmp;
            }
        rewinddir(dirp);
    }
    closedir(dirp);
    return result; // Return the found name (may be null)
    return "";    // No match was found
}

Deleted by MR 595 by vz,97/11/15,approved [Stop source search at 1st match]
MR 467 by dla,97/9/21,integrated [Find source using list of suffixes]
"findsource.c", line 15 of 23
```

Fig. 4. VE view with recent deletions underlined, additions bold

Our second example scenario is taken from a real development environment where many developers make changes in parallel to the code, and the order of inclusion of the changes into product versions does not necessarily match the order in which the changes were made.

In this example, we need to make a change to a function that is called when a file is closed in a version editor. As originally designed, the function to be changed just releases the resources used for the file buffer in the editor: the version table object and the array of Line objects. Testing and investigation have shown that only the storage for the pointers to the Line objects is being released, not the storage for the Line objects themselves. Our task is to modify the function to properly release the Line objects. A natural implementation would be to loop over the Line objects, releasing each one in turn.

When we use VE to edit the function, we see the view presented in Figure 5 and find exactly the loop that we need. However, in this view, other developer's changes which are not yet approved for the official version of the product are highlighted in italics. This highlighting shows us that the loop over the Line objects is code that is still under development — it is part of a change that has not yet been submitted for inclusion in the final product.

Knowing that the code we see highlighted is not yet approved is very important information in our decision about whether to use the loop. If we add code within the loop, our new change will be dependent on the unapproved (and not even submitted) change. That is, it will be necessary to include both changes in order for our change to compile and work properly. Since VE shows us the

```
extern Version *vTable;   // The version table
extern Line * lines[];    // Array of pointers to the line objects

void CloseTheFile()
{
    // Calculate lines inserted, deleted
    int inserted = 0, deleted = 0;
    for (int i = 0; i ¡ nlines; ++i) {
        if (lines[i]->InsertingDelta() == vTable->CurrentDelta())
            ++inserted;
        if (lines[i]->DeletingDelta() == vTable->CurrentDelta())
            ++deleted;
    }
    cerr << inserted << " lines inserted, " << deleted << " deleted";

    // Release resources for the file
    delete vTable;
    delete [] lines;
}

MR 526 by tball,97/11/11,assigned [Report size of change at file close]
"close.c"   line 10 of 26
```

Fig. 5. VE view with unapproved changes highlighted in italics

author of the other change, we can contact the author to find out if his change will be submitted soon. If not, we must be careful to keep our implementation from becoming dependent on his change by coding our own loop to traverse the array of lines. In any case, the knowledge about the status of other code is important in our coding decisions. Having this information available as we are editing permits us to adjust our coding appropriately, and avoids unpleasant surprises about dependencies that we would otherwise encounter after the completion of coding.

5   Notes About the Interface and Implementation

One of the most important principles guiding the design of the Version Editor was ease of use. In order for the tool to be accepted, developers must be able to use it in existing environments with no re-training. So, rather than design a new editing interface, VE very faithfully emulates existing editing interfaces. This allows new users to immediately begin to edit with VE (possibly without even realizing it is not their normal editor). Some of the extra functionality of VE can be made available for "free". E.g., the highlighting of the current changes just happens without requiring any user action. Another example is the standard Vi command (Control-G) to display the current line number. In VE, the same command not only displays the line number, but also displays the line's change history: originator, date, and MR abstract. Other commands for version specific functionality are modeled after standard editor commands. For example, version search semantics are like standard text search semantics, allowing forward and backward searches and remembering the object of the last search.

The Version Editor can even be used with ordinary text files so that users do not have to shift tool sets. Of course, for an ordinary file there is no version history, but editing can still benefit from the highlighting of the current changes.

The Version Editor accesses the underlying SCCS files of the VCS directly so that it has all available data about the change history of the file. Additional change information maintained by the VCS is also correlated to the delta information stored by SCCS. Each line in a file has an associated set of version attributes. These attributes consist of the delta that inserted the line and zero or more deltas that deleted the line. Each delta in turn has a set of attributes: when it was made, by whom, a possible delta comment, and a corresponding MR (for SABLIME and ECMS VCSs). The MR then has its own set of attributes: the status of the MR, when the status last changed, and the abstract of the MR. Taken together, each line of the file has a rich set of version attributes.

The "version" of a line is its delta set. This notion of version enables VE to compare lines for their version so that all lines changed at the same time may be grouped together and meaningful views of the file can be created. However, since all attributes directly or indirectly associated with a line may be used to control visibility, artificial views of the file (e.g., showing both the old and new versions of a line) may be created.

VE re-implements the Vi and Emacs text editors. Although this may at first seem unnecessary, the version information is needed at such a low level in editing that performance might not be acceptable if VE were implemented as a layer on top of a plain text editor. In particular, every keystroke would have to be intercepted as well as every display update by the plain editor. Since VE was initially designed, more powerful programmable editors such as GNU Emacs[Gli97] are now available, and it is possible that such an editor could be extended with knowledge of the VCS to provide version sensitive editing like VE.

6   Related Work

The term version is often used to describe two different aspects of variations of a source file. It may refer to flavors of the file extracted for different purposes, e.g., different code constructs needed for distinct operating system platforms. The term also may refer to the sequence of changes over time as the source code is developed. The editor P-EDIT[Kru84] addresses the problem of dealing with multiple code variants. This tool hides the variant selection constructs and allows the user to view and edit different versions within a single editing session. The Version Editor provides similar capabilities by automating the creation of the variant control constructs of ECMS that are embedded in the source and these capabilities have been described elsewhere[Pal89] . However, P-EDIT does not address the problem of dealing with changes over time and interfacing to the VCS. Some editors (e.g., GNU Emacs[Cam96]) provide an interface to the VCS.

However, this interface is a convenience limited to executing VCS commands with the editor's buffer and does not integrate the change history into the editor. Microsoft Word[Cat97] implements some degree of revision control, but this is restricted to the file edited and does not incorporate any information from an external VCS. The editor EH[Fra87] provides sophisticated management of the version tree but does not deal with accessing the change history of a file stored under a conventional VCS.

7   Summary

Version Control Systems can be a rich source of information about the history of change that has led to the current state of a program's source. Knowledge of this change history can improve the understanding of the code and aid in the design of enhancements and problem solutions. Programmers often ignore the version data because it requires too much effort or it is too distracting to unearth the history during the coding process. By integrating the version data into the code editing environment, the information can be made available when it is likely to be of the most use.

The Version Editor is a tool that puts the change history into the editor where it can be instantly accessed and used to control editing and convey version information in the editor's display. The easy availability and disposition of the change history benefits the coding process. Problem areas in code may be identified more readily, unwanted dependencies may be avoided, and the version dimension can increase comprehension of code.

The Version Editor was originally designed to work with existing SCCS based VCSs whose purpose is the administration and safe storage of program source. The VCS only stores changes at the line level using a file comparison algorithm, but the usefulness of the version information during editing suggests that it would be more desirable for a VCS to capture more of the editing intent. That is, a VCS that stored a finer unit of change that corresponds to the actual editing could provide even more version context to enhance the coding process.

8   Acknowledgments

The Version Editor traces its roots to early work by Coplien on an experimental Delta Editor[Cop87] . The initial implementation with SCCS files was done by Maria Thompson and Pat Baldwin. Anil Pal collaborated on much of the design of the Version Editor and Joe Steffen provided the implementation of the Emacs interface. Special thanks are due to Tom Ball and Audris Mockus for all of their suggestions about this paper.

References

[Bal96] Thomas Ball and Stephen G. Eick, Software Visualization in the Large. *IEEE Computer*, 29(4):33–43, April 1996.

[Bal97] T. Ball, J.-M. Kim, A. Porter, and H. Siy, If Your Version Control System Could Talk... , *ICSE '97 Workshop on Modeling and Empirical Studies of Software Engineering*, May 1997.

[Cam96] Debra Cameron, Bill Rosenblatt, and Eric Raymond, *Learning GNU Emacs*, O'Reilly & Associates, 1996.

[Cat97] Catapult, Inc., *Microsoft Word 97 Step by Step, Advanced Topics*, Microsoft Press, 1997.

[Cop87] J. O. Coplien, D. L. DeBruler, and M. B. Thompson, The Delta System: A Nontraditional Approach to Software Version Management, *AT&T Technical Papers*, International Switching Symposium, March 1987.

[Fra87] Christopher W. Fraser and Eugene W. Myer, An Editor for Revision Control, *ACM Transactions on Programming Languages and Systems*, 9(2), April 1987.

[Gli97] Bob Glickstein, *Writing GNU Emacs Extensions*, O'Reilly & Associates, 1997.

[Kru84] Vincent Kruskal, Managing multi-version programs with an editor, *IBM Journal of Research and Development*, 28(1), January 1984.

[Mid97] Anil K. Midha, Software Configuration Management for the 21st Century, *Bell Labs Technical Journal*, 2(1):154–165, Winter 1997.

[Pal89] Anil Pal and Maria Thompson, An Advanced Interface to a Switching Software Version Management System, *Seventh International Conference on Software Engineering for Telecommunications Switching Systems*, Bournemouth, UK, July 1989.

[Roc75] Marc J. Rochkind, The Source Code Control System, *IEEE Transactions on Software Engineering*, SE-1(4):364–370, December 1975.

[Tic85] Walter F. Tichy, RCS — A System for Version Control, *Software — Practice and Experience*, 15(7):637–654, July 1985.

Coordinated Editing of Versioned Packages in the JP Programming Environment

Michael L. Van De Vanter

Sun Microsystems Laboratories
901 San Antonio Road
Palo Alto, CA 94303 USA
Michael.VanDeVanter@Eng.Sun.COM

Abstract. As part of an investigation of scalable development techniques for systems written in the Java™ programming language, the Forest Project is building JP, a prototype distributed programming environment. For extensibility and usability, a mechanism is required to coordinate the activity of multiple editor programs (each specializing in particular source types) with the JP versioning system. The JP architecture makes it possible, using a very simple framework, to coordinate loosely coupled Java-implemented editors that share no data representations with one another or with the versioning system. This framework also supports a streamlined user model for editing that keeps users' version awareness to an absolute minimum during routine development tasks. This architecture relies on two key technologies: orthogonally persistent object storage, and orthogonal versioning of hierarchical, immutable, source objects.

1 Introduction

Constructing and maintaining large software systems demands aggressive use of versioning and configuration management for source artifacts such as program code and documentation. This requirement conflicts in practice with another important requirement, namely that developers can view, modify, and build sources with as little distraction and delay as possible. The difficulty increases when the requirement is added that source objects be edited and versioned as hierarchical aggregations of parts, and that it be possible for new types of sources (along with appropriate editors) to be added during the lifetime of a development environment. A new coordination framework, developed as part of the JP programming environment by the Forest Project at Sun Microsystems Laboratories, addresses all of these requirements.

The JP programming environment specifically addresses problems of scale in software development: large systems are constructed from parts, usually in multiple configurations, developed by teams, possibly at diverse locations. Central to the JP approach is the notion of a uniquely named, reusable, independently versioned package. Each package contains, along with a hierarchical aggregation of sources, information describing how to build it. JP packages unify important aspects of large system development: system structure, storage management, building, and configuration management. Tools exploit this unity to simplify the developer's task, even while providing stronger guarantees of reliable and repeatable system builds than is now common.

The first and most important set of tools includes those which permit developers to view and modify sources and to create new source versions to be built. Editing and

B. Magnusson (Ed.): ECOOP 98, SCM-8, LNCS 1439, pp. 158-173, 1998

versioning are coordinated with a framework that is simple, easily extended to new type-specific editor types, and supportive of a streamlined user model that minimizes the need for version awareness by developers. Simplicity in the framework is made possible in large part by orthogonality in the JP architecture:

- orthogonal object persistence removes storage concerns from the framework; and
- a versioning model is orthogonal to version content.

Section 2 of this paper introduces the JP environment and points out the particular problem that is solved by the editor coordination framework. Section 3 walks through this framework, discussing the implication of each part at the level of editor implementation and visible user model. Section 4 compares this approach with other work. Section 5 summarizes current project status, followed by acknowledgments and conclusions based on the work so far.

2 JP Overview

JP is an integrated development environment being developed to explore fundamental solutions to the problems of scale that plague development of large software systems [10]. Although the JP approach is general, the current prototype targets systems written in the Java™ programming language [9] and encourages a development style that will result in simpler and more reliable construction of large Java systems [11].

This section reviews the JP approach and describes requirements that motivate the framework for coordinated editing presented in Section 3.

2.1 Package-Centric Development

Central to JP's design is replacement of one of the weakest links in current development environments: the *make* [8] program for system building. JP's adaptation of the Vesta approach [14], a fundamentally more sound and scalable technology, unifies four roles, described below, more commonly supported by disconnected services.

The JP approach is based on independently *versioned Java packages*: collections of classes (as well as other resources) that exist in stable, immutable, versioned configurations. Each version includes a build script: a system model that is also a parameterized program for building the package. The JP environment abstracts away details of package location, contents, and construction, affording developers the luxury of a single package naming scheme in most situations. The following overview describes the four roles played by JP packages.

System Structure. Packages play the role of software *modules*: the developer assembles large systems by constructing packages whose build scripts import other packages. Each import specifies a particular version of an imported package, and the builder's import mechanism abstracts away conventional distinctions between source (uncompiled) and binary (compiled) reuse. Build script imports do not affect the semantics of the Java language (in particular the Java import statement).

Storage. The developer manages sources in terms of the package namespace, with the addition of package-level versioning; tools abstract away details of underlying storage and distribution. The build system invisibly manages derived objects (class files and other objects created by invoking build scripts), thereby reducing name clutter and eliminating confusion among objects derived in alternate variants.

System Building. The developer builds a package by evaluating its associated build script using a special interpreter; imported packages are incorporated by recursive script invocation. The developer gains access to derived objects (for example executables) by invoking tools that abstract away the complexity of the script's result. The developer can supply parameters that cause variants to be built (even of imported packages, possibly remotely located) without perturbing package sources. Build script results contain extensive information that is both precise and complete, enabling straightforward access by tools that extract, analyze, and display particular kinds of information to developers. Build results are guaranteed repeatable, as discussed in the Vesta literature [14], enabling derived information to be managed as a cache within the build interpreter; further discussion of build scripts is beyond the scope of this paper.

Configuration Management. The developer creates configurations as packages whose role is to import particular versions of other packages, including other configurations. Each version of such a package specifies transitively and immutably an arbitrarily large, buildable aggregation of packages comprising some version of an application, applet, library of classes, or other deliverable. Completeness and precision are crucial to the repeatable build guarantee. A configuration manager permits concurrent non-interfering work by multiple developers.

2.2 Strong Object-Oriented Abstractions

The JP architecture achieves simplicity and robustness through object-oriented design as well as a strong separation of concerns among subsystems. An important technique for decoupling subsystems in JP is reliance on Java *interfaces*. A Java interface defines a new reference type without implementation, but which can be implemented by otherwise unrelated classes that provide implementations for the interface's methods [9]. The editor coordination framework described in Section 3 is based on a Java interface.

Interfaces isolate implementation choices, and even permit multiple implementation choices to coexist. JP subsystems such as the builder, the versioning system, and source viewing and editing are quite independent. Multiple versioning mechanisms could coexist in a single JP store.

2.3 Orthogonal Persistence

Crucial to the independence of subsystems is JP's replacement of a second weak link in current development environments: reliance on simple file systems to store complex, long-lived application data. An implementation of orthogonal persistence for Java [3] permits all JP objects to live as long as needed. Most importantly, it does so nearly transparently, without degrading JP subsystem boundaries.

Objects persist by reachability from a privileged named root, for example a table of versioned packages that reside in a particular store. Object persistence is independent of object type and independent of how objects are created [2]. New object types, added after construction of a programming environment, can persist as well, without any special modifications. This makes all JP objects potentially persistent in a uniform way, much as Java's automatic memory management reclaims storage from unused objects in a uniform, transparent way.

As a consequence, the objects that populate a JP store (for example those representing Java sources) have not been complicated (nor have their interfaces been twisted) by the need to store them as anything other than the objects they are. A second consequence of making objects first class (and not some external file-based representation of them) is that tools such as editors normally run as Java programs on a simple objects-in, objects-out basis. A third consequence is the difficulty inherent in revising the code that implements an installed JP store; this is an instance of the *schema evolution problem,* whose discussion is beyond the scope of this paper.

2.4 Simple Versioning and Configuration Management

Although versioning and configuration management are at the heart of the JP environment, as described in Section 2.1, the JP versioning/CM system is relatively simple. It can be thought of as a monotonically growing map that permanently binds names and immutable content.

Uniform Versioning. All versioning takes place at the granularity of packages. JP configurations, which aggregate package versions, are themselves versioned packages and can recursively represent systems of any size with precision.

Orthogonal Content. JP versioning is orthogonal to content, as suggested by Conradi and Westfechtel [6]. Objects of new types, added after original programming environment construction, can be versioned as well.

Immutable Content. Objects to be versioned must implement a special interface (Mutability) that permits the versioning system to ensure, before creating a new version, that the transitive closure of its proposed content is immutable.

Version Accretion. A developer commits changes (prerequisite to building) by creating new versions. JP's versioning model[1] permits versions to be added subject to rules based on named branches with numbered entries. For example, a developer who wishes to work on version 3 of package named com.sun.pkg must first invoke a *Checkout* operation on version com.sun.pkg.3. Unlike conventional systems, which treat checked out data as mutable, JP creates a new branch, for example beginning with version com.sun.pkg.3.checkout-mlvdv.0 (whose content is identical to that of sun.pkg.3). The developer may add successively numbered ver-

---

[1]This duplicates the Vesta model, although other models could be added.

sions, typically one for each attempted build,[2] with an *Advance* operation. This work might conclude with version com.sun.pkg.3.checkout-mlvdv.14, at which the developer would invoke a `Checkin` operation to create com.sun.pkg.4. JP also supports a *Branch* operation; this could be used to create a branch beginning with version com.sun.pkg.4.mytest.0. Experiments might be performed on this branch by a series of Checkout, Advance, and Checkin operations, and a merging tool would help migrate changes back to a main branch.

Content Hierarchy. Package contents are typically hierarchical aggregates of objects, analogous to folders and text files in simple cases, but possibly more like compound documents in other cases. Such objects, called *parts* in JP, are by definition immutable and by convention constructed to be independent of context; this permits parts to be treated as pure values that can be safely shared among versions.

Lightweight Versions. Version creation, being little more than extension of a naming data structure, is very light weight. The coordination framework, described in Section 3, takes care to share parts among versions when possible.

Limitations. This simple but robust approach to versioning omits some commonly supported mechanisms, for example dynamically bound names such as "`latest`". Such functionality is supplied in JP by tools. For example, a tool might help create new configurations according to higher level intentions, such as "update all imports to latest versions." Other policy-oriented tools might control visibility and access.

2.5 The Coordinated Editing Problem

A developer makes progress in JP by routinely creating and building new versions. This involves creation of new source objects, based on recent edits, as well as new folder-like containers that represent changed contents. Editing in JP is supported by Java-implemented editors that specialize in particular types of source objects, including containers. Starting with an initial part, a JP editor allows the developer to make changes (as in the mutable *buffer* of a text editor) and eventually to create a new object of the same type. The problem is how to coordinate editors working on various parts, and how to progress smoothly as the developer advances through successive versions.

The coordinated editing framework described in the next section addresses this problem. The intended effect is that developers have the freedom to edit what needs to be edited, to build when desired, and to be able to understand the versioning status of a package on those occasions (preferably few) when it is important. This approximates the kind of freedom offered by single-user integrated development environments, but which is difficult to achieve in a scalable development environment based on strong versioning and configuration management. To summarize, this means that in JP:

---

[2] The justification for this apparently profligate storage policy is beyond the scope of this paper, but experience with both Vesta and JP support it.

- new versions of packages must be created quickly and unobtrusively;
- what's being edited is a hierarchy of parts, in which parts may contain other parts of possibly different type, requiring services of type-specific editors;
- contained types are generally opaque, whose implementation is known only to an open-ended collection of editors that collaborate through generic interfaces; and
- developers must be able to ascertain at a glance the relationship among editors and their version-related status.

3   The Coordinated Editing Framework

Coordinated editing in JP is based on the Java interface PartHandler.[3] This section walks through the interface, describing how coordination works and discussing implications for implementations and for developers working in JP.

```
Public interface PartHandler {
  // Context and Coordination methods
  void initialize(VersionHandler vh);
  boolean setPart(Mutability part);
  void edit();
  PartHandler getPartHandler(Path name);
  // Versioning methods
  Mutability advance();
  void revert();
  // Usability methods
  void setEditable(boolean isEditable);
  void setModified(boolean isModified);
  void setVersionName(String name);
  void setPartName(String name);
}
```

3.1 Context and Coordination

A part handler (an object implementing the PartHandler interface) is not an editor itself, but a coordinator. It collaborates with four types of objects:

- a single version handler,
- a single part within the package version being edited,
- possibly views/editors for that part, and
- possibly part handlers for contained subparts.

---

[3] The interface presented here has been simplified for exposition; it omits issues of concurrency, event management, and editor start-up/shutdown.

Figure 1 shows an example of these relationships; here rectangles represent object instances and arrows represent object references. In the example a developer is viewing and preparing to edit a part named b.d in version 3 of package com.sun.pkg. The leftmost part of this diagram represents a JP versioned store, where mutation is narrowly constrained: versions may be added, but once created never change; parts, once included in a version, likewise never change. All access to and mutation of the versioned store (in the form of new version creation) is managed by the handlers in the middle part of the diagram. All of the relationships shown in this figure will be discussed in this section.

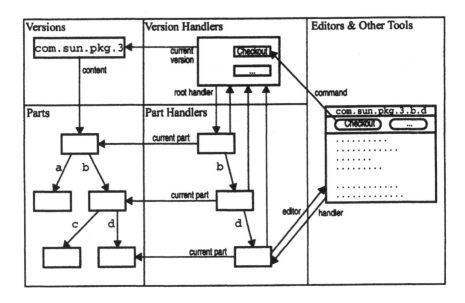

Fig. 1. Example Object Instance Relationships

Four methods in the PartHandler interface establish contextual relationships. The first creates a permanent relationship with an object of type VersionHandler:

```
void initialize(VersionHandler vh);
```

A version handler plays several, central roles. It:

— is the point of access into the JP versioned store for tools in the environment;

— provides access to its *current* package version;

— implements command objects, which use the versioning system to create new versions (e.g. Checkout, Advance);

— reassociates itself with any newly created version, thus tracking successive versions of the developer's work; and

— notifies its part handlers of version-related state changes.

These roles will become more clear in the following discussion. It is significant that versioning operations are not implemented in any part handler or editor. This is a direct consequence of orthogonality in both the versioning and storage systems. Developers can invoke versioning commands (for example the Checkout command in the figure) from any editor, where they might appear as buttons or menu items, but such command objects are opaque to the editors. Although not strictly required (a separate tool could make versioning commands available), direct access to the commands from every editor reduces distraction and eliminates confusion concerning which editors are associated with which versions.

The next method establishes the fundamental relationship between a handler and a part in the versioned store:

```
boolean setPart(Mutability part);
```

This returns `false` if the part is not of the implementation type for which the handler is specialized (this is a system error). Although this method is normally invoked only during part handler creation, the part associated with a handler changes during the handler's lifetime as new parts are created during Advance operations. The part represents the version content a developer wants to see when browsing; when the user is editing, the current part represents the most recently versioned instance of the named part.

Each part handler implementation is responsible for creating an editor appropriate to the implementation type of its associated part (for simplicity we assume that all editors appear as top level windows). In a simple realization of the framework, this is done by a call to a method on the part handler:

```
void edit();
```

An editor communicates only with its associated part handler via a comparably simple interface that can be private to the pair. In the most flexible realization of the framework, using the Model-View-Controller approach, the part handler holds the (possibly mutable) *data model* for the associated part, and editors are *views*. Other editor implementations may manage their own mutable buffers, into which the data content of the current part is initially copied. In any case, the division of responsibility between part handler and editor is private to the two implementation types, hidden by the `PartHandler` interface. Finally, a part handler is responsible for passing to its editor the set of command objects associated with its version handler. The editor can make these available to the developer, for example as buttons or menu items.

A fourth relationship is with handlers for parts that are children of the current part. Tools in the environment gain access to parts by first locating a version handler associated with the desired package version, and then requesting a part handler for each part of interest. A version handler supplies part handlers by recursive calls down the part handler hierarchy of the following method, based on the name of the part:

```
PartHandler getPartHandler(Path name);
```

Typical implementations create handlers for subparts only when needed, as suggested in Figure 1 where not all potential handlers appear. The implementation types of subparts need not be known to a container or its part handler. Part handlers are created by a shared abstract factory object that embodies the desired binding (possibly configured by individual developers) between part types and handler types (which in turn implies editor types in the simple case).

The net effect of this collaboration is that each version of a package being accessed by tools in the environment is associated with a single version handler; the version handler manages a tree of part handlers which partially mirror the version's content. A developer can conveniently and safely view multiple versions of a package at the same time, *even in situations where a part is contained in multiple versions.* Such sharing is common, since unchanged parts are typically shared by successive versions (see below). Each version's handler group maintains context for viewing parts, which are immutable and independent of the contexts in which they are included.

3.2 Versioning

Versioning operations include Checkout, Advance, Checkin, and Branch. Each adds a new version to a JP package according to rules of the versioning model. Checkout, Checkin, and Branch operations create new versions with content identical to their predecessors, as in the example of Section 2.4.

A developer's changes are committed by the Advance command, implemented within the version handler. This command creates a new version, makes it the successor to the current version with a call to the versioning system, and then causes the new version to become version handler's current version. The Advance command obtains the content for a new version by calling the following method on the root part handler:

```
Mutability advance();
```

This returns a part that represents the current "value" of the handler's data model. A newly created part also becomes the handler's current part. In cases where the developer has made no changes, then the handler returns its current part, without creating a new one. Parts can be shared safely among versions when they are designed to be independent of context.

A handler for a container part must implement this method recursively, for example advancing each child handler and creating a new container part if any of its children have produced new parts. This amounts to a distributed implementation of the simple path-copying approach to versioning large objects, for example as used for Exodus "storage objects" [4]. It is not required that handler/editor pairs follow this approach, but doing so effectively constrains storage consumption.

It is worth noting that all this takes places via interfaces that hide part representations, which are generally considered private to handler/editor implementations and possibly some privileged clients of them. This permits alternate implementations of similar parts. For example, editor implementations are free to represent versioned parts as deltas that refer to predecessor parts (whether or not all the predecessors were actually versioned directly), either in the name of compact storage or to implement editor-specific history mechanisms. Such history mechanisms are orthogonal to package-level history maintained in package version histories; history-guided undo can be supported at both levels, but always by advancing to newly created versions, not by removing versions.

This separation of concerns is greatly enhanced by the absence from this interface of any negotiation for persistent storage: a handler (or its editor) simply creates an object, which is then passed to the versioning system where it becomes permanent.

The handler framework itself supports a crude but familiar kind of undo. A Revert action recursively instructs a group of part handlers to discard changes made relative to the current version (i.e. since the most recent Advance).

```
void revert();
```

3.3 Usability

Only those aspects described above are strictly required for the JP coordination framework to function correctly. For it to function effectively, however, attention must be paid to the look and feel of the system in operation. Four methods in the `PartHandler` interface are used to ensure smooth, unobtrusive interaction between editing and versioning.

A common, frustrating usability failure occurs in many environments when changes made in one or more edit buffers cannot be conveniently committed because of inappropriate versioning state. Each JP editor is made aware whether editing should be permitted.[4] Notification is propagated from version handler to part handlers by calls on the method:

```
void setEditable(boolean isEditable);
```

Editors display this status (ideally using a visual theme shared with other editors) and refuse to make changes when this permission has not been granted. For example, a developer viewing package version `com.sun.pkg.3`, as shown in Figure 1, would not be allowed to make changes without first clicking on the Checkout button, invoking the Checkout operation in the associated version handler. The version handler uses the versioning system to create a checkout branch and then notifies part handlers, which in turn notify editors that editing is permitted. At this point the version handler's current version changes to the newly created version (`3.checkout-mlvdv.0`, for example). Part handler and editors make no changes, however, because the content of the newly created version is identical to its predecessor.

Confusion arises from misunderstanding the status of uncommitted editing changes. In keeping with JP's versioning model, any change to a part is treated as a change to the whole version. Each version handler keeps a "dirty" bit and notifies its part handlers when it changes:

```
void setModified(boolean isModified);
```

Editors display this status, ideally using a visual theme shared with other editors. The coordination framework requires that any editor about to permit a change must check the dirty bit; when the dirty bit is off, the editor must notify its part handler, which in turn notifies the version handler, which then notifies all part handlers that the dirty bit has come on.

---

[4] In the current versioning model, permission to edit is defined by whether the current version is the latest on a checkout branch.

It can be confusing to have parts visible from more than one version, so each editors is made aware of the name for its current version. This name changes when versioning actions occur, as in the Checkout example mentioned above, following which the version handler notifies all part handlers with calls on the method:

```
void setVersionName(String name);
```

Editors display this name, for example in the window bar as shown in Figure 1.

Hierarchical naming of parts within a package is natural for source objects, although not strictly required. Each editor is made aware of the current name of its associated part. The name of a part can change, for example when the developer renames an enclosing folder, in which case the affected part handlers must notify handlers for child parts with calls on the method:

```
void setPartName(String name);
```

3.4 Coordination in Action: The Edit-Build Loop

An important consequence of this framework is the smoothness with which work gets done. Here is a summary of how it appears to a developer.

— A developer opens one or more editors on parts of a package version, for example com.sun.pkg.3. Parts might include both folders and source objects.

— The editors visually indicate that editing is not permitted and, of course, that the contents of the version are not "dirty".

— Deciding to make changes, the developer presses the Checkout button on any of the associated editors. Every editor shows the new version name (for example com.sun.pkg.3.checkout-mlvdv.0), and every editor indicates that editing is now permitted.

— The developer begins to edit. The first change in any editor causes all editors to show that the dirty bit has turned on.

— The developer decides to try a build by pressing a build button on any editor, which automatically invokes an Advance before the actual build. All editors show that the dirty bit has gone off and that there is a new version name (for example com.sun.pkg.3.checkout-mlvdv.1).

— When finished with the session, the developer presses the Checkin button and enters some version comments. The version name changes yet again (for example to com.sun.pkg.4), and editors show that editing is no longer permitted.

It is significant that the developer pays no attention to versioning, other than the decision to invoke Checkout and Checkin operations. At the same time, the progression through versions is visible in every editing context, and the developer benefits from a complete history of every build performed, along with the JP guarantee that all build are repeatable.

The developer may ask to view another version, for which a new version handler and associated editors would be created. These editors are managed separately, since they have distinct version handlers, even in situations where the same part might be shared between the two versions in view.

In practice developers often work concurrently on many packages, which in JP are independently versioned. Coordination among version handlers is an important issue that lies beyond the scope of this paper.

4   Related Work

4.1 Vesta

The JP environment is based heavily on design principles from the Vesta project [14], which takes the position that configuration management, building, and storage management must be aligned for reliability and scalability. Building takes place in the store in both JP and Vesta; in JP, however, editing also takes place in the store, whereas it does not in Vesta. A Vesta Checkout operation copies the hierarchical content of a package version into a file system tree where it may be edited with conventional editors; a Vesta build requires creation of a new version by copying files back into the store.

Vesta makes no provision for coordination among file-based editors and versioning system, as there is in JP. Furthermore, Vesta package contents are limited by what can be represented as files (Vesta stored sources are byte arrays) and directories, in contrast to JP's flexible use of arbitrary objects.

4.2 POEM

The POEM environment [15], developed concurrently with the first JP prototype and with a similar strong influence from Vesta, shares many goals with JP.

Key implementation strategies differ, however. POEM keeps meta-data in an OODB, leaving storage of parts to a conventional file-based versioning system. In contrast, JP represents all data as persistent objects in a simple object-oriented versioning framework. As in most systems, POEM permits editing by creating mutable files; JP supports editing in the store through direct object interaction in the handler framework (although integration with separate editors can be supported by particular implementations of the `PartHandler` interface). Building in POEM is encapsulated as an operation within software units, whereas the JP approach separates the two more strongly: JP parts are treated as immutable values, and the JP builder is a single interpreter (with generic caching behavior) that computes over a space of values that includes those parts as well as derived objects.

4.3 Compound Document Editing

The JP approach to coordinated editing has much in common with compound document frameworks such as OpenDoc [7]. Compound documents can contain other documents whose types are unknown, the only requirement being adherence to a coordination framework by appropriate editors. JP departs most notably from compound document frameworks with its support for versioning (without requiring any version awareness in editor implementations).

Compound document frameworks deal with other issues as well. For example, parts of their protocols concern GUI-related resources (for example screen real estate and access to a shared menu bar), so that editors for embedded parts can be visually embedded within a containing editor; such support is absent in JP, but could in principle be added. Compound document protocols must also deal with the sticky problem of storage management, a problem solved transparently in JP through its reliance on orthogonally persistent objects.

4.4 COOP/Orm

JP's editor coordination has the most in common with work on fine-grained collaborative editing and version control by Magnusson et. al. [16][17]. Both start from the position that a software development environment must be focused on concurrent, collaborative, and distributed development; both projects place version and configuration management mechanisms at the heart of the respective systems.

Differences between the systems reflect different project emphasis:

— *Point of Departure*: JP starts with the requirement for reliable, scalable system building, whereas COOP/Orm suggests that software development is an important special case of collaborative document development.

— *Versioning*: COOP/Orm emphasizes fine-grained versioning, whereas versioning in JP is defined to coincide with the granularity of building (language packages).

— *Editing*: COOP/Orm emphasizes fine-grained collaborative editing, whereas JP approximates file-granularity editing (finer grained editing is a JP goal) with collaboration permitted only by concurrent package checkouts.

— *Distribution*: COOP/Orm emphasizes distributed, collaborative editing, whereas JP emphasizes reliable, distributed building.

— *Editor Integration*: COOP/Orm editors must be strongly versioning-aware and participate in a collective representation scheme, where JP editors have no such requirements. JP editors are free to represent the parts they manage in any way. JP storage is made straightforward by a combination of orthogonal persistence and orthogonally versioned store objects.

None of these differences appear to reflect fundamental incompatibilities between the COOP/Orm and JP approaches.

4.5 ClearCase

Although there is no direct counterpart in ClearCase, a commercial Configuration Management product [5], to the editor coordination framework that is the focus of this paper, the case study of ClearCase by Asklund and Magnusson [1] invites a broader comparison. The dominant distinction is in fundamental technology: ClearCase is designed to work within the semantics of conventional file systems and the *make* [8] program for system building.

The JP approach abandons both of these in favor of technologies believed to be fundamentally more reliable and scalable: persistent object storage combined with Vesta-style functional programming for building. This shift potentially addresses most shortcomings mentioned in the case study, by making needed mechanisms either more reliable, easier to implement, or unnecessary. Specific limitations addressed by the current, limited prototype of the JP approach include:

- Support for versioned sub-systems;
- "Light-weight" branch types;
- Fine-grained "micro-versions"; and
- A more powerful support for configurations than "labels".

5   Project Status

The architectural principles behind the JP environment were first explored in a prototype implemented in C++ using an object-oriented database [12][13]; that first prototype included editor coordination as described here. The architectural complexity (and accompanying fragility) added by the OODB, although less severe than in file-based implementations, drove us to seek truly orthogonal persistence.

A second, file-based prototype has been in daily use for several years, supporting both its own development and that of its successor. Editor coordination is missing in this second prototype, and it is sorely missed.

A third prototype is being constructed in Java using PJama [3] for object storage, an implementation of orthogonal persistence [2] for Java. PJama is being developed through a collaboration between the Forest Project at Sun Microsystems Laboratories and the Persistence and Distribution Group at the University of Glasgow. The third JP prototype is dedicated specifically to building large systems in Java [11], and the editor coordination scheme reported here is at its core.

Our immediate goal is to put into daily use the PJama-based JP prototype. On that platform we intend to push source editing in several directions:

- Finer granularity: decompose Java source objects into smaller language-oriented parts, for example as is done in COOP/Orm [17].
- Higher-level sources: build or import tools that create higher-level source objects from which Java sources are generated through building. Examples include GUI builders and OO modeling tools. The main difficulty here is adapting file-centric applications to the much simpler "objects-in, objects-out" interface.
- Add a layer for software process tracking and management.
- Add a more rich view architecture, for example supporting editing in place in the style of compound documents.
- Language-based editing: make available to editors the results of recent builds, so that suitably equipped editors can exploit language information to drive high-productivity editing [18].

6 Conclusions and Further Work

Our very limited experience with coordinated editing suggests this approach does indeed enable a smooth edit-build loop for developers, with absolutely minimal need for version awareness until such time as a versioning-specific action such as Checkin is desired. Lack of editor coordination in the second prototype has been both a constant irritation and reminder of its success in the first prototype. We are confident that this framework will be a key component in our efforts to make convenient an otherwise inconvenient environment that creates a completely new versioned configuration with every build.

Implementation experience so far confirms our intuition that the need to deal with issues of storage and versioning complicates the construction of editors tremendously; the overhead of creating new editors for particular objects is sufficiently low in JP that it makes sense to construct an editor in this framework for tasks as simple as setting a boolean value (the first prototype indeed had such an editor).

We will be able to evaluate and validate this framework more thoroughly as we pursue the editing-related goals mentioned in the previous section.

7 Acknowledgments

This work benefits greatly from the vision of Mick Jordan, Principal Investigator of the Forest Project at Sun Microsystems Laboratories. The delightful opportunity to use an increasingly practical, highly orthogonal persistent object system owes much to Prof. Malcolm Atkinson and his band of persistent researchers in Glasgow. Helpful comments on drafts of this paper were contributed by Huw Evans, Tobias Murer, Yuval Peduel, and anonymous reviewers.

8 Trademarks

Sun, Sun Microsystems, and Java are trademarks or registered trademarks of Sun Microsystems Inc. in the United States and other countries.

References

1. Asklund, U, Magnusson, B.: A Case-Study of Configuration Management with ClearCase in an Industrial Environment. In: Conradi, R. (ed.): Software Configuration Management, Proceedings of the ICSE '97 SCM-7 Workshop, Boston. Lecture Notes in Computer Science, Vol. 1235. Springer-Verlag, Berlin Heidelberg New York (1997) 201-221

2. Atkinson, M., Morrison, R: Orthogonally Persistent Object Systems. VLDB Journal **4** (1995)

3. Atkinson, M., Daynès, L., Jordan, M., Printezis, T., Spence, S.: An Orthogonally Persistent Java. In: ACM SIGMOD Record **25** (1996) 68-75

4. Carey, M., DeWitt, D., Richardson, J., Shekita, E., Lochovsky, F.: Storage Management for Objects in EXODUS. In: Kim, W. (ed.): Object-Oriented Concepts, Databases, and Applications. Addison Wesley, Reading, Massachusetts (1989) 341-369

5. ClearCase Concepts Manual. Atria Software (1992). See also http://www.rational.com/products/clearcase/

6. Conradi, R., Westfechtel, B.: Towards a Uniform Version Model for Software Configuration Management. In: Conradi, R. (ed.): Software Configuration Management, Proceedings of the ICSE '97 SCM-7 Workshop, Boston. Lecture Notes in Computer Science, Vol. 1235. Springer-Verlag, Berlin Heidelberg New York (1997) 1-17

7. Feiler, J., Meadow, A.: Essential OpenDoc. Addison Wesley, Reading, Massachusetts (1996)

8. Feldman, S.: Make -- A Program for Maintaining Computer Programs. Software--Practice & Experience **9** (1979) 255-265

9. Gosling, J., Joy, W., Steele, G.: The Java Language Specification. Addison-Wesley (1996)

10. Jordan, M., Van De Vanter, M.: Large Scale Software Development in Java. (In Preparation) Sun Microsystems Laboratories Technical Report (1998)

11. Jordan, M., Van De Vanter, M.: Modular System Building With Java Packages. In: Ebert, J., Lewerentz, C. (eds.): Proceedings 8th Conference on Software Engineering Environments, Cottbus, Germany (1997) 155-163

12. Jordan, M., Van De Vanter, M.: Software Configuration Management in an Object-Oriented Database. In: USENIX Conference on Object-Oriented Technologies (COOTS), Monterey, CA, June 26-29 (1995)

13. Lamb, C., Orenstein, J., Weinreb, D.: The ObjectStore Database System. Communications of the ACM **4** (1991) 50-63

14. Levin, R., McJones, P.: The Vesta Approach to Configuration Management. Research Report 105. Digital Equipment Corporation Systems Research Center (1993)

15. Lin, Y., Reiss, S.: Configuration Management in Terms of Modules. In: Estublier, J. (ed.): Software Configuration Management. Lecture Notes in Computer Science, Vol. 1005. Springer-Verlag, Berlin Heidelberg New York (1995) 101-117

16. Magnusson, B., Asklund, U., Minör, S.: Fine-Grained Revision Control for Collaborative Software Development. In: Proceedings of the First ACM SIGSOFT Symposium on the Foundations of Software Engineering, Los Angeles, California (1993) 33-41

17. Magnusson. B.: Fine-Grained Version Control in COOP/Orm. In: Workshop on Version Control in CSCW Applications at the European Conference on Computer Supported Cooperative Work, Stockholm (1995)

18. Van De Vanter, M.: Practical Language-Based Editing for Software Engineers. In: Taylor, R., Coutaz, J. (Eds.): Software Engineering and Human-Computer Interaction. Lecture Notes in Computer Science, Vol. 896. Springer-Verlag, Berlin Heidelberg New York (1995)

CoEd – A Tool for Versioning of Hierarchical Documents

Lars Bendix[1], Per Nygaard Larsen[1], Anders Ingemann Nielsen[1],
Jesper Lai Søndergaard Petersen[1]

[1] Department of Computer Science, Aalborg University,
Fredrik Bajers Vej 7E, DK-9220 Aalborg Øst, Denmark
bendix@cs.auc.dk

Abstract. In this paper, we report on our experiences from developing and using a tool to provide optimal version control support during co-operative development of hierarchical documents. The main problem in co-operative work is to maintain an overview of how the document is evolving, and at the same time to maintain a complete version history. We extend traditional version control in the sense that we provide version control on both the entire structures of the document and its constituent parts. This enables us to establish natural baselines of the document that have actually existed, and furthermore our system is capable of manipulating directly the structure of the document while retaining complete version history. CoEd consists of four browsers, which show the configuration, version, hierarchy and text aspects of the document. We describe the analysis and considerations that led us to the actual design and implementation of the two prototypes of CoEd. Furthermore, we detail the experiences we have gained from actually using these prototypes, compare our work with that of others, and generalise our results to the field of software development.

1   Introduction

In this paper, we report on our experiences from developing a tool to provide optimal support for our students during their co-operative development of textual documents. We also discuss the results we have obtained from groups of students actually working with our tool.

For years the students at our department have encountered numerous problems when they have had to work together to write reports. Each semester our students spend the major part of their time developing a system, enabling them to put the theory they are taught during the courses into practice. They work in groups of 3-7 people and the theory and the process, as well as the final product, have to be documented in a report which is usually between 80 and 120 pages long.

Our students experience problems, not so much during the programming process where existing tools seem to be of sufficient help, as during the writing process which is usually short and hectic and characterised by a very dynamic organisation of tasks

B. Magnusson (Ed.): ECOOP 98, SCM-8, LNCS 1439, pp. 174–187, 1998

and responsibilities. They especially have problems in keeping an overview of the document and how its structure develops through new versions. This causes problems in establishing baselines and in finding proper use of version histories. Finally, communication of information about the development is important as our students often work in a distributed way. Some students in a group may work at home, while others work in the room that each group has at the university, and others yet work in the computer labs at the department. Some students even prefer to work at night.

About a year ago we set out to improve the situation for our students by providing them with a tool which was better suited for their specific problems than the ones previously used. Instead of buying a new tool or trying to solve a general problem, our strategy was to try to solve the specific problems of our students in their given context, and to gain experiences from the students actually using a prototype of the tool. During and after this process we would try to see where and how well our results would generalise to the wider field of software development.

All groups of students use Latex for producing their project reports. Some groups have so far used manually imposed group discipline to be able to manage the development, dividing the document up into disjoint units with respect to responsibility. They have, however, usually encountered serious problems, both because units are inherently interdependent and because of the complete absence of versioning. Most groups have used either RCS [Tichy85] or CVS [Berliner90] as their tool of choice to manage the development, usually based on whether they liked a strict locking mechanism or not. This has enabled them to version the development of the single parts of the document, but they have still had problems in keeping an overview of the entire document and to manipulate its structure.

The tool, which we design and implement, should provide:
- overview of the document (contents and structure)
- versioning (baselining and version histories)

Our hypothesis is that by providing versioning of the document as a whole, instead of just as single units to be composed, we will be able to improve overview and communication in co-operative efforts as well as in individual ones. We test this hypothesis by letting groups of students carry out experiments with a prototype of our system.

In our design, we were very much inspired by the COOP/Orm system [MA96] for our general approach. They look at a program as a hierarchically structured collection of units that has to be versioned as a whole. Their basic approach is, however, slightly different from ours and has some shortcomings which are both general and specific to the context of our students. Therefore, we want to maintain COOP/Orm's qualities, while extending its functionality and improving on its shortcomings.

Some factors must be taken into consideration when designing the tool. Firstly, the tool must have a low overhead in both learning and use. Secondly, it must represent a significant improvement on previous tools, and, finally, it must be flexible and open with respect to other tools. These factors are very important if we want to convince our students of the benefits of changing tool.

The rest of this paper is organised in the following way: In the next section, we dedicate ourselves to a more in-depth analysis of the situation of our students and the cause of their specific problems. Where appropriate we also discuss problems from literature to enrich the analysis. Based on this analysis we then propose our solutions to the problems. We give a short, basic description of COOP/Orm and go into more details with the discussion of the actual design of the fundamental model for CoEd and the four browsers of its GUI. We also briefly mention some of the alternatives which where discarded. In section four we describe the two prototypes we have implemented and report on the results and lessons learned from our experiments. This is followed by an evaluation of the CoEd prototype with respect to the initial goals and problems, and a comparison with similar systems. Finally, we generalise our results where possible or point out where they are specific to our context, and conclude on the whole effort with some pointers to future work to be carried out.

2   Analysis of the Problems

This problem analysis takes it origin in the problems that our students have reported from their co-operative work on developing textual documents. Through examples we will describe a number of problems that the students have experienced. We will analyse the cause and nature of these problems and how they interrelate. The students also had a lot of demands to the system, which together with the results from the above analysis make up the requirements for the system to be designed.

The problems of our students are many and varied, but can roughly be grouped in three categories. One that has to do with lack of overview, both of the document and of what everyone else is doing. Another category has to do with problems doing version control the way that they want and need. And, finally, problems that have to do with the communication.

Problems that have to do with lack of overview manifest themselves in several ways. Students complain that it is very difficult to organise the structure of the report and to have the structure visualised while working in front of the screen. Much paper is wasted printing out indices or entire reports just to gain overview, and much work is lost in manually changing Latex-commands (and/or file names) to reflect a reorganisation of the report. This of course implies that groups rarely change their way of working. If they work in a top-down fashion, the structure of the paper remains fixed right from the start. Groups working in a bottom-up way remain in a limbo until the last moment where all the pieces are finally put together. A mixed and flexible approach would obviously be desirable.

These problems are in part due to the fact that the version control tool (or the file system) is treating the document just as single pieces and not as a whole too. In part the problems are due to the lack of a proper GUI which can visualise the structure of the document. Version control tools permit us to divide up the document in logic entities, like chapters and sections, and put them on separate files organised in a hierarchical directory structure. But without a proper GUI it is difficult to get a quick overview of the entire document. Furthermore, the fact that the structure is not manifest, but only implied by a directory structure, means that we must manually change this structure every time the organisation of the document is to be changed.

To remedy this problem it would be desirable if our system had knowledge of Latex, such that it could automatically create (and maintain) the storage organisation from that implied by the Latex code. Furthermore, a GUI, which can visualise structures, is indispensable. Finally, it should be possible to visualise - and work with - the document both as a whole and as individual parts.

In the second category of problems we find misfits between the version control needs of our students and the functionality provided by the tools they use. Our students do not have very sophisticated needs, they do not develop variants and do not have to maintain old releases, as is usual in software development. Still they have troubles in using version control tools. They find difficulties in retrieving old versions. Often confusion arises when the supervisor comments on the document and the students find out that this is not the version they printed out just before the meeting. When a section or a chapter is split up into two, the version history for one of the parts is lost. They also have problems in following which changes have been carried out and which are still pending. These problems are very similar to the problems in version selection, baselining and change tracking pointed out by [Tichy88].

Again, the problems are in part due to the lack of a GUI and in part to problems with the data model that the version tool builds on. A GUI will make version selection far easier because one immediately sees what one selects. At least with versions of the individual parts. When we come to baselining the entire document it is a cumbersome and sometimes error prone process. This is due to the fact that it is a manual task where the document is viewed as a collection of versioned parts. As such there is no explicit versioning of the entire collection as a whole. Furthermore, as the tools are unaware of operations like splitting a unit, this becomes something that is unsupported and has to be carried out outside the tool.

To avoid these problems we have to make the construction and versioning of baselines an integrated part of the tool, treated on equal footing with the versioning of the individual parts. Furthermore, we must support splitting of units as a basic functionality. Finally, the GUI should enable version selection and visualise the result immediately.

As can be seen from the discussion above, many of the requirements regard a GUI to visualise information which, in part, is already present in the tools our students presently use for version control. The tool we want to design can be considered as consisting of three layers as seen in figure 1. In the model layer goes requirements like versioning of wholes, split of units and automatic creation of the hierarchy. At the engine level we find the basic versioning and storage capabilities.

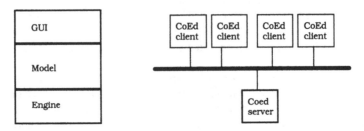

Figure 1. CoEd's layered model.   Figure 2. The client-server architecture of CoEd.

Finally, we would like to return to some of the constraints that the students have put on the system to be developed. They wanted to be able to work in a distributed way and preferably with a system, which is platform independent. Based on an analysis using the categorisations of [KSM93], we have chosen a client/server architecture, as shown in figure 2, as the most suitable for CoEd. This also allows us to make a nice separation of functionality into GUI aspects, which are handled by the clients, and the model and engine aspects, which are handled by the server. Furthermore, we program CoEd in Java to obtain easy platform independence. Another must for our students is that they want to be able to continue to use their favourite editors. And, as we were not particularly happy with the thought of having to write an editor, there is no editor in CoEd. This means that text has to be exported in order to be edited and then re-imported into the system again. Beneficial side-effects of this approach is that it makes CoEd open towards other tools like compilers, and that pre-written text can be put under the control of CoEd at no costs.

3   Design of CoEd

Before we go on to describe the design of CoEd, we want to give a brief description and analysis of the COOP/Orm system [MA96], as this was our starting point of inspiration.

The COOP/Orm system can be characterised as an editor with integrated storage representation, version control and group awareness. In their system, documents and programs are viewed as hierarchical structures of logic units (chapters and sections or classes and methods). The structure is considered a whole and version control is carried out in steps of the logic units. To visualise these structures they use folders in their GUI - very similar to the GUI of the Macintosh. A folder can be opened to see its contents. Every time a new version of a unit is made, it creates conceptually a new version of the whole structure, which is the new baseline. Awareness is obtained by annotating the folders with symbols showing their status.

The power of versioning the structure as a whole, and thus working with automatically created baselines, which can be easily identified, was quite apparent. We found, however, some shortcomings in the application, some of which were general while others were specific to our context.

The fact that a new baseline is created for every little change to the logical units means that a lot of baselines will be created in a short time. COOP/Orm, as it is, does therefore not scale with respect to the number of changes to a document or program. This, and the way version graphs are presented, gives serious problems with overview after some time. In our context, where we treat only documents, we can make some further improvements both with respect to presenting the hierarchy and with respect to allowing direct manipulation of the hierarchy. This is because the pieces of a document are naturally ordered, while classes in a program are not.

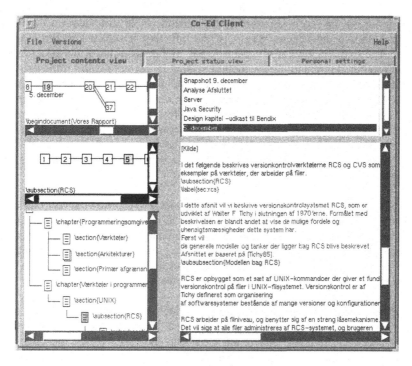

Figure 3. The user interface of a CoEd client.

Returning now to CoEd, we will describe its design by giving a guided tour of the GUI of the CoEd client, which can be seen in figure 3. CoEd consists of four browsers showing different aspects of the document at different levels of details. All browsers have windows, which are scrollable in both the vertical and the horizontal plane.

At the bottom left, we find the *hierarchy browser*. This browser shows the hierarchical structure of the document as it is implied by the Latex commands in the text. The design is inspired by the Pathfinder of Windows95 and icons can be expanded and compressed by double-clicking on them. This makes it very easy to get a quick overview of the whole or parts of the document at the desired level of detail.

At the bottom right, we find the *text browser.* Here is shown the text that corresponds to the icon selected in the hierarchy browser. As documents, in contrast to programs, consist of contiguous pieces of text it is possible to scroll this text and thus arrive at the text that precedes or follows the selection. If a selection is made in the text browser, by double-clicking anywhere in the text of a logic unit, the entire text is highlighted and the corresponding icon in the hierarchy browser is highlighted too.

At the top left, we find the *version browser,* which has two windows. The top window shows all the versions of the baseline, which is equivalent to showing the version group of the root's structure as we version whole structures. In the bottom window is shown the version graph for the unit that is selected in the hierarchy browser. The two windows are "synchronised" in the sense that if we select another baseline version, it might highlight another version in the unit graph - if the version of that unit is not the same in the two baselines. If another version is selected in the unit graph, it will definitely highlight another baseline version - as a change in a unit will always cause a new baseline. The hierarchy browser is a "slave" of the version browser as it always shows the structure that corresponds to the current baseline selection. Through the hierarchy browser also the text browser is a "slave" of the version browser and thus always shows the text which corresponds to the current baseline selection.

At the top right, we find the *configuration browser.* This browser was introduced in order to solve the lack of overview caused by the high number of baselines. As can be seen in the version browser window, baselines can also be named to distinguish important ones. These named baselines are the ones that appear in the configuration browser. The selection of one of these baselines will cause the icon of the same baseline to be selected and highlighted in the version browser.

A typical scenario for the use of CoEd will find us with (a piece of) a document which we want to continue to develop using CoEd. Using the file menu, we will ask CoEd to check in the file(s) containing the document. CoEd parses the Latex code and if successful constructs the implied hierarchical structure, otherwise it refuses the text. Using the version browser, we can now select the baseline to be changed (usually the latest). We can use either the hierarchy browser or the text browser to select the contiguous piece of text in question (it can span several logic units) and ask CoEd to check it out to a file. This file we edit using our favourite editor and when we have finished editing the text, we ask CoEd to check it in again. CoEd automatically discovers which units have been changed - creating new versions - and which have not - leaving them untouched. It will even discover if units have been added or deleted and react correspondingly.

The way that CoEd discovers which units have been changed is by matching the checked in units with the ones that were checked out. In the normal case, this is quite straightforward. However, when there are changes to the structure too, things become much more complicated. Such changes could be the addition or the deletion of a section or the permutation of a number of sections. In these cases too, CoEd must be able to automatically keep track of things in order to maintain a proper version history for all units. If a new section is added, its place must be properly identified and this goes for deleted and permuted sections too. Had there only been performed structural changes this would still not cause any problems, but the point is that we allow people to perform changes to *both* the structure *and* the contents in the same session. Thus, if we check out sections A, B, C and D, we can make changes to sections A, B and D, obtaining A', B' and D'. We can then delete section C, swap sections A' and D' and insert a new section X before section B'. The result which we want to be checked in is D', X, B', A'. Now CoEd should discover that the new first section D' is in reality a modification of the old last section D, and so on.

To solve this problem, we designed a matching operation which uses a score function. What CoEd will do is to match D' with the old sections A, B, C and D to see which is most similar to it, and then assume that D' (in its new place in the structure) is a new version of that one and therefore has to be put in the version group of that section. To find the best match it uses a sentence based score function, which awards points based on similarity in title and sentences of a unit. Our first score function was line based, but we soon discovered that for documents the formatting of the raw Latex code is irrelevant - and is sometimes changed without changing the actual text - and changed to a sentence based function. In order to discover new units, like section X in the example, we use cut-off values and not best fit values. Otherwise, the new section X would not be discovered in this specific case where another section has been deleted, but would be matched with one of the old sections A, B, C or D.

The matching operation is the price we must pay in order to satisfy our students' requirement that CoEd should be open with respect to the editor, such that they can use their favourite editor. This means that text is taken outside of CoEd's control while it is being edited, and when it is brought back in, CoEd must find out what has been going on. An alternative to this approach would be to check each unit out to a separate file. This was quickly discarded, both because it would mean complete loss of overview and because it would be against the idea of working on structures and wholes.

CoEd also has some more advanced functions, which work at the structural level of the document. These are split of a unit, creation of compressed versions and direct manipulation of the structure. Let us assume that we have sections A, B and C, and want to split section A into two sections A1 and A2. When we check in the result - A1, A2, B' and C' - CoEd will discover that there is one more section than was checked out. It will, however, also recognise that A1 and A2 were parts of the original section A and create two new version groups and connect them with the version group of A in a seamless way, such as not to loose the continuity in the compound version history. Again we use cut-off values to recognise the situation.

Compressed versions is another way to reduce the number of baselines, such that it becomes manageable (the configuration browser has the same objective). The mechanism we have adapted for versioning in CoEd (the engine part of CoEd's model) means that each change in a unit creates not only a new version of that unit, but also a new version for all units on the path to the root of the structure. This is done because we consider also structure and not just contents of singular units. So if we have chapter 3 with sections A, B and C, and make changes to sections A and C, there will be created *two* new versions of chapter 3. One containing sections A', B and C and one containing sections A', B and C'. It is easy to imagine how many baseline versions a document with many units in a hierarchy would create when changed frequently. We did not want to change the basic versioning mechanism of the engine such that it would create only the latter version of chapter 3. Instead, we made a change to the model at the higher level, such that these versions would automatically be grouped together into a single compressed version, representing a whole session. Compressed versions can be opened such that the single versions can be seen and accessed.

Direct manipulation of the structure is another way to permute units. It is possible to move both single units and parts of the structure. We simply select what has to be moved and drag it to the place where it has to be inserted. In this way we can change a chapter to a section (including its sub-structure) or vice versa, and CoEd will make the necessary changes to the Latex code for us. In the implementation of direct manipulation, we profit from the automatically created compressed versions. This is because the engine implements a move operation as a number of inserts followed by a number of deletes, which would otherwise quickly generate an awful lot of baseline versions.

4   The Two Prototypes and the Experiments

What we have described in the previous section is the latest of two prototypes, which have been developed and used for performing experiments. We deliberately planned to make two prototypes such that experiences from using the first one could be fed into the development of the second one.

The CoEd project ran from September '96 through June '97 and the two prototypes were used by various groups of students during the two semesters of 96/97. The first prototype was operational in November '96, while the second was finished in April '97. As expected the requirements - as well as the problems - of the students were many, varied - and vague. It was, therefore, very valuable to have a working prototype to be able to discover the potential of this new way of working on whole structures.

The first prototype focused on the following aspects:
- GUI and the browsers
- versioning capabilities
- client/server architecture

Our target group carried out experiments with this prototype, and small corrective and perfective changes were made during the experiments. In the experiment with the first prototype, the average size of documents was 50 pages. The average number of units was close to 100 and the number of baseline versions created was 2-6 times the number of units in the document (just bringing a document into CoEd will generate the same number of baseline versions as there are units). Version graphs were mostly linear with few branches and merges.

Our students were particularly satisfied with the way in which the baseline browser and the hierarchy browser work together to show the development in the structure of the document. Going through the baseline versions "it was like watching a movie". In addition, the text browser received acclaim, as it was now possible to actually browse through pieces of text in their proper context, without having to go through all the work of checking them out and putting them together.

What they found not so successful was the support for splitting up units. It was indeed possible, but as in existing version control tools, the version history was lost for one of the new units. They also complained that the support for bottom-up work - though improved - was still not satisfactory. It was cumbersome to permute units using an editor and they suggested to have a pool of units that could then be inserted when and where needed. We were quite surprised to experience the great number of baseline versions created, but that did not seem to confuse our students. This can be taken as an indication of the configuration browser doing its job well. Finally, we were amused when the students started to complain about the text browser being read-only. Especially for small changes, they wanted to carry them out on the spot.

We used these experiences to develop an enhanced prototype that focused on the following aspects:
- splitting up units
- direct manipulation
- reduce the number of baseline versions

Again, groups of students carried out experiments using the new prototype (which, by the way, was able to use the old data sets). This time the average number of pages managed by CoEd was 90 per document, which can be taken as a sign of the students using CoEd more seriously and not just playing around with it. The splitting capability was used from 2 to 7 times, probably depending on the working style of each group. The size of the automatically created compressed versions was on average 9 baseline versions, but compressed versions of 20-30 were also seen (especially for the groups that started to use CoEd when a lot of text had already been produced). Finally, the capability to directly manipulate the structure was extensively used.

Students were very pleased with the support for splitting up units and the possibility to directly manipulate the structure. The automatically created compressed versions were appreciated, but not considered an important enhancement over the previous prototype. They proposed to visualise more status information through the icons (now checked out units are shown in red). The direct manipulation can presently only be used to *move* units. It was suggested that we implemented also the possibility to create (empty) units and to delete units from within CoEd. Finally, one group would like to see the possibility of supporting graphs instead of only trees, because they had a piece of text which had to appear several places in their report - and in identical form.

Generally our students were very happy with CoEd and found it a very useful improvement to what they had previously experienced. Because of the GUI it was immediate to use and the learning phase was very short. Although CoEd is implemented in interpreted Java, because we did not have access to a compiler, it is not particularly slow. However, the students found out that our department does not have an unlimited number of powerful workstations with colour screens.

5 Evaluation and Comparisons

We set out to implement a system to give our students help in their co-operative development of documents. In particular we wanted to provide support for:
  • overview of the document (contents and structure)
  • versioning (baselining and version histories)

Furthermore, our hypothesis was that providing versioning of the document as a whole, instead of as single parts to be composed, we will be able to improve overview and communication. In this section, we will evaluate the developed prototype of CoEd against our initial goals. We will also render probable our hypothesis, and finally we will compare CoEd with similar systems.

Overview of the document is obtained through the browsers. The text browser takes care of creating overview of the contents of the document. It does so by not only showing the text of a selected unit, but also the surrounding text when we scroll. In extremis, we can scroll through the whole document in the text browser. The hierarchy browser takes care of structural overview. It does so by showing the hierarchy implied by the Latex code of the document. The hierarchy can be opened and collapsed, so different degrees of details can be obtained.

Versioning is carried out at two levels. As in traditional systems, each single unit is versioned giving rise to a version group. We extend this by versioning also the entire document as a whole, thus obtaining automatic versioning of baselines. Version histories are maintained for all version groups throughout the entire development - even when units are moved or split up.

As can be seen from the discussion above and from the feedback we have had from our students, CoEd greatly improves the overview of the co-operative development effort. To some extent it also improves the communication - or we could say that it eliminates some of the *need* for communication. One of the basic and fundamental aspects of CoEd is that of versioning structures, and we can therefore claim to have demonstrated our hypothesis. This is further strengthened by similar observations in Ragnarok [Christensen97] where a spatial metaphor is used as the central concept.

In comparing CoEd with other systems it is obvious to choose CVS [Berliner90], which is one of the tools the students used prior to CoEd, and COOP/Orm [MA96], which served as an inspiration for CoEd (especially for versioning of structures).

With respect to CVS, CoEd has the obvious advantage of its GUI and its browsers. As we have seen above, this plays a great part in providing overview. However, also on other aspects we find that CoEd improves on the model of CVS. Under CVS, the structure of the document becomes very static, as it requires a lot of work to change. In CoEd instead, we can change the structure of the document by direct manipulation. Split of units in CVS is not supported and therefore the version history is lost. This is in part caused by the fact that the granularity in CVS is files, which discourages users from having small units. CoEd, having its own data structure, encourages users to use the logic units of Latex. Even more so as it provides mechanisms to maintain overview also when a small granularity is used.

COOP/Orm suffers from some of the same things. Units cannot be moved in the structure and split is not supported. Furthermore, our target group found the fixed editor of COOP/Orm to be a problem. With respect to versioning of structures, the approach of COOP/Orm is slightly different from ours. When a change is made somewhere, COOP/Orm creates a new version in *all* version groups. In CoEd, a new version is created only in the version groups on the path to the root. This means that - except from the leaves in CoEd - new versions can be caused either by a change in contents or by a change in the underlying structure. Our students sometimes had problems making this distinction and would have liked it to be visualised through the use of different icons. However, this problem is far smaller in CoEd than in COOP/Orm, where also the leaf groups are "swamped by irrelevant versions". It also means that the version explosion happens in all version groups in COOP/Orm, while in CoEd it happens only for the version groups of the root - and here we have the configuration browser to alleviate the problem.

6   Generalisation and Conclusions

In this paper, we have shown that the idea of versioning hierarchical documents both at a structural and a textual level brings many benefits in the development effort. We have designed and implemented such a system showing proof of concept. Through experiments carried out, we have demonstrated the hypothesis that this leads to better overview and fewer problems in the development of documents

Of new concepts, we have introduced and implemented split of units, compressed versions and direct manipulation of the structures. Furthermore, we are using match and merge operations, which are both based on sentences rather than being line based as in traditional tools. Match is a completely new concept and although potentially fallible, we have never experienced any errors during our experiments.

Much of CoEd's strength is due to the fact that it is specifically targeted to a particular group and to a specific context. We see few problems, however, in extending CoEd such that it can work with programs too. Programs are hierarchical structures and they can be parsed such that CoEd can build their structure. As for the size of the groups, CoEd should have no problems in supporting more numerous groups. We never found the server to be the bottleneck in the system.

It is interesting to note that CoEd's baseline versions have a close resemblance to ordinary instantiated Makefiles. They give a complete description of the structure of a specific version of the entire document. In the present implementation, baseline versions can also contain text besides the structural information because we are dealing with Latex documents. When generalising CoEd to be used to support the development of programs, this is of great help. Most programming languages with modularization mechanisms have the same structure. A module is a body of text with some structural information added to describe the dependencies of the module.

CoEd as a programming environment would thus need to be extended with a parser that allows it to parse and extract the dependency information. Once this is done, CoEd will be able to keep track of all structural changes, just as it does now with Latex documents. This creates an environment with a seamless integration between a build tool like Make [Feldman79] and a versioning tool like RCS [Tichy85]. In CoEd, we furthermore avoid the usual problem of versioning Makefiles that other such integrations have.

Two problems remain to be solved if CoEd has to be used for programs too. We should be able to support graphs, as program hierarchies are not always tree structures. Direct manipulation has little sense for programs, instead we need a mechanism for manually selecting a new baseline version from pieces of older ones.

The first problem is a matter of presentation only, as CoEd can already represent graphs internally. We need to change the hierarchy browser in such a way that it can visualise graphs. The second problem does not require extensive changes, as direct manipulation and selection are quite similar in nature. In the former, we are working exclusively within one single baseline version. In the latter we are working between several baseline versions, but still using the principle of moving around specific units.

We are currently working on a prototype implementation of CoEd, which will be able to support development of programs. In this implementation we are also investigating the potential benefits of using the VTML format [VD95] as our basic data structure at the engine level. This should give us better possibilities for visualising differences between baseline versions, both in contents as well as in structure.

Acknowledgement

This research is supported, in part, by the Danish Natural Science Research Council, grants no. 9701013 and 9701406.

References

[Berliner90]: Brian Berliner: *CVS II: Parallelizing Software Development*, in Proceedings of USENIX Winter 1990, Washington D.C.

[Christensen97]: Henrik B¾rbak Christensen: *Context-Preserving Software Configuration Management*, in Supplementary Proceedings of the Seventh International Workshop on Software Configuration Management, Boston, Massachusetts, May 18-19, 1997.

[Feldman79]: Stuart I. Feldman: *Make - A Program for Maintaining Computer Programs*, Software - Practice and Experience, Vol. 9, April 1979.

[KSM93]: J¿rgen Lindskov Knudsen, Elmer Sandvad, Sten Minšr: *Grammar based architectures*, in J. Lindskov Knudsen, M. Lšfgren, O. Lehrmann Madsen (eds.) Object-Oriented Environments, The Mj¿lner Approach, Prentice Hall, 1993.

[MA96]: Boris Magnusson, Ulf Asklund: *Fine Grained Version Control of Configurations in COOP/Orm*, in Proceedings of the Sixth International Workshop on Software Configuration Management, Berlin, Germany, March 25-26, 1996.

[Tichy85]: Walter F. Tichy: *RCS - A System for Version Control*, Software - Practice and Experience, Vol. 15 (7), July 1985.

[Tichy88]: Walter F. Tichy: *Tools for Software Configuration Management*, in Proceedings of the International Workshop on Software Version and Configuration Control, Grassau, Germany, January 1988.

[VD95]: Fabio Vitali, David G. Durand: *Using versioning to support collaboration on the WWW*, in Proceedings of the IV World Wide Web Conference, The World Wide Web journal, 1 (1), O'Reilly, December 1995.

Modelling Versioned Hypertext Documents*

Mária Bieliková and Pavol Návrat

Slovak University of Technology, Dept. of Computer Science and Engineering,
Ilkovičova 3, 812 19 Bratislava, Slovakia

Abstract. Versioning of hypertext documents is in many aspects very similar to versioning of software systems (and their components). In the paper we concentrate on an analysis of similarities and differences between them with the intention of possibly finding in the area of software configuration management a starting point for a new method of version control in hypertext systems. Then, we have proposed a model of a hypertext document which takes into account the perspective of its permanent change. Hypertext documents are modelled by two kinds of nodes in an AND/OR graph. The model forms a basis for building a configuration.

Keywords: hypertext document, hypertext document model, version, configuration.

1   Introduction

Version control has been identified as one of the critical research areas in the hypertext field [8]. It is important especially for hypertext documents published on the web.

Methods of support to versioning hypertext systems have been subject of intensive research for some time [9,12,14,7]. However, the problem has quite naturally been related by many to versioning software systems which is being studied in software engineering.

Software configuration management (SCM) is a very active research area of software engineering today. In spite of many contributions to finding a way how to manage (large) software systems which evolve, researching a framework for unified version model which integrates extensional and intensional versioning, state-based and change-based versioning, revisions and variants, etc. remains on the agenda [4,15].

Although we can consider a hypertext document as a software system (and consequently apply principles of SCM to versioning and configuration management of hypertext documents) there are several specific features of hypertext documents which deserve attention when efficient CM is to be implemented. We will discuss them later in the paper.

---

* The work reported here was partially supported by Slovak Science Grant Agency, grant No. G1/4289/97.

B. Magnusson (Ed.): ECOOP 98, SCM-8, LNCS 1439, pp. 188–197, 1998.

It becomes increasingly important to make explicit the structure and the relations between parts of the document because there is often a need to build a *configuration* of the (part of) document as a whole.

Documents are typically highly interrelated and often have an implicit structure (e.g., order of chapters, content of document, index, etc.). Therefore the process of building a hypertext document configuration is itself a complex one. Bookkeeping of attributes and relations of thousands of objects alone, not to speak of the frequency of their changes is a task which can best be handled by a computer. A support from a computer should further be sought in freeing the author(s) of document from the burden of a too detailed configuration specification. Instead, the author should have means to write higher level requirements which specify the configuration implicitly. Ultimately, this leads to employing relevant knowledge which would be represented explicitly and used by the computer. This can be considered as an approach to automating the above mentioned part of the hypertext documents management.

Any progress in automating is hard to imagine without further formalisation in describing the objects and processes. In this paper, we discuss the problem of modelling a versioned hypertext document. A model is used to express its structure, respecting in our case the viewpoint of building the hypertext document configuration. We have adopted the *AND/OR* graph model used in software configuration management [1]. Semantics of the model is specified according to specific properties of hypertext documents.

2   Hypertext Documents vs. Software Systems

A hypertext document is in contrast to a traditional text (as a book) nonsequential (nonlinear), i.e. there is no single order that determines the sequence in which the text is to be read.

When reflecting on hypertext documents, two perspectives are especially worth mentioning: (1) *user perspective* where a navigational character of the hypertext document is important (for a document to be a hypertext, it must allow the users to take control over a set of links among units of information interactively [11]); (2) *developer perspective* where a life cycle, an architecture, a model, etc. are important features.

Our main interest is to capture the developer perspective. From this point of view a hypertext document has many similarities with the notion of software as it is traditionally understood:

- both consist of many components (nodes in the hypertext) which may undergo changes;
- both usually consist of many content types of components (e.g., in a WWW site the contents can range from HTML pages to Java programs, or sound files);
- components of both of them can be either static i.e., source (known in advance) or dynamic i.e., computed, or derived i.e., generated by the system;

- components of both of them are interrelated in several various ways (here, e.g. composition and dependency relationships in a software system specialize to links in a corresponding hypertext document). Relationships can be in both of them represented either explicitly in the sense that their instances have been marked in the document, or implicitly when the instances can be inferred from the contents of the document;
- both of them are under computer control;
- both of them are very often created and maintained by teams, so it may be desirable to maintain different versions;
- the components are in both of them managed using file systems, relational databases, and object-oriented databases;
- both are often developed in teams by multiple developers (e.g., when they are large).

Usually, the material in a hypertext document (e.g., WWW site) is authored by several teams. Since many documents can be integration points for various departments or functions, each of these departments use their own authoring teams to prepare the information for the hypertext documents. However, overall document has to present a consistent, navigable hypertext that is made up of material supplied by these teams. The problem is similar to the integration and testing step performed in software development. Teams may want to "install" or "stage" delivery of information in hypertext by swapping different configurations for different uses at different times.

Therefore collaborative development leads naturally to versioning. However, we do not discuss this issue in the paper. In [5] there is presented an interesting approach to modelling versions in a collaborative work by so called 'modal model' which takes into account a context of the use of versions.

The primary purpose of a software system development is to build executable software from its components (i.e., a configuration) which can be used for automated support of some task. The primary purpose of a hypertext document is to convey information by being browsed and consequently read (or heard, watched, etc, in case of hypermedia). In case of internet, or intranet hypertext documents there is a *new* interesting goal of browse (or download) specific configuration of the visited site.

Specific properties of hypertext documents enable the use of more specific structures and processes for configuration management. They are based on the characteristic properties and occurence of components and relationships between them:

- a structure of hypertext documents is more dynamic and subject to change than with most software systems. This means that hypertext document has great flexibility, which is normally an advantage but can also be a disadvantage [11]. Structure of software systems is typically restricted to a strict hierarchy which can be modelled by a tree or by an acyclic directed graph. A model of hypertext document may contain cycles;
- a hypertext document often requires that there are represented dependencies which are finer grained than in a traditional software;

– a hypertext document contains fewer types of relationships between components (nodes). Relationships are represented by links which often express explicit navigation ("activate this link to visit that related resource") or the position of a document within a series of documents.

3 Model of Hypertext Document

Solving various problems related to building hypertext document configurations requires describing the actual hypertext document in the simplest possible way, but still sufficiently rich to reflect the principal relations and properties which are decisive in the building process.

In spite of mentioned specific properties of a hypertext document we can with advantage use the analogy of the hypertext document with a software system. Generally, various kinds of graphs are being used to model software systems. The model is often provided by AND/OR graphs [13,6,1].

We attempt to describe a hypertext document with the specific purpose in mind, i.e. to be used during development and maintenance, and specifically in building the hypertext document configuration. Therefore, our model encompasses those parts of the document and those relations among them which are important for building a configuration. Due to many similar properties of software systems and hypertext documents we find the intertwinded AND/OR graphs suitable for modelling a hypertext document.

Note that we adopted the version oriented model (as an alternative to a change oriented one) where *explicit versions* of components are used to construct configurations. "Intensional vs. extensional versioning" is orthogonal to a model of the system [4], thus this is not a restriction for the proposed model.

3.1   Elements of the Model

Throughout the rest of the paper we use the term *hypertext component* as any kind of identifiable entity put under configuration management control (i.e., hypertext nodes – elementary units as well as parts of a hypertext document – composite units). Creating a hypertext component version can be done in one of two possible ways. First, versions are created to represent alternative solutions of the same purpose. They differ in some attributes. Such 'parallel' versions, or variants, are frequently results of different specializations. Second, versions are created to represent improvements of previous ones, or as modifications caused by error correction, content enhancement, and/or adaptation to changes in an environment. Such 'serial' versions, or revisions, are frequently results of concretizations of the same variant. A *family* of hypertext components comprises all components which are versions of one another.

When defining a model of a hypertext document, relations between hypertext components should be considered. They can be either development-induced, for example *is_variant* and *has_revision*, or navigational, i.e. hypertext *links*. We identify several types of links based on the location of the source and destination:

intra-component links are links with both the source and destination located in the same component; *inter-family* links are links with both the source and destination located in different components within different families; *inter-document* links are links with both the source and destination located in different documents. We distinguish also *implicit* links which mirror the predefined structure of the document such as *next, previous, home,* etc.

We found useful to consider *variant* as a set of hypertext components. This conceptual design choice does not impose any serious limitations in most cases. On the contrary, it provides a considerable flexibility to the configuration management process. It offers a useful abstraction that should simplify the process. In order to describe variants, we define a binary relation *is_variant* which determines a set of hypertext components with the same (1) navigational relations, (2) variant attributes and (3) constraints (in the sense of combining components to configurations) within a given family.

Let us note that the distribution of hypertext components to variants depends on a decision which properties are considered as variant properties and as revision properties, i.e. unique properties of the actual hypertext component. Decision about distributing attributes is left open in our approach because it depends on the project, its size, problem domain, etc. Typical recommendations applicable in many cases are to consider as variant attributes the following properties: specific characteristics of the document being presented, characteristics of the development environment (language, formalism for text formating), etc. This means in our terminology that their change leads to a new variant. Properties related to the development process such as state, change description, author, date, time are often considered as revision attributes, i.e. their change leads to a new revision.

One consequence of our design decision of taking variants to be sets of components is that from the two kinds of versions of components, only revisions are left to represent actual single hypertext components (e.g., nodes of a hypertext network).

As an example, let us present a part of a hypertext document which includes versions of (some of) its components. The example is taken from Maria's home page where – among other things – the subject Knowledge Based Systems is presented. Hypertext components are shown in Figure 1 along with navigational relations between them (implicit links and intra-component links are not illustrated).

Let us reflect the concept of variants once more by viewing of this figure. Assuming a branch in the version tree of REQUIREMENTS family resulted just from changing the author and the attribute "author" is considered a revision attribute, this family consists of just a single variant. Although there is a branch in the version tree, it does not give rise to another variant.
Consider now the ASSIGNMENTS family. Assuming a branch resulted from changing a graphic mode and the attribute "graphic" is considered a variant attribute, the family consists of two variants.

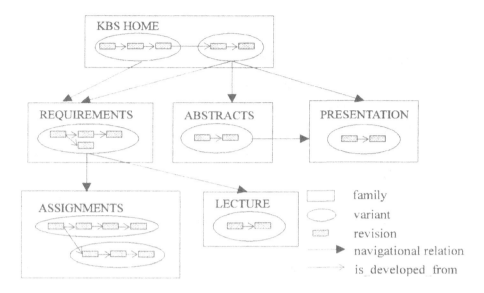

Fig. 1. An example hypertext document: partial hierarchy of elements.

Finally, a change of the navigational relation in the family KBS HOME gives rise to another variant even if there is no branch.

3.2   AND/OR Graph Model

The concepts introduced above will let us to formulate a model of a hypertext document which supports the process of configuration building. In the case of a software system a configuration is often defined as a collection of components tailored to a specific purpose. This definition can be adopted to a hypertext document, too.

Our method of modelling a hypertext document H is to describe it by an oriented graph $M_H = (N, E)$, with nodes representing reference to families and variants in such a way that these two kinds of nodes alternate on every path and every maximal connected subgraph has at least one root.

Any element of $E, (e_1, e_2) \in E$, called an edge, is of one from among the two mutually exclusive kinds. Either $e_1 \in VARIANT_H$ (a set of variants of a hypertext document H) and $e_2 \in F_S$ (a set of family names of a hypertext document H); in this case, the node e_1 (variant) is called the AND-node. Or $e_1 \in F_S, e_2 \in VARIANT_H$; in this case, the node e_1 (reference to family) is called the OR-node. Revisions are covered in the model through AND-nodes which represent variants, i.e. sets of revisions.

We remark that the binary relation originating at AND node stands for navigational relations (relating variants to families) Implicit links and intra-component links are not captured by the model. The relation originating at OR node mirrors *has_variant* relation. In case when composite nodes are in-

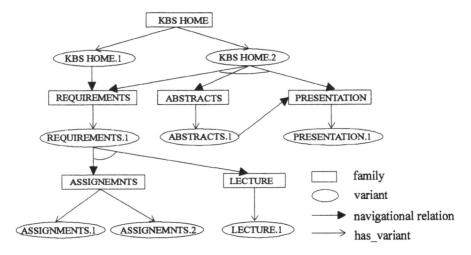

Fig. 2. Model of the hypertext document from Figure 1 represented as an *AND/OR* graph.

corporated in the model the former relation can represent also the composition relationship.

The requirement that a model of a hypertext document should have at least one root is motivated by the fact that the model should serve the purpose of building a hypertext document configuration. When there is no root in a model, then it is not possible to determine which components are to be selected for a configuration.

Actually, this requirement is not a restriction in our case as a document commonly has an entry point to start reading from. Moreover, the hypertext document model captures the notion of a definite hypertext document. In the case of WWW hypertext documents we do not have ambition to model the whole hypertext network. Rather, a WWW network is to be modelled as a collection of hypertext documents all of which are treated independently from the others. This may seem as a restriction and thus a disadvantage but as a consequence it highly simplifies the model. Inter-document (external) links are not represented in the model, so their change does not give rise to a new variant. Moreover, such a model is typically formed by an acyclic AND/OR graph.

The example hypertext document depicted in Figure 1 can be expressed by an *AND/OR* graph in Figure 2. For the sake of simplicity, variants are given names which are derived from the name of the corresponding family by suffixing it with a natural number. Formal definition of such a model is presented in [1] where modelling a software system is considered. The difference lies in the interpretation of specific parts of the model which were described above.

Note that in such a model of a hypertext document, versions of links are represented by a new variant in the family of components. A hypertext component need not to be a file. For example, in many cases it is advantageous to consider a page (in a WWW site) together with all graphical objects included in it as a hypertext document node.

3.3   Building of a Hypertext Document Configuration

When building a configuration, for each family already included in a configuration there must be selected at least one variant. For each variant already included in a configuration, there must be included all the families related by architectural relations to that variant. Taking into account that a software component is determined completely only after a revision has been selected, the resulting configuration is built by selecting precisely one revision for each selected variant.

Note that not precisely one variant for each family included in a hypertext document configuration is to be selected but instead *at least one*. This is a consequence of the specific characteristics of the hypertext document and of our defintion of its model. Variants can for example represent sets of revisions in different languages (Slovak, English, etc.). Sometimes there is a requirement to have the document written in several languages so more than one variant for a particular family should be incorporated into the configuration.

There can be built several different configurations from a model of a hypertext document, usually based on different required purposes of the desired configuration. There can be desired a configuration for the end user, a configuration for further development, etc. Such configurations can be specified by different configuration requirements.

In order to build a configuration, our method that was designed originally for software systems can be used [2] together with a programming technique of implementing search of AND/OR graphs with constraints [3]. This technique uses markings to maintain consistency and identification the reason for a deadend. It attempts to find a place in the graph where the search for an alternative solution should be resumed.

The method takes into account the knowledge about the navigational relations between components, about selecting components (families) and also about selecting a variant and revision for each family. Selection of a variant and a revision can be accomplished by our method for version selection [10]. Our strategy of version selection is based on a sequence of heuristic functions which reduce the set of suitable versions. By changing the order in which the heuristic functions are applied we can vary the importance of the evaluation criterion which the given function embodies.

4   Conclusion

We have presented an AND/OR graph model of hypertext document. The model is based on the similarities of software systems and hypertext documents and on specific characteristics of hypertext documents. Main strengths of our approach to modelling hypertext documents for configuration management are (1) considering of the conceptual distinction between variants and revisions,

(2) considerating of navigational relations at the variant level, (3) abstarcting from implicit and intra-component links in the model which results in simpler model, and (4) allowing more than one hypertext component from a particular family to be in a configuration. In the case of web documents we propose an atomic hypertext document to be in most cases of greater granularity than a file.

Our way of modelling a hypertext document is limited by the fact that every change (leading to a new version) of variant attributes, constraints or navigational relations outside the component but within the hypertext document results in a new variant regardless to the real nature of the change.

The area of hypertext documents versioning and configuration building requires further research. Open problem is acquiring knowledge on the suitability of component versions. In case when attributes of components are not known for no matter what reason, methods of reverse engineering could be attempted to supply them.

The proposed model together with a method for configuration building could be incorporated into a hypertext system. At the moment we have started with prototyping for modelling versioned web pages. We concentrate on a developer perspective as was indicated in the paper. At the implementation level it is advantageous to use results from research in versioning databases.

References

1. M. Bieliková and P. Návrat. Modelling software systems in configuration management. *Applied Mathematics and Computer Science*, 5(4):751–764, 1995.
2. M. Bieliková and P. Návrat. A knowledge based method for building a software system configuration. *Knowledge Based Systems*, 9(1):61–65, 1996.
3. M. Bieliková and P. Návrat. A Prolog technique of implementing search of A/O graphs with constraints. *Computers and Artificial Intelligence*, 16(4):377–400, 1997.
4. R. Conradi and B. Westfechtel. Version models for software configuration management. *ACM Computing Surveys (to appear)*.
5. A. Dix, T. Rodden, and I. Sommerivlle. Modelling versions in collaborative work. *IEE Proc. Softw. Eng.*, 144(4):195–205, August 1997.
6. J. Estublier. Configuration management: the notion and the tools. In *Proc. Int. Workshop on Software Version and Configuration Control*, pages 38–61, Stuttgart, 1988.
7. A. Haake and D. Hiks. VerSE: Towards hypertext versioning styles. In *7th ACM Conference on Hypertext*, Online Proceedings (http://www.cs.unc.edu/~barman/HT96/), Washington DC, USA, March, 1996.
8. F.G. Halasz. Reflections on NoteCards: seven issues for the next generation of hypermedia systems. *Commun. ACM*, 31(7):836–852, July 1988.
9. C.Y. Lo. Comparison of two approaches of managing links in multiple versions of documents. In *Proc. of the Workshop on Versioning in Hypertext Systems*, Edinburgh, September, 1994.
10. P. Návrat and M. Bieliková. Knowledge controlled version selection in software configuration management. *Software - Concepts and Tools*, 17:40–48, 1996.

11. J. Nielsen. *Hypertext & hypermedia*. Academic Press, Boston, 1990.
12. L.F.G. Soares and M.A. Casanova. Nested composite nodes and version control in hypermedia systems. In *Proc. of the Workshop on Versioning in Hypertext Systems*, Edinburgh, September, 1994.
13. W.F. Tichy. A data model for programming support environments and its application. In B. Langefors, A.A. Verrijn-Stuart, and G. Bracchi, editors, *Trends in Information Systems*, pages 219–236. North Holland, 1986.
14. F. Vitali and D.G. Durand. Using versioning to support collaboration on the WWW. In *Fourth World Wide Web conference*, 1995.
15. A. Zeller and G. Snelting. Unified versioning through feature logic. *ACM Transactions on Software Engineering and Methodology*, 6(4):397–440, 1997.
16. B.R. Schmerl and C.D. Marlin. Versioning and Consistency for Dynamically Composed Configurations In *Proc. of SCM-7*, Springer LNCS 1235, pages 49–65, 1997.

Requirements for Software Deployment Languages and Schema

Richard S. Hall, Dennis Heimbigner, Alexander L. Wolf

Software Engineering Research Laboratory
Department of Computer Science
University of Colorado
Boulder, CO 80309 USA
{rickhall, dennis, alw}@cs.colorado.edu

Abstract. Software distribution via networks provides timeliness and continual evolution that is not possible with physical media distribution methods. Organizations such as Microsoft, Marimba, and the Desktop Management Task Force are strengthening their efforts to package software systems in ways that are conducive to network distribution. The result of these efforts has led to the creation of software description languages and schema, but they do not address deployment issues in a complete, systematic fashion. The contribution of this paper is to define and explore the requirements for software deployment languages and schema.

1   Introduction

Software distribution methods are evolving constantly. The once preferred floppy disk has given way to the CD-ROM, which is now being challenged by wide-area networks as a software distribution mechanism. Current bandwidth considerations limit the volume of data that can be distributed over a network connection, but it is clear that software distribution via a network connection is growing in importance.

Given benefits such as timeliness, continual evolution, and market access, it is evident that technologies to support network software distribution are important and must be created. One area in particular that is starting to see activity is software deployment languages and schema. Efforts such as the Software Dock [3], the Desktop Management Task Force (DMTF) [1], and the Open Software Description (OSD) [5] are trying to create standard syntax and schema for describing software systems in order to facilitate deployment over networks. These technologies share a common approach with other work, such PCL [7], Adele [2], DCDL [6], in that they are trying to define a standard terminology that can be used to reason about software for specific tasks.

The contribution of this paper is to define and explore what is required in a software description language or schema in order to support software deployment. Additional details and an evaluation of OSD and MIF can be found in [4].

B. Magnusson (Ed.): ECOOP 98, SCM-8, LNCS 1439, pp. 198-203, 1998

2   Software Deployment Language and Schema Requirements

Software deployment is a collection of interrelated activities, referred to as the software deployment life cycle, that address all of the issues of interfacing a deployed software system to the ongoing usage of the consumer as well as the ongoing development efforts of the producer. The software deployment activities include release, install, update, adapt, activate, de-activate, de-install, and de-release. These activities define the scope of the software deployment problem space; a space for which software deployment languages and schema must provide coverage.

The purpose of software deployment language and schema technologies is to provide semantic knowledge that is rich and rigorous enough to support the automation of the software deployment life cycle. Given such semantic descriptions, generic solutions to software deployment tasks are possible by combining software product knowledge with consumer site knowledge.

In order to provide such semantic descriptions of software systems and consumer sites it is necessary to adopt a semantic model. A common approach, and one that is assumed in this paper, is that software systems and computing sites are objects that can be modeled as a collection of attributes or properties. These collections of properties may have internal structure, but at the base level they map to primitive data types (e.g., integer, string). This model is used throughout this paper and, in general, is used by both OSD and MIF.

2.1   Consumer Site Description

There are two classes of participants in the software deployment problem space, namely producers and consumers. The purpose of the consumer description is to provide a context about the site into which a software system is to be situated; this is essential to fully describe a software system or component. The consumer site description and the software system description, should be viewed as two halves to a whole, rather than two distinct entities.

In the end, the consumer site description is combined with the software system description to determine how deployment processes should be performed. The result of such deployment activities is a modification to the consumer site description in order to record the results of the deployment activity.

2.2   Software System and Component Description

The other half of the deployment puzzle is represented by producer descriptions of software systems and components. These descriptions define an interface to the products and services provided by software producers. The goal for the software system description is to provide enough semantic information about a particular software system so that it can be deployed in an automated fashion. The responsibility of describing a software system lies solely with the producer of the software system since it has the most knowledge about the system.

We have identified five classes of semantic information that must be described for a software system or component, these are outlined in the following subsections.

Assert constraints: The correct operation of a software system is dependent upon values of properties at the site where the software is to be deployed; these types of constraints are assertions and they cannot be resolved in the presence of a conflict. Some possible examples of assertions are the requirement that the operating system be Windows 95" and the screen resolution be greater than 800 pixels by 600 pixels.

Assertions are used for two different purposes: to select a properly configured software system for deployment and to maintain the proper operation of a deployed software system. Two common examples of the former type of assertions are hardware architecture and operating system; upon determining the operating system and architecture for a consumer site it is possible to select the artifacts to install.

The second use of assertions is best described with an example. Imagine a particular deployed software system that requires version 1.0.2 of the Java Virtual Machine. This constraint was, by definition, true at the time of installation, but anytime after installation this constraint may be violated if the Java Virtual Machine is upgraded. The result is that the deployed software system will no longer function properly since its constraint on the Java Virtual Machine has been violated.

Assertions can be used to alleviate this situation by not allowing changes that violate existing constraints. Assertions are generally discarded after they are used to select a properly configured software system. In order to guarantee operational correctness, assertions must be maintained and managed at the consumer site, thus a consumer site description is essential for deploying software systems.

Complications may arise from these inherited assertions. For example, a deployed software system may be constrained by version 1.0.2 of the Java Virtual Machine. A new software system that is being deployed may be constrained by version 1.1.4 of the Java Virtual Machine. These constraints are in conflict and any attempt to deploy the second software system will fail because there is no way to resolve the constraint conflict. Using assertions, such a situation is guaranteed to fail even though it might be possible to install multiple versions of the Java Virtual Machine. This last point illustrates the need for treating dependency constraints distinctly from assertion constraints.

Dependency constraints: Dependency constraints have a means for resolution if a conflict arises. The more general assert constraint is still necessary, though, because not all constraints are solvable and even those that are solvable should not be solved in all cases. A common dependency constraint can be found in a Web page-based software system. This type of system depends on the existence of a Web browser in order for it to operate. It is very likely that a Web browser could be retrieved and installed if one does not exist, thus subsystem dependencies are one type of dependency constraint.

The line dividing assert constraints from dependency constraints is subjective, though. Recall the previous example of two systems requiring different versions of the Java Virtual Machine. In this scenario the second software system being deployed could retrieve and deploy its required version of the Java Virtual Machine since the two versions of the Java Virtual Machine do not conflict with each other. Since the Java Virtual Machine consumes a relatively small amount of resources it may make sense to allow multiple copies. In other scenarios, though, multiple copies of a subsystem might not make sense because of incompatibilities or impracticalities.

These scenarios emphasize the importance of having distinct notions of an assert constraint and a dependency constraint; assert constraints only assert that the constraint must be true while dependency constraints try to find a resolution. If assert constraints were not treated separately from dependency constraints, each constraint conflict on a subsystem, for example, would be resolved by simply requesting that a new copy of the subsystem be deployed to meet the new constraint specification. It is clear that this is not a desirable situation; the resulting consumer site would be littered with various versions and configurations of the same subsystem.

The discussion of dependency constraints thus far has centered on the notion of a dependent subsystem and its version number. This is only one possible example of a dependency constraint. Within subsystem dependencies one might wish to constrain the subsystem based on some functional configuration, rather than the version number. Given a conflict it may be possible to attempt to reconfigure the functional aspects of the dependent subsystem. As another example, a dependency constraint may be placed on the configuration of the consumer site operating system. In such a case it might be possible to resolve a conflict by reconfiguring the operating system. The notion of a dependency constraint must be flexible.

Dependency constraints are also complicated because there are different types of dependency constraints. By expanding beyond the notion of corequisite dependencies, a class of temporal dependency constraints is found. Temporal dependency constraints exist at particular time during a software system's deployment life cycle, but they are not integral pieces of the software system's time invariant definition. For example, a software system being deployed at a particular site may have a prerequisite dependency on a specific tool during installation, such as an unarchiving tool. The unarchiving tool is only required during installation and may be removed after the software system is installed without affecting the proper operation of the software system.

The notion of an abstract dependency constraint is also a common requirement. A software system that has documentation files in HTML format has an abstract dependency on an HTML viewer. From the software system's perspective it does not matter which HTML viewer is available, it is just concerned with the availability of the abstract capability of viewing HTML formatted documents. These types of abstract descriptions of software systems are very important and a complementary schema for describing abstract capabilities should be considered separately.

Artifacts: When describing a software system it is necessary to describe the actual, physical components that make up the system. The physical components of a system are the collection of executables, libraries, data sets, and documentation that are used to compose the software system. Not all software systems will have all of the aforementioned types of component files, but they serve to illustrate the general classes of artifacts for a software system. This information may include the location, description, and type of the artifacts included in the software system.

Configuration: There are two types of configuration information that describe a software system or component. The simpler of the two is the settings or configurable properties of a software system. A software system can generally be configured in many ways. The various configurations may determine simple aesthetic issues or they may be used to determine various levels of performance or functionality. It is therefore imperative that the variability of the software system configuration be described so that it can be examined and possibly changed by other software systems that, in some way, depend on the particular software system. By fully identifying and recording this configuration information it is then possible to uniquely identify the existence and exact state of the deployed software system.

The second type of configuration information regards a higher level description of the system components. While a description of the software system artifacts is necessary to perform most of the basic software deployment tasks, a higher level description of the software system is required to perform some of the more abstract software deployment tasks. This high-level description of the software system's configuration can be partly thought of as an architectural description, but specifically it describes special relationships between specific software system components. For example, a client/server system must describe the relationship between the client program and the server program so that the activation activity of the software deployment life cycle can understand that the server must be activated before the client can be activated. In addition to relationships between components, the interfaces and capabilities provided by those components must also be described. These interfaces may include management-related functionality as well as service-related functionality.

The relationship information provided in the configuration description is not used in isolation. The relationship information details *how* a software system can be configured. This information then affects all other aspects of the software system description. For example, a software system may have many possible configurations. Choosing one configuration over another may result in changes to the specific set of constraints, artifacts, and activities for the given software system.

Activities: Despite the fact that the previous classes of semantic information describe a large portion of a software system for deployment, it is still not possible to know all the specialized activities that need to be performed during various processes of the software deployment life cycle.

Full support of software deployment requires support for specialized activities that are required during the various software deployment processes. For an example, consider a software system that maintains an index on an evolving collection of Web pages. Each time any of the software deployment life cycle processes modify the collection of Web pages, by addition, update, or removal, it is necessary to re-index the Web page collection. This type of activity cannot be easily inferred from the previous classes of semantic information and must be described separately.

No matter how well thought out a deployment language or schema is, it will not be possible to anticipate every specialized activity that a specific deployment process might require. Also, by supporting activity descriptions it is possible to understand the relationships between the activities and the deployment processes in order to reduce redundancy and increase correctness in the overall deployment solution.

3   Conclusion

The use of networks, such as the Internet, to distribute software to consumers is proving to be very beneficial for both the consumer as well as the software producer. In order to realize the potential of network software distribution, though, the definition and standardization of software system and component description must be introduced. Describing software systems and components in a complete and rigorous manner is required for the creation of a general infrastructure to support the software deployment life cycle. Such a software description definition must include ways to describe system assert constraints, dependency constraints, artifacts, configurations, and specialized deployment activities. Combining such a definition with a semantic description of consumer sites makes it possible to create general solutions to the various deployment tasks.

Further effort in these areas is being researched by the University of Colorado's Software Dock [3] project. The main purpose of this project is to create a standard, rigorous schema for describing software systems and consumers sites and to create a software deployment framework to utilize these descriptions. The approach taken by the Software Dock is to develop a distributed framework where various agents are used to interpret semantic deployment information and to then automate the software deployment life cycle tasks.

Acknowledgements: This work was supported in part by the Air Force Material Command, Rome Laboratories, and the Defense Advanced Research Projects Agency under Contract Number F30602-94-C-0253. The content of the information does not necessarily reflect the position or the policy of the Government and no official endorsement should be inferred.

References

1. Desktop Management Task Force, Software Standard Groups Definition, Version 2.0, November 29, 1995. (http://www.dmtf.org/tech/apps.html)
2. J. Estublier, R. Casallas.   „The Adele Configuration Manager,„ Configuration Management, Wiley, 1994, pp. 99-134.
3. R. S. Hall, D. Heimbigner, A. van der Hoek, A. L. Wolf. „An architecture for Post-Development Configuration Management in a Wide-Area Network,„ Proceedings of the 1997 International Conference on Distributed Configurable Systems, IEEE Computing Society, May 1997, pp. 269-278.
4. R. S. Hall, D. Heimbigner, A. L. Wolf. „Software Deployment Languages and Schema.„ Technical Report CU-SERL-203-97, University of Colorado, Dec. 18, 1997. (http://www.cs.colorado.edu/serl/cm/Papers.html#Schema)
5. A. van Hoff, H. Partovi, T. Thai. „The Open Software Description Format (OSD),„ Microsoft Corp. and Marimba, Inc. (http://www.w3.org/TR/NOTE-OSD.html)
6. B. R. Schmerl, C. D. Marlin. „Versioning and Consistency for Dynamically Composed Configurations,„ Proceedings of the 1997 International Symposium on System Configuration Management, Springer, 1997, pp. 49-65.
7. E. Tryggeseth, B. Gulla, R. Conradi. „Modeling Systems with Variability using the PROTEUS Configuration Language,„ Proceedings of the 1995 International Symposium on System Configuration Management, Springer, 1995, pp. 216-240.

The Agony and Ecstasy of Configuration Management

Susan Dart

Dart Technology Strategies, Inc.,
1280 Bison, Suite B9-510, Newport Beach, CA, USA
sdart@earthlink.net

Tutorial Extened Abstract

This tutorial is designed to expose the agony and ecstasy of configuration management (CM) based on industrial experience in finding a CM solution. The agony comes from the challenges in adopting a good CM solution. Typical challenging questions that companies ask are: how do we know we have a CM problem? How do we get sponsorship to get a new CM tool? How do we avoid politics and affecting production deadlines? Which tool is best? Will engineers accept it? What CM process should be followed? How will the tool support distributed development. And so on.

The ecstasies come from the benefits of having a well-thought out and optimally implemented CM solution. They include: improved release cycles, less bugs found in the field, quality control by default, management of change complexity and its evolution, repeatable builds, ability to support more variant baselines, and able to be more responsive to customers' growing need for bug fixes and enhancements.

Many companies realize that CM is a vital part of their business strategy. In fact, it is a key part in keeping them competitive as well as expanding their product lines. But, most companies struggle with adopting a CM solution or improving their existing approach. There are many reasons for this. But essentially, it all relates to poor technology adoption practice. Regardless of whether a company is small or large, mistakes are made in selecting the right tool and in its deployment which could have been avoided.

This tutorial presents a process that companies can follow in order to successfully select and deploy a CM tool. Such a process involves understanding the CM problems, gathering the CM requirements, and developing various plans such as the evaluation strategy, proof of concept pilot project plan, risk management plan, and deployment plan.

One of the initial steps is to understand what CM is. Within a company there generally is a multitude of definitions of CM. This tutorial will look at the spectrum of CM operational elements which includes: version control, build and release management, change tracking, process control, workspace and repository management, parallel and distributed development, and audit control. Highlighted will be the more challenging aspects of CM which include: release planning, change sets, distributed development, people issues, risk management, ties with related tools such as document management, and process issues. An overview of CM tools providing different levels of support will be given.

This tutorial is suited to practitioners who want broader exposure to the operational issues regarding CM and for those who seek a comprehensive introduction to CM.

B. Magnusson (Ed.): ECOOP 98, SCM-8, LNCS 1439, pp. 204-205, 1998

Biography

Susan Dart is President and CEO of Dart Technology Strategies, Inc., an independent consulting firm that helps companies achieve process improvement via the adoption of technology. Her firm specializes in configuration management (CM). Ms Dart has 22 years of experience in industry and academia, focusing on software tools and software development environments. She has over 40 international publications, including co-author of the Ovum book on Evaluating Configuration Management Tools. Ms Dart also participates on the United States' Federal Aviation Authority panel on developing CM for Explosives Detection Systems at airports and has done over 25 workshops/ seminars throughout the world.

Before starting her own company, Ms Dart was Vice President of Process Technology at Continuus Software Corporation, a CM vendor, where she developed adoption services to assist strategic customers in achieving the best possible CM solution. Previous to that, she spent 7 years at the Software Engineering Institute (SEI) of Carnegie Mellon University (CMU), developing models for CM and environments. Prior to the SEI, Ms Dart developed compilers at Tartan, Inc. and telecommunications software and standards for Telstra, Australia. Ms Dart has a Master's Degree in Software Engineering from CMU and a Bachelor's Degree with Distinction from RMIT.

Author Index

Springer
and the
environment

At Springer we firmly believe that an
international science publisher has a
special obligation to the environment,
and our corporate policies consistently
reflect this conviction.
We also expect our business partners –
paper mills, printers, packaging
manufacturers, etc. – to commit
themselves to using materials and
production processes that do not harm
the environment. The paper in this
book is made from low- or no-chlorine
pulp and is acid free, in conformance
with international standards for paper
permanency.

 Springer

Lecture Notes in Computer Science

For information about Vols. 1–1361

please contact your bookseller or Springer-Verlag